WHO KILLED EPSTEIN?

PRINCE ANDREW OR BILL CLINTON

WAR ON DRUGS BOOK 5

SHAUN ATTWOOD

ACKNOWLEDGEMENTS

A big thank you to Lee Williams (researching, text-editing),
Mark Swift (proof-reading), Jane Dixon-Smith
(typesetting, book-jacket design)

SPELLING DIFFERENCES: UK V USA

This book was written in UK English, so USA readers may notice some spelling differences with American English: e.g. color = colour, meter = metre and pedophile = paedophile

SHAUN'S BOOKS

English Shaun Trilogy
Party Time
Hard Time
Prison Time

War on Drugs Series
Pablo Escobar: Beyond Narcos
American Made: Who Killed Barry Seal? Pablo Escobar or George HW Bush
The Cali Cartel: Beyond Narcos
Clinton Bush and CIA Conspiracies: From the Boys on the Tracks to Jeffrey Epstein

Un-Making a Murderer: The Framing of Steven Avery and Brendan Dassey
The Mafia Philosopher: Two Tonys
Life Lessons

Pablo Escobar's Story (4-book series 2019-21)
T-Bone (Expected 2022)

SOCIAL-MEDIA LINKS

Email: attwood.shaun@hotmail.co.uk
YouTube: Shaun Attwood
Blog: Jon's Jail Journal
Website: shaunattwood.com
Instagram: @shaunattwood
Twitter: @shaunattwood
LinkedIn: Shaun Attwood
Goodreads: Shaun Attwood
Facebook: Shaun Attwood, Jon's Jail Journal,
T-Bone Appreciation Society

Shaun welcomes feedback on any of
his books and YouTube videos.
Thank you for the Amazon and Goodreads reviews and to
all of the people who have subscribed to Shaun's YouTube
channel!

CONTENTS

AUTHOR'S INTRODUCTION

You may be wondering: how does Epstein fit into a War on Drugs series of books? In part three of this series, *American Made*, I told the story of Barry Seal, who flew cocaine into America and weapons out of America to Nicaragua for the CIA, under instructions from George H. W. Bush and Oliver North. Prior to his assassination, Barry's goal was to run Southern Air Transport (SAT) over Mexico, with CIA pilot Terry Reed – whose book, *Compromised*, documents Terry's discovery of CIA drug trafficking and the deadly consequences he faced when he blew the whistle. On February 19, 1986, Barry's SAT dream died after he was shot by a Colombian hit team in front of the Salvation Army's Community Treatment Center in Baton Rouge.

Drug trafficking allegations led to the CIA investigating itself. On October 1, 1998, the CIA inspector general issued a report linking SAT to allegations of trafficking cocaine to finance the Contra rebels in Nicaragua in the 1980s. On the exact same day, SAT went bankrupt in Columbus, Ohio. What was it doing in Ohio? None other than Jeffrey Epstein had arranged for SAT to establish itself at Rickenbacker Air Force Base in Columbus, Ohio. Epstein was working for Leslie Wexner, whom Epstein survivor Maria Farmer described as "the head of the snake" for the US honeytrap operation.

The arrival of SAT in Ohio was publicised as a boost for the local economy, the same spiel Governor Bill Clinton had used when promoting the Arkansas Development Finance Authority, which according to ex-employee Larry Nichols was washing drug money. As suspicion grew about its real purpose, SAT collapsed under massive debt.

Researching the War on Drugs has revealed that the biggest

players are governments, the military and intelligence agencies – and that honeytrap operations such as Epstein's are tentacles of the same forces at work, or as Charlie Robinson described when titling his book: *The Octopus of Global Control.*

CHAPTER 1
THE MURDER

On July 6, 2019, Jeffrey Epstein was arrested at New York's Teterboro Airport, following a trip to France. During a raid on his mansion, the FBI found nude photos, including images of teenage girls. Charged with sex trafficking and conspiracy to traffic minors for sex, he offered to pay a $600 million bail bond, which the judge denied because he was a flight risk, an acute danger to the community and a threat to the witnesses.

With his case under scrutiny, his former protectors – including Prince Andrew and Bill Clinton, whom he had attempted to compromise in a honeytrap scheme – began to pull away. Facing a life sentence, he hoped to win a double-jeopardy motion or to cut a deal with the prosecutor, which would have required naming his accomplices. As his legal difficulties multiplied, so did the risk to his powerful co-conspirators. If their activity was documented in court, certain government agencies would be forced to act. Epstein had to be eliminated.

On August 3, 2019, I posted a video on YouTube: Has Bill Clinton Scheduled Jeffrey Epstein For Prison Death To Cover Up Lolita Scandal? I stated that Epstein would be killed and that it would probably be made to look like a suicide. On August 10, 2019, the news reported that he had died.

Just ten days before his death, on July 23, an incident happened that suggested his time was limited: in the Metropolitan Correctional Center, he was found unconscious with injuries to his neck. He had been assigned a cellmate called Nicholas Tartaglione, a musclebound ex-cop turned gangster accused of killing four men in his brother's bar after a drug deal soured. Facing the death penalty, Tartaglione had access to the outside world through an illegal cell phone. Under normal circumstances, sex offenders would never be housed with murderers and gangsters, because the convict code dictates that they should be killed on sight (KOS). Epstein complained to one of his lawyers that he had been attacked by Tartaglione. Naturally, when questioned by investigators, his cellmate denied having had anything to do with the injuries.

Whatever had prevented the first attempt on his life, Epstein was placed on suicide watch. On July 29, he was removed from suicide watch and put in a special housing unit with another cellmate. Every thirty minutes, a guard was supposed to check on him. The night before his murder, August 9, his cellmate was conveniently removed. The cameras monitoring the area malfunctioned and the guards on duty had supposedly fallen asleep or been so engrossed in online shopping that they were oblivious to the man dying a short distance from the guard station. The two guards, Tova Noel, thirty-one, and Michael Thomas, forty-one, would later be charged with falsifying records and conspiracy because for eight hours – from 10.30 p.m. on August 9 to 6.30 a.m. on August 10 – they had not gone to his cell door.

The indictment against the guards stated: They sat at their desks, browsed online and moved about the common area for a substantial portion of their shift instead of completing the required checks. Noel and Thomas allegedly appeared to be asleep at their desks for about two hours. Noel used her computer to search for furniture sales and benefit websites during her shift. Thomas allegedly searched online for motorcycle sales and sports news briefly at 1 a.m., 4 a.m. and 6 a.m. The pair were only 15 feet away from Epstein when he died. They found him dead when they went to serve him breakfast at 6.30 a.m. The last time they had checked on him was at 10.30 p.m. the night before.

Noel allegedly told a supervisor: "We did not complete the 3 a.m. and 5 a.m. rounds."

Thomas added "We messed up" and "I messed up, she's not to blame, we didn't do any rounds."

According to Nick Tartaglione's lawyer, "Nobody heard anything. It was a silent act."

The autopsy revealed that various neck bones had been fractured, including the hyoid, which most medical experts commenting on the case have stated is more common in homicide than suicide. Life is cheap in prison. A small amount of heroin is enough to get somebody killed. To get away with a professional hit, the victim would have to die in a way that would look like suicide.

Out of the methods that prisoners use to commit suicide or to die accidentally, a professional would probably go with hanging or a hotshot. Guards who have killed prisoners have been known to rope somebody up. Gang members often employ the hotshot because a prisoner found overdosed on heroin appears to be just another dead addict, which requires no further investigation.

In 2008, teenager Ronnie White, who was charged with killing a cop, was found dead in a Washington jail. After the medical examiner found a broken hyoid, the cause of death was changed from suicide to homicide. The examiners suspected that he had been strangled with a sheet, towel or the crux of an elbow. The guard who had moved his body was found guilty of obstruction, but no charges were filed for his murder. In 2013, a federal judge declared the cause of death a mystery.

One of the lawyers representing victims of Epstein, Spencer Kuvin, spoke to a staff member at the jail and told the media:

"I received a call from a supervisor at the MCC, which is the jail that Mr Epstein was held in. The first words out of his mouth to be honest were: 'Don't believe what you are hearing in regards to Epstein's death.' I had a lengthy conversation with him about the issue of security within MCC and he gave me a fairly detailed description of the interior of the jail, which led me to believe that he was credible. He told me how the SHU (Special Housing Unit) where Mr Epstein was kept was basically designed to be a jail within the jail. And then there was a separate, even more secure unit, inside the SHU, where the highest value targets were kept. He said every square inch of that place is covered by cameras. It was designed that way because of super-high-value targets that are kept there such as terrorists, drug dealers and other extremely high-value targets or suspects like Mr Epstein.

"If reports that there is no CCTV are true, it would mean that they'd either shut the cameras off or they were not functioning in some way. He says there's no way that they would not have been able to see what was going on. What my source found very suspicious was that his cellmate was pulled the day before. The purpose of a cellmate for someone who either was on suicide watch or is on suicide watch is to notify guards if something is happening. So, the fact that they pulled the cellmate is not only one level above negligent, it also appears intentional. Really, he should have been on suicide watch. Not only was he not on suicide watch, they pulled the one person that could have notified guards if something untoward was about to occur. It was almost as though they did it so that no one could see what was going to happen the following day.

"I met [Epstein] on three separate occasions and he never seemed to me to be a remorseful individual. He always seemed highly intelligent, arrogant, self-assured, confident; never thought he did anything wrong, even in light of all the evidence against him. He basically just blamed the victims and had an incredible ego about himself, and someone with that type of ego just never struck me as someone that could possibly commit suicide. I didn't think he was that brave to be perfectly honest. He always hid behind lawyers upon lawyers upon lawyers in his civil and criminal cases. I mean, you can't even count the number of people he hired to protect him from any allegations, both civil and criminal. This type of an act requires a certain amount of resolve, and he just never struck me as someone that could do that.

"I think the most likely scenario if it's not suicide is that somebody on the inside of the prison was paid essentially to make it look like a suicide, and the guards were paid to disappear and not be there, and his cellmate was taken away on Friday, so there'd be no witness. So, someone went in there in the early morning hours, tied him around the neck with a bed sheet, tied the bed sheet to the bed and pushed him down effectively and held him down until he choked to death.

"For something like this, you would expect to see some type of bruising or whatever around his shoulders if he was being held down against his will. So that would be the most likely scenario to make it appear as though he had done the act himself. With the fracture of the bone in his neck it suggests a high amount of force pushing down on him. I think the most likely scenario if it is not suicide is that there were too many people that were afraid that he would talk about what he may have done with them and others. They just paid off someone to go into the jail and take care of him."

Even with the most baffling assassinations, those responsible sometimes reveal themselves during the cover-up. The person assigned to investigate Epstein's death was Attorney General William Barr, whose headmaster father had hired Epstein in 1974 to teach teenagers mathematics and physics at the exclusive Dalton School on the Upper East Side of Manhattan. From 1973 to 1977, Barr worked for the CIA, starting out as an analyst and then becoming the assistant legislative counsel. From 1991 to 1993, he was the Attorney General for George H. W. Bush. According to the journalist Whitney Webb, while Barr was in the CIA's Office of Legislative Counsel, he stonewalled the Church and Pike committees, which were investigating the wrongdoing of the CIA, including sexual blackmail operations carried out in the 1970s. While working for the Bush administration, he pardoned several controversial Iran-Contra figures, including people linked to sexual blackmail operations involving children. Barr worked for Kirkland & Ellis, a law firm that defended Epstein. Stating that he didn't specifically work on the Epstein case, Barr refused to recuse himself from the investigation. His history of covering things up for the CIA suggests that the agency may have been used to coordinate the assassination.

If those responsible for Epstein's death were able to order an intelligence agency to perform the hit, then the suspect list must be comprised of people far more powerful and wealthier than the deceased. The next question that must be asked is: who had the most to gain from silencing Epstein? Which could be rephrased: who had the most to lose if Epstein remained alive?

CHAPTER 2
PRINCE ANDREW

Survivors of Epstein's sexual abuse were incensed by his first lenient sentence and his sweetheart deal, which included immunity from prosecution for his co-conspirators. By agreeing to a conviction for procuring a prostitute under the age of eighteen, Epstein had legalistically converted vulnerable teenagers into sex workers. In 2015, Virginia Roberts fought back against the sweetheart deal by filing a civil lawsuit stating that Epstein and Maxwell had sexually abused her and groomed her into becoming a sex slave to serve elites including Prince Andrew and Alan Dershowitz. Everyone she accused denied her claims and counter-suits were filed. Dershowitz called his accusers liars and prostitutes. An out-of-court settlement was reached with Epstein.

The court document filed in 2015 by Virginia Roberts stated:

Epstein made me have sex with Prince Andrew several times. Prince Andrew, Maxwell and I are shown in the photograph below. I had sex with him three times, including one orgy. I knew he was a member of the British Royal Family, but I just called him Andy.

One day when I was in London (specifically in a townhouse that is under Maxwell's name), I got news from Maxwell that I would be meeting a prince. Later that day, Epstein told me I was meeting a "major prince". Epstein told me "to exceed" everything I had been taught. He emphasized that whatever Prince Andrew wanted, I was to make sure he got.

Eventually, Prince Andrew arrived, along with his security guards. The guards then went out of the house and stayed out front in their car. It was just Epstein, Maxwell and me inside alone with Andy. I was introduced to the prince, and we kissed formally, cheek to cheek.

There was a lot of legal discussion about Andy and his ex-wife ("Fergie"). Then the discussion turned to me. Maxwell said: "Guess how old she is?" Prince Andrew guessed seventeen.

Then we all went to a Chinese restaurant for dinner and then to Club Tramp, a fancy "members only" nightclub in central London. Andy arranged for alcohol to be provided to me at the club. Eventually, we left. I rode with Epstein and Maxwell back to the townhouse.

On the way there, Epstein and Maxwell informed me that the prince wanted to see "more of me" that night. Andy travelled in a separate car with his guards.

We all arrived back at the townhouse and went upstairs. Epstein took a picture of me and Andy with my own camera. The picture above is that picture, which has been widely circulated on the Internet. Andy has his left arm around my waist and is smiling. The picture was developed on March 13, 2001, and was taken sometime shortly before I had it developed. I was seventeen years old at the time.

I wanted a picture with the prince because I was keeping in contact with my family. I had told my mom and my grandma that I was meeting Prince Andrew and that I'd take a picture for them. They told me to "be careful".

After the picture, Epstein and Maxwell kissed me and said to "have fun". They left Andy and me alone upstairs. We went to the bathroom and bedroom, which were just steps away from where the picture was taken. We engaged in sexual activities there. Afterwards, Andy left quickly with his security.

I chatted with Epstein about this the next day. I told him: "It went great." Epstein said something to the effect of: "You did well. The prince had fun." I felt like I was being graded. It was horrible to have to recount all these events and have to try to meet all these needs and wants. I told Epstein about Andy's sexual interest in feet. Epstein thought it was very funny. Epstein appeared to be collecting private information about Andy.

When I got back from my trip, Epstein paid me more than he had paid me to be with anyone else – approximately $15,000. That money was for what I had done and to keep my mouth shut about "working" with the prince.

The second time I had sex with Prince Andrew was in Epstein's New York mansion in spring 2001. I was seventeen at the time. Epstein called me down to his office. When I got there, Epstein was there, along with Maxwell, Johanna Sjoberg and Andy. I was very surprised to see him again. Epstein and Maxwell were making lewd jokes about "Randy Andy".

I had the impression that Andy had come there to see Epstein and to have sex with me. There was no other apparent purpose for Andy to be there. I was told to go upstairs with Andy and to go to the room I thought of as the "dungeon" (the massage room, but it is really scary-looking). I had sex with Andy there. I was only paid $400 from Epstein for servicing Andy that time.

The third time I had sex with Andy was in an orgy on Epstein's private island in the US Virgin Islands. I was around eighteen at the time. Epstein, Andy, approximately eight other young girls and I had sex together. The other girls all seemed and appeared to be under the age of eighteen and didn't really speak English. Epstein laughed about the fact they couldn't really communicate, saying that they are the "easiest" girls to get along with. My assumption was that Jean-Luc Brunel got the girls from Eastern Europe (as he procured many young foreign girls for Epstein). They were young and European-looking and -sounding.

Afterwards, we all had dinner by the cabanas. The other girls were chatting away among themselves, and Epstein and the prince chatted together. I felt disgusted and went quickly to my own cabana that night and went to sleep. Prince Andrew must have flown out early the next morning, as I did not see him when I got up.

I have seen Buckingham Palace's recent "emphatic" denial that Prince Andrew had sexual contact with me. That denial is false and hurtful to me. I did have sexual contact with him as I have described here – under oath. Given what he knows and has seen, I was hoping that he would simply voluntarily tell the truth about everything. I hope my attorneys can interview Prince Andrew under oath about the contacts and that he will tell the truth.

In late 2019, news headlines about Prince Andrew, Epstein and Virginia Roberts went parabolic in the UK. Hoping to dodge the storm, Prince Andrew fled to Spain with his "partner in crime" for many years, Fergie. While they sunbathed in Málaga, the *Daily Mail* published a video of Andrew peeping out of Epstein's front door and waving at a young woman departing from the nine-storey, 21,000 square foot mansion. The video also showed Epstein leaving the house in the company of a shivering young blonde. The footage was dated December 6, 2010, when Prince Andrew was supposed to be operating as the UK's Special Representative for International Trade.

After questioning a source close to the Royal Family, I was told that Andrew had been advised to drop Epstein after his first conviction, but that he had refused to listen. Supposedly, there had been a heated discussion, but he had continued his relationship with the paedophile anyway.

The source claimed that in late 2019, the Queen had been at Balmoral Castle in Scotland, where she spends the summer. Andrew and Fergie had arrived, but with Prince Philip – who dislikes Fergie – scheduled to arrive, the Duchess of York was informed that she had to leave. As a show of good faith, the Queen made a public appearance with Andrew at a church. Then the Epstein story heated up and Prince Philip's arrival was imminent, so Andrew and Fergie flew to a £38-million mansion in Málaga. They got a flight from Farnborough Airport, which is thirty minutes from where I live. A source at the airport disclosed that Fergie and Andrew refused to speak to anybody and were spirited away by a small army of bodyguards and secret service guys.

The royal PR machine stated, "It is emphatically denied that the Duke of York had any form of sexual contact or relationship with Virginia Roberts. Any claim to the contrary is false and without foundation," and added that, "Any suggestion of impropriety with underage minors is categorically untrue." Andrew and Fergie fled in a hurry, hoping that the Epstein news would settle down while they enjoyed the Spanish sunshine.

The *Daily Mail* quoted a source with inside knowledge of Andrew's visit to Manhattan: "The prince looked entirely at ease in Epstein's house. There were girls coming and going. One, who came out of the house with Epstein about an hour before Prince Andrew said goodbye to the brunette, was tiny and shivering. It was a particularly cold New York December day. What I remember most is the constant procession of girls and women going to and from the house. It was chilling to see. Everyone knew by that point that Epstein was a convicted paedophile, yet he was flaunting his lifestyle in plain sight.

"When the prince came to the door I was stunned. He looked totally at ease. He said a few words to the girl, who was very pretty, and then she walked off down the street in the direction of Central Park. If I hadn't known it was Prince Andrew, I would have thought he owned the place. He looked so comfortable and relaxed as he stood there at the door. He didn't appear to have a concern in the world as he smiled and waved goodbye to the girl. It was only as the girl walked off that he glanced around the door frame, almost as if to check no one was watching."

According to *Vanity Fair* writer Vicky Ward, the interior of the mansion was weird and twisted. The entry foyer where Prince Andrew had stood was decorated with rows of individually framed artificial eyeballs. Video footage showed Epstein's initials on the wall next to the front door. Outside, he had installed a heating system below the pavement to melt the snow. On the wall was a portrait of Bill Clinton in red heels and the semen-stained blue dress worn by Monica Lewinsky on the day of the world-famous blowjob, which Bill had initially denied, but had then appeared repentant on TV and confessed – which distracted the media from the true story of the cocaine that had been smuggled into Arkansas by the CIA under George H. W. Bush and Oliver North, an operation that Arkansas Governor Bill Clinton had protected with his state police force (documented in my book, *American Made*).

There was a huge painting of Epstein as a convict surrounded by razor wire, by a gun tower with armed guards, which he said was "to remind me that I could go back to prison at any time". Hanging from a chandelier was a human-size female doll. A bathroom had prosthetic breasts on its wall, which according to a survivor, enabled Epstein to "play with the nipples as he took a bath". He had a giant stuffed tiger and at the bottom of the main staircase, a chessboard with human-size pieces modelled on his female staff. He had a twice-life-size statue of a naked African warrior and a leather room. He advertised his closeness to his elite friends through numerous photos of him posing with people such as Bill and Hillary Clinton, Woody Allen and Saudi Arabia's crown prince, Mohammed bin Salman.

How did Prince Andrew miss the procession of girls? Police officers who investigated the case claimed that anyone who had attended Epstein's properties knew full well that he was abusing teenagers. Some of their photos were on the walls. During an FBI raid, thousands of indecent images of teenage girls were found on hard drives.

The video published by the media showed Epstein emerging from his mansion at 3.35 p.m., wearing a thick white fur-lined winter coat, followed by a girl dressed in a gray top carrying his glasses. Barely as tall as Epstein's shoulders, she appears cold and trembling, while walking him to his Bentley. While he gets into the back of the vehicle, she stands on the street, with an obedient expression as if receiving instructions. Passers-by glance at them. After two minutes, she jogs back to the house. Trembling, she stands on the step and presses the doorbell. The door is opened by a professional-looking brunette resembling Sarah Kellen, Epstein's former assistant who several survivors have alleged to be a co-conspirator. Operating as Maxwell's lieutenant, Kellen allegedly had a list of girls whom she contacted to arrange meetings with Epstein. When questioned in court, she exercised her right to remain silent. Now married to US race car driver, Brian Vickers, Kellen has not publicly commented on the case.

In the video at 4.30 p.m., the door opens and a brunette emerges. She stops to gaze back at Prince Andrew at the door. They chat for a few seconds before she walks away, leaving Andrew watching the street before closing the door. She was later identified as Katherine Keating, the daughter of Paul Keating, a former Australian prime minister, who violated protocol by putting his arm around the Queen in 1992, earning him the nickname "Lizard of Oz". At the time of the video, Katherine was in her late twenties.

In 2013, at a Dom Pérignon-sponsored event, Katherine was photographed with Ghislaine Maxwell at her home for the launch of a social network called Ideapod, a publishing and education platform. Also in the photo were the prime minister of Iceland, Ólafur Ragnar Grímsson, his wife and their daughter. In 2014, Katherine helped to push Maxwell's ocean-conservation agenda by interviewing Epstein's procurer for the *Huffington Post*. In 2015, at the opening of the Whitney Museum of American Art, Katherine was photographed with Misha Nonoo, the British-Iraqi fashion designer who it is believed played a role as a matchmaker for Prince Harry and Meghan Markle. At Nonoo's fall 2014 New York Fashion Week show, Katherine was photographed with Princess Eugenie.

CHAPTER 3
METHODS OF SUICIDING

Life is cheap in prison. Killing a high-profile sex offender like Epstein is a means to advance convict status. Having spent almost six years in the Arizona state prison system for Ecstasy trafficking, I met people prepared to kill for as little as $50 worth of heroin. With most of the inmate population addicted to hard drugs, there are always desperate people willing to do anything to get their next fix.

Guards have the ability and the knowledge to kill prisoners and to get away with it. They are ideally placed to frustrate investigations and to coordinate cover-ups. Being on the front line for little pay, some guards succumb to the temptation to supplement their incomes by facilitating or participating in hits. In Mexico and Colombia, the cartels have so much money that they often pay to have prisoners eliminated. Sometimes, the guards perform the hits directly; other times, the guards "fall asleep" or move a prisoner to an area where enemies are waiting.

Epstein was in the federal, not the state, prison system. The feds have got more money and their prisoners are supposed to be better protected. To suicide someone in any prison system in America, it's got to look like an actual suicide. Epstein's assassins must have considered the various ways prisoners commit suicide and mimicked one of those ways. In the Arizona system, I became aware of six methods of prisoner suicide, including hanging.

New prison arrivals are given certain items known as property, including a towel, clothes, a skinny mattress, a sheet and maybe a blanket. Ripped sheets can be converted into rope. Cell ceilings have no fixtures to hang anything from. The highest point to attach a rope would be the top bunk. The cells I experienced were originally designed for one person, but over the years, additional bunks were added until there was a maximum of three bunks. If the rope is attached to the top bunk, depending upon the height of the prisoner, his feet may still be on the floor. You may be wondering: how can someone hang himself from a bunk if there's not enough room and his feet are touching the ground?

For expertise on this subject, I interviewed Neil Samworth, who for eleven years worked at HMP Manchester and published a book called *Strangeways: A Prison Officer's Story*. He gave a horrific account of finding the corpse of a prisoner who had hung himself, but his feet weren't off the ground. The deceased had tied the rope and leaned forward. They found the corpse at an angle and determined that the force on his neck had choked him to death.

Among the various methods of hanging, some prisoners put the rope down the toilet, flush it until it is anchored, and then use the leverage to lean away from it. I interviewed Michael Maisey, who wrote the book *Young Offender: My Life from Armed Robber to Local Hero*. Michael described a hanging suicide method whereby the prisoner rolls sideways off his bunk and by the time he hits the floor, his neck has already snapped.

Murder in prison can easily be disguised as a suicide.

After my documentary was broadcast on the National Geographic Channel as an episode of *Locked Up Abroad* (called *Banged Up Abroad* in the UK) titled "Raving Arizona", I was contacted by a viewer:

Dear Shaun, I just watched your story on 4/23/13 … a little about me, I have four brothers that did time. My older brother's name is James T Larkin, the cops killed him, they said he hung himself with a pair of blue jeans that was brand new. It happened at the 26th police district in Philadelphia PA, a friend of his was in the jail when they brought him in, he was lifeless. Nothing was done to the cop that killed him, that was in 1976. My other brother

Michael Kevin Larkin hung himself in great ford prison in Penn, feeling a little down, talk later.

The hot-shot method is favoured by gangs such as the Aryan Brotherhood. In Arizona state prison, the majority are injecting drugs, mostly heroin and crystal meth. The widespread drug usage is no secret to the guards, who use the threat of a urine test to try to keep the prisoners from misbehaving. If a corpse is found with a needle at the scene, there is an immediate assumption that the deceased has overdosed. The paperwork will document the death as an accident or maybe even a suicide. Such a conclusion minimises the amount of paperwork to be filed by the staff versus the work required if there were a murder investigation, so the staff members are incentivised to not explore any options other than suicide.

I interviewed ex-cop Neil Woods, author of *Drug Wars: The Terrifying Inside Story of Britain's Drug Trade*. Neil described how drug gangs in Brighton terrorised the lowest level street people by inflicting hot shots on any they suspected of becoming police informants. This caused a record amount of accidental overdoses to be reported. Emergency responders finding a needle and drugs at the scene naturally assumed that the deaths were accidental or maybe suicides. The anomaly was only discovered by comparing the numbers over time and in other cities.

Another method of suicide in prison is by jumping from a height. Prisoners are often housed in tiers on multiple storeys. When they emerge from their cells, there are upper-tier railings blocking a steep drop into the day room. This particularly brutal method doesn't always end in death. Some drop, hit a table or the floor, and remain alive with a broken leg or a snapped spine.

There is a method called suicide by cop or suicide by guard. Prior to coming to Arizona prison, a friend I made in prison became depressed after his girlfriend died from lung cancer. He decided to commit suicide by cop. Attempting to rob his own bank, he waited in line, went to a familiar teller, extracted a note that said he had a gun and demanded cash. Outside, he waited for the police to arrive so that he could go down in a hail of bullets. Thirty minutes later, they calmly showed up and asked him why he had stolen less money than his own balance at that bank. After getting arrested, he was told that the only way they might have shot him dead were if he had a hostage.

One day, I was in my cell reading on my bunk when a prisoner with a neckerchief tied around his face dashed past, wielding a lengthy home-made knife. After running around yelling, the guards coaxed him to a fence. On the other side of the fence, a SWAT team arrived with live ammunition. He was told to drop the shank. After refusing, he was told they were going to count down from ten to zero, and if he had not dropped the shank by zero, they were going to shoot him dead. Observing from my cell with my heart rate elevated, I prayed he would drop the weapon, which he did during the countdown.

Overdosing on pills is another method. The prison system is one of the biggest customers for the pharmaceutical companies. Nurses perform pill calls throughout the day. Many of the prisoners pretend to swallow the pills, while hiding them in their mouths, so that they can be illegally traded. Suicidal prisoners stockpile the pills until they think they have enough to kill themselves.

The next method is wrist-slashing. Every thirty minutes or so, a guard does a security walk. He (the guards are mostly male) comes into the building and walks around. If the inmates are locked down, he looks into each cell to ensure they are still alive. Due to the time it takes to bleed out, a suicidal prisoner would have to do it immediately after a guard does a security walk.

In my second year in the Maricopa County jail, when the prosecutor said that I was facing a maximum 200-year sentence, I became suicidal. With cockroaches crawling over my skin at night, I couldn't sleep, a condition aggravated by the itchiness from heat-induced skin infections and bedsores. After the prosecutor stopped my girlfriend from visiting the jail, I became depressed and planned to slash my wrists. Looking at the photos of my mum, girlfriend and sister prevented me from attempting suicide. I couldn't bear the thought of my mum getting a call saying that her son had killed himself in a foreign jail. Cutting and wrist slashing happen more in prison than in the outside world. Some inmates even eat razorblades or employ methods such as drinking bleach.

Before my release from prison in December of 2007, I sometimes sat in the chow hall with Grim, a baldheaded giant with tattoos on his skull. After my release, he and a group of accomplices tried to kill someone over a drug debt. They poisoned his hooch, but he didn't die. They injected him with a hot shot, but he didn't die. They ended up successfully hanging him in his cell from the top bunk. The guards grew suspicious and reviewed the security camera footage, which showed the co-conspirators leaving the cell with the deceased's property: TV, clothes, etc.

After my release, a friend who was serving multiple life sentences became so sick from cancer that he wanted to die. He injected a hot shot, but because he had been on opiates for so long, his tolerance was so high that he didn't die.

In the context of my experience, the official version of Epstein's death seems farcical. Guards are constantly doing headcounts and security checks. As Epstein was so high profile, the staff should have been extra vigilant and aware that their careers were on the line if something were to happen during their shift. For them to do the opposite – to fall asleep and do online shopping and leave Epstein unchecked for hours – suggests that they were ordered or compensated in some way.

Most murderers follow certain rules, including: no witnesses, no crime. With Epstein's cellmate removed, the guards conveniently oblivious, and the security cameras malfunctioning, conditions were perfect for homicide. When a government agency such as the CIA commits a murder, it will often employ the rule of investigating itself. With a desired outcome in mind, the authorities will put someone in charge of the investigation who will announce whatever they want the public to hear. "We will get to the bottom of what happened, and there will be accountability," Attorney General William Barr said.

A third rule is to have fall guys: in Epstein's case, the guards. Blame was immediately apportioned to them for not performing a check on Epstein every thirty minutes and for making false entries in the logbook. According to a jail employee, one of the sleepy guards was a former correctional officer whose new position did not include guarding inmates. He had volunteered to resume his former job for overtime pay. The second sleepy guard had been assigned to Epstein's wing because the MCC was short-staffed. The Justice Department announced that the MCC's warden, Lamine N'Diaye, would be transferred to a Bureau of Prisons office in Philadelphia while the FBI and the Justice Department's inspector general conducted inquiries.

Prison staff union leaders criticized Bill Barr's decision to allow the MCC's boss to keep working while two staff members were put on leave. "It makes me angry that they reassigned the warden," said Jose Rojas, a prison employees' union official and a teacher at the Coleman prison complex in Sumterville, Florida. "They didn't put him on administrative leave like the others. The warden made the call to take Epstein off suicide watch and to remove his cellmate. That is egregious." Of course, the fall guys were sacrificed, while the warden was allowed to remain to keep the cover-up going and to tie up any loose ends.

A fourth rule is to have the mainstream media repeatedly publish a false narrative: "Prison staff discovered Epstein dead in his cell at Metropolitan Correctional Center at 6.30 a.m. on Saturday, an official said." "He had apparently hanged himself with a bed sheet, likely fastening the sheet to a top bunk and pitching himself forward, law enforcement and prison officials said." The suicide fit a pattern of behavior already reported by the media, who had claimed that the previous injuries Epstein had sustained had arisen from a failed suicide attempt – a version of events disputed by Epstein's lawyers.

In Epstein's case, all the rules were followed, implying that powerful people had wanted him dead. Who were they and what had the paedophile done to get on the wrong side of them? To begin answering those questions, we need to look at Epstein's past.

CHAPTER 4
WHO WAS JEFFREY EPSTEIN?

Journalist Edward Jay Epstein described the first time he saw beneath the veneer of Jeffrey Epstein. The two had met at a Halloween party in New York in 1987. Finding out that Edward Epstein (no relation) was flying to Spain the following week, Epstein offered to upgrade his ticket to first class. As instructed, Edward dropped his luggage off at Epstein's one-bedroom apartment on East 66th Street and his flight was duly upgraded. Epstein aided Edward with similar upgrades until a year later when, trying to board an All Nippon Airways flight, Edward was told his ticket was not valid and he was moved unceremoniously to economy. Edward later found out from a friend of Epstein's that the high-flying financier had obtained a bunch of first-class stickers from a friend, which he merely stuck onto the luggage to fool the check-in attendants. The scam apparently only worked one in three times and Edward had finally got unlucky.

It's a typical Epstein story and one that sums up the contradictions in his character. Described by some as generous to a fault, to others he was a cheapskate and a fraud. Charming, sweet, funny and kind to some; to others he was dark, calculating and ruthless – a cruel trickster with no emotions or empathy. Many who met him were bowled over by the brilliance of his mind, while others saw only a fake. Surrounded by every kind of opulence, he was nearly always seen in clothes so casual that they bordered on scruffy. Touted by many as a financial genius, others questioned where all his clients were.

Whatever the true character behind his ever-changing façade, there was no arguing about Epstein's wealth and influence. Private jets and helicopters – including a converted commercial Boeing

727 – properties that included the largest private residence in Manhattan, a 10,000-acre ranch in New Mexico, and his own private island in the Caribbean, and friends like Bill Clinton and Prince Andrew – somewhere along the line this supposed Wall Street whizz-kid had garnered some serious power.

But when? And how?

There was certainly nothing in his background or childhood that hinted at the person Epstein would become. Born on January 20, 1953 in Sea Gate, a gated community on Brooklyn's Coney Island, Jeffrey Epstein was the first son of distinctly lower middle-class parents. His mother, Pauline, was a school assistant and his father, Seymour, a gardener for the New York City Department of Parks and Recreation. Both parents were the children of Jewish immigrants from Europe who, according to the book, *Epstein: Dead Men Tell No Tales*, had lost several family members in the Holocaust.

Epstein's brother, Mark, was born a year later and within four years the two were attending a local public school. Epstein began studying the piano at the age of five and showed an aptitude for learning with a specific talent for Mathematics, joining the Mathematics team in Lafayette High School in Brooklyn, where he graduated in 1969. He studied Mathematics at Manhattan's Cooper Union College before dropping out in 1971, then attended New York University's Courant Institute of Mathematical Sciences before dropping out again in 1974. Epstein never earned a degree. It's somewhat of a mystery why he dropped out of both colleges, but it would be the start of a trend that would follow him his whole life. All his endeavours seemed to end with him pulling out early, being fired, leaving in disgrace or, often, with the organisation itself going down in flames. Was there already a hint of the monster he would become in those hasty college departures?

Another pattern in Epstein's tumultuous life was that each disaster ironically seemed to lead to greater opportunities, as if he were being rewarded rather than punished for his failures.

This trend also started early. After his premature departure from New York University, the qualification-less young man somehow landed a job as a Physics and Mathematics teacher at Dalton, one of Manhattan's most prestigious private schools. Journalist Edward Jay Epstein was told by a private detective from the Kroll agency, hired by a board member of Leslie Wexner's company Limited Brands to investigate Epstein, that he had faked his résumé to get the role at Dalton.

With hindsight, it's appalling to think of the paedophile monster having access to so many underage girls at Dalton. There were no formal complaints of sexual misconduct against him during his time at the school. However, some pupils reported him hanging around students socially in a manner that they thought "inappropriate", according to a *New York Times* article, with Epstein even turning up to student parties. Whether or not he was involved in sexual abuse, Epstein didn't last long at Dalton. In 1976, just two years after he had started, he was fired, his performance deemed substandard.

Again, the failure metamorphosed into an opportunity. A friend of Bear Stearns bank head, Alan Greenberg, was a parent at the school. At a parent-teacher conference, Epstein turned on the charm and the financier father was so dazzled that he recommended Epstein to Greenberg for a job. Epstein's career at Bear Stearns began later that year as a lowly junior assistant to a floor trader. However, Greenberg took Epstein under his wing, introducing him to every area of the business, and within four years he had risen to become a limited partner. Epstein quickly became a millionaire and grew a network of wealthy and influential clients including, according to *Epstein: Dead Men Tell No Tales*, Edgar Bronfman, president of Seagram and a friend and associate of Leslie Wexner, a man who would become intimately linked with Epstein's future exploits.

But in the meantime, the familiar pattern was re-emerging. In 1981, Epstein was fined for lending money to a friend and using his insider knowledge to guide him in how to invest it.

Soon afterwards, a Securities and Exchange Commission (SEC) investigation into Epstein's client, Bronfman, led to Epstein leaving the bank under a cloud of suspicion. According to Epstein, he quit, but others say he was fired.

The next period of his life is one of the most clouded and mysterious. During much of the Eighties, he travelled widely and often lived outside the US, mostly in Europe. He flew on an Austrian passport with a fake name that listed him as living in Saudi Arabia. He had set up his own consulting firm, Intercontinental Assets Group (IAG), which operated out of a building on East 66th Street in Manhattan. Claiming he was a kind of financial bounty hunter who recovered stolen money for clients, he also during this period said that he worked for the CIA, which he later denied.

He was certainly dealing with some unusual characters. One of his clients was Adnan Khashoggi, the Saudi international arms dealer who had been heavily involved in the Iran-Contra scandal where US weapons sales to Iran were used to fund and import cocaine from the Contra rebels in Nicaragua. Steven Hoffenberg, who would employ Epstein later in the Eighties, said Epstein was working for Sir Douglas Leese, a shadowy British arms dealer who was in part responsible for British arms deals with Saudi Arabia. Hoffenberg claims that most of Epstein's work at the time was illegal, involving money laundering, spying and illegal arms sales including that of the AWACS spy plane. One of the stories about Epstein from around this time, according to an article in the *Evening Standard*, was that he turned up at Leese's house carrying a New York-police-issue pump action riot gun. "God knows how he got it into the country," a friend commented, according to the report.

It was also during this period that ex-Israeli intelligence agent, Ari Ben-Menashe, claims Epstein first met Robert Maxwell, the millionaire media mogul. Aside from his above-board enterprises, Maxwell was operating for Israeli Intelligence, selling arms, laundering money and spying on foreign governments. Ben-Menashe says Maxwell recruited Epstein for Israeli intelligence and this would fit in with his many covert movements and dealings at the time. It has been speculated that much of Epstein's funds came directly from Maxwell and it may be that Maxwell was eying him up as a kind of successor within the intelligence world, especially as, according to Menashe, Epstein had already begun a relationship with his daughter Ghislaine (official accounts are that Epstein and Ghislaine Maxwell didn't meet until the early Nineties, when the heiress moved to New York, but Ben-Menashe claims they were already romantically involved during the late Eighties).

Another key figure Epstein met during this time was billionaire businessman, Leslie Wexner, the founder and CEO of Limited Brands, a fashion conglomerate that included Victoria's Secret and Bath & Body Works. But according to independent journalist, Whitney Webb, Wexner also had ties to organised crime via the Mega Group, a consortium of Jewish billionaires which he had co-founded with Edgar Bronfman who, as we saw earlier, was already linked to Epstein and some dodgy dealings at Bear Stearns.

According to Webb, Wexner and Epstein were involved in the relocation of cargo firm Southern Air Transport (SAT) from Florida to Ohio, Wexner's home state, where he could use it to shift goods to and from the Far East. SAT had been a CIA front company that had transported arms, money and drugs in the Iran-Contra affair, so Wexner and Epstein's interest in the air company could point to the CIA links that Epstein boasted about. Webb also points out that many of the individuals Epstein was working with had links to the Bank of Credit and Commerce International (BCCI). Otherwise known as the Bank of Crooks and Criminals International, BCCI was also reputed to have CIA and Mossad links, and to be involved in money laundering, arms dealing and even child trafficking.

During this time, there seems to be no evidence of paedophilia or child abuse. Epstein had a string of girlfriends and affairs, but they were all with adult women. He referred to one "illicit affair" with a secretary at Bear Stearns in his testimony to the SEC. Longer-term relationships came with Paula Heil Fisher, another Bear Stearns colleague, and Eva Andersson (later Andersson-Dubin), a doctor and one-time Miss Sweden. Neither has ever mentioned anything wayward about Epstein's sexuality, but there is a hint of something untoward that came from the relationship with Andersson-Dubin. According to several reports in 2019, Epstein was said to have had a very close relationship with Eva Andersson-Dubin's daughter, Celina, and although there have been no allegations of sexual improprieties, he was reported to have declared his desire to marry the teenager. It is interesting to note that Eva Andersson-Dubin's husband, hedge fund billionaire Glenn Dubin, is one of the men Epstein victim Virginia Giuffre claims she was forced to have sex with.

Whatever activities Epstein was involved in throughout the Eighties, his rise to prominence continued. In 1987, he was hired by Steven Hoffenberg, founder and CEO of Towers Financial, a corporate debt collection agency. Hoffenberg says Epstein was recommended to him by British arms dealer Douglas Leese. Hoffenberg agreed to meet him and was immediately impressed by Epstein's ability to understand complex financial concepts, his charm, his knack for salesmanship and his roguery. Hoffenberg went so far as to call Epstein a "mastermind in criminality" and a "master manipulator", according to an interview with the authors of *Epstein: Dead Men Tell No Tales*. He also said that despite Epstein's many unusual dealings throughout the Eighties, the international player was stone broke, intimating that – once again – Epstein had gotten into undisclosed trouble in Europe. One story tells how at the time, Epstein was living rent-free in one of the East 66th Street apartments while holding parties on the roof, so that guests would assume that he owned the penthouse suite.

Despite, or perhaps because of, Epstein's criminal talents, Hoffenberg decided to hire him, paying him $25,000 a month and setting him up in offices in the historic Villard Houses on Manhattan's Madison Avenue. At first, Epstein and Hoffenberg attempted to use Towers Financial as a corporate raiding vessel, but they were completely unsuccessful, failing in attempts to take over Pan American Airways in 1987 and Emery Air Freight Corporation in 1988. They then switched efforts to less savoury enterprises, raising money from investors to pay off other investors in a corporate scam that has been labelled one of the biggest Ponzi schemes in American history, losing investors over $450 million.

Epstein left Towers Financial in 1989, but in 1993, the firm was investigated for corruption. Hoffenberg was found guilty and sentenced to twenty years in jail with a $1 million fine and $463 million in restitution. Epstein, however, who was deeply bound up in the fraud according to Hoffenberg, walked away scot-free. According to Hoffenberg, the trustee in charge of the case, Alan Cohen, hired lawyers Indyke and Kahn to investigate Epstein's role in the affair. This is remarkable because both Indyke and Kahn were long-term friends of Epstein. Indeed, the lawyer and accountant became joint executors of Epstein's estate after his death, so perhaps it is no wonder that he escaped without charges. Even better (for Epstein), Hoffenberg claimed in an interview with the authors of *Epstein: Dead Men Tell No Tales*, Epstein was able to keep the money he had illegally earned from the Ponzi scheme and used it to set up his companies J Epstein and Company and Intercontinental Assets Group.

Leaving the ashes of another disaster scene smoldering behind, Epstein moved blithely on. It was now that his connection with Leslie Wexner deepened. Wexner became a client – in fact the only known client – of J Epstein & Company, a financial management firm that boasted of only taking on billion-dollar customers. Epstein reportedly tidied up Wexner's fortunes, saving him a lot of money. But the relationship went much deeper. In 1991, Wexner granted Epstein full power of attorney over his affairs. If this wasn't enough, the billionaire purchased the Herbert N. Straus mansion on 71st Street in Manhattan for $13.2 million, completely refurbishing it with closed circuit TV cameras in every room and a special room for monitoring them. Wexner then gifted this property to Epstein for free or – as Maria Farmer reported Epstein saying – for just one dollar.

The fact that Wexner would spend so much time and money setting up a mansion that was rigged for total monitoring adds credence to the claims that Wexner and Epstein were working together on a honeytrap scheme to blackmail prominent US and international figures for intelligence, most likely on behalf of Israel. But other testimony points to an even closer clandestine relationship. Maria Farmer claims that the two were allegedly involved in an illicit love affair. She says she was told this by Epstein's long-time personal chef, who had previously worked as a private chef for Wexner. Whatever the truth about the relationship, Wexner certainly had total trust in Epstein, not only granting him power of attorney but also making him a director of the Wexner Foundation.

Once the New York mansion had been refurbished, Epstein moved in. The sheer size and opulence of the property gives some indication of the kind of lifestyle the ex-high school teacher was now living in, as well as his quirky sense of humour. The nine-floor, forty-room ex-school building is reportedly Manhattan's largest private residence. It was described by journalist Vicky Ward, who was invited inside as part of her profile on Epstein for *Vanity Fair*, as a "private Xanadu".

The entrance hall, according to Ward, was filled with individually framed eyeballs that were imported from Britain, where they had been made for wounded soldiers. Perhaps there was a mischievous hint here at the monitoring operation going on throughout the property, a brazen yet tongue-in-cheek warning that guests were being watched. Moving on into the marble foyer, guests were overwhelmed by a twice-larger-than-life statue of a naked African warrior. Ward was served tea in the so-called "Leather Room", with leopard print chairs and a huge painting of a woman "holding an opium pipe and caressing a snarling lionskin". Ward was then taken upstairs to Epstein's office, which she described as "an enormous gallery spanning the width of the house". Strangely, the office had no computer, but did contain a huge gilded desk that once belonged to J P Morgan, a nine-foot Steinway grand piano and a Persian rug so huge that, according to Epstein, "It must have come from a mosque."

Amidst all the exotic grandeur, however, was an incongruous detail – a stuffed black poodle standing on the grand piano. It was another example of Epstein's perverse sense of humour – summed up by his characteristic stand-offish smirk – that suggested he was secretly laughing at everyone around him. One feature Ward didn't mention was a secret bathroom, described by a *New York Times* article as: "Reminiscent of James Bond movies: hidden beneath a stairway, lined with lead to provide shelter from attack and supplied with closed-circuit television screens and a telephone, both concealed in a cabinet beneath the sink."

It was around this time that Epstein *officially* met Ghislaine Maxwell, the British socialite and daughter of media mogul Robert Maxwell, who had died in suspicious circumstances aboard his superyacht, the *Lady Ghislaine*. Ghislaine Maxwell had recently moved to New York following her father's death in 1991. Epstein and Maxwell supposedly met at a New York party following her break-up with Count Gianfranco Cicogna Mozzoni of the CIGA Hotels dynasty. However, as already mentioned, there is evidence that Epstein had already met, and may even have been having an affair with Maxwell, since the mid-to-late Eighties. Indeed, the same sources claim that it was Maxwell's Mossad-connected father who introduced Epstein to the world of espionage and set him up in a role with Israeli intelligence. This leads to speculation that Epstein could have been the benefactor of some of the missing millions that Robert Maxwell stole from his Mirror Group pension funds, which would certainly explain Epstein's meteoric rise to wealth.

Whatever the case, Epstein and Maxwell were soon inseparable and holding lavish parties at the camera-riddled Manhattan mansion provided by Wexner – parties attended by large numbers of young-looking foreign models who were ostensibly recruited for Wexner's Victoria's Secret brand. It seems highly likely that Epstein and Maxwell's careers as sexual blackmailers of the rich, famous and influential had begun in earnest. One guest at Epstein's town house described it as being filled with foreign women who were dressed "rather bizarrely". And the same woman mentioned a cocktail party attended by Epstein's friend, Prince Andrew, where there were young Russian models everywhere. "Some of the guests were horrified," reported the scandalised woman.

If Epstein wanted to attract the rich and famous for his blackmail operation, he was certainly beginning to succeed. Around this time, he acquired his private jet, a refurbished Boeing 727 later referred to as the "*Lolita Express*". He had the former commercial airliner fitted with padded floors, a circular lounge area, a dining area with attached galley kitchen, and even a private bedroom with double bed and en-suite shower. It's alleged by his victims that the jet was used for secret sex parties. Flight logs show dozens of celebrity guests including Prince Andrew, Kevin Spacey, Naomi Campbell, Chris Tucker, David Blaine, Bill Gates, Ehud Barak and Tony Blair. One of the biggest and most frequent names on the Lolita flight logs was Bill Clinton.

The former US president flew on the jet no less than twenty-seven times, despite claiming he had only done four trips. Indeed, Epstein and Clinton may have had a relationship that was far closer, and longer, than the official records suggest. Epstein survivor Maria Farmer claims that Clinton was a frequent visitor to the Manhattan mansion in the early Nineties, when he was still president. Yet his visits were without a security detail and everyone was ordered to clear the house except for the chef and two Filipino maids. Epstein made substantial donations to the Clinton Foundation and even helped set up the Clinton Global Initiative. He also visited the White House during Clinton's administration on four recorded occasions. Could it be that Clinton was one of the highest-profile – perhaps *the* highest-profile – "victim" of Epstein's honeypot blackmail scheme? As a later chapter will show, there is certainly evidence to believe so.

Another presidential name on the flight logs was Donald J Trump, another high-profile friendship of Epstein's that had murky beginnings some time in the Eighties. Trump and Epstein may first have met at a boat party thrown aboard the *Lady Ghislaine* by Robert Maxwell, but like so many of Epstein's acquaintanceships, there are different stories depending on who you speak to. What is certain is that the two were neighbours in Palm Beach, Florida from 1990, when Epstein bought a property on El Brillo Way for $2.5 million. Trump owned the nearby Mar-a-Lago resort, and the two tycoons were often seen partying together.

Described by friends and acquaintances as "tight", "each other's wingmen" and (together with Trump's friend Tom Barrack) "a set of nightlife musketeers", Trump and Epstein were even captured on video at one Mar-a-Lago party where Trump is pointing out to Epstein a woman he finds attractive. In 2002, Trump was quoted in *New York Magazine* as saying of Epstein: "He's a terrific guy. It is even said that he likes beautiful women as much as I do, and many of them are on the younger side."

Later, the two fell out in 2004 over a bidding war for a Palm Beach property which Trump won. In 2008, Trump reportedly threw Epstein out of Mar-a-Lago, following his first sex abuse trial, and in 2019 Trump told the press he wasn't "a fan" of Epstein. However, whatever had come between them, Trump clearly had associated with Epstein. There is even testimony from Maria Farmer that Trump's ex-wife Ivana had accompanied Ghislaine Maxwell on expeditions around New York, when Maxwell was hunting for young girls for Epstein.

Another high-rolling friend of Epstein's was Prince Andrew, the Duke of York and second son of the Queen of England. Andrew and Epstein were apparently introduced by Ghislaine Maxwell, who had been friends with the prince since her Oxford University days. The trio began hanging around together in the late Nineties and soon appeared inseparable, turning up to parties all over the globe, including a combined royal birthday party at

Windsor Castle attended by the Queen, followed by a weekend at Sandringham, the Queen's country estate, for Ghislaine's 39th birthday. The same year, 2000, Epstein and Andrew were seen together on no fewer than five occasions, including on a luxury yacht in Thailand, where they were photographed surrounded by topless women.

But holidaying with Epstein wasn't the only thing Andrew got up to. According to Epstein survivor Virginia Giuffre, in court documents, she was paid to have sex with Andrew on three occasions when she was just seventeen, one of which was an orgy that included underage Russian girls. Andrew continued to be friends with Epstein after his 2008 conviction for sexual abuse and even attended Epstein's release-from-prison party in 2010 at his New York mansion, where the prince stayed for four days. Andrew was photographed standing in the doorway of the building, waving surreptitiously goodbye to a young-looking girl. The prince later said he had flown to New York to say goodbye to Epstein and terminate their friendship in person because he could no longer associate with the convicted felon.

It was Epstein's 2008 Florida conviction that first exposed the sordid underbelly of his glamorous lifestyle. In 2005, Palm Beach police were notified of a teenage girl who had been given $300 to strip naked and massage the fifty-two-year-old Epstein. Detective Joseph Recarey began an undercover investigation of the businessman which interviewed thirty-four victims, all of whom had similar testimonies – either they were asked to strip naked and massage Epstein while he pleasured himself or they were sexually abused or raped by him. All the girls were underage, some as young as fourteen, many having been recruited from a local public high school.

In October 2005, Recarey and his team raided Epstein's Palm Beach home, finding several computers had been removed with the leads left dangling. It seemed somehow that Epstein had been tipped off. Even so, the police had enough evidence to accuse the financier. The FBI soon joined in, launching their own investigation into Epstein, which led to his indictment in June 2007. However, Epstein's star-studded team of lawyers (which included Alan Dershowitz of O. J. Simpson trial fame) somehow cut a plea deal with State Attorney Alex Acosta, that granted Epstein immunity from all federal criminal charges, along with four named co-conspirators and any unnamed potential co-conspirators. Epstein now faced just state charges of procuring for prostitution a girl below the age of eighteen. Incredibly, the sweetheart deal had not only rescued Epstein from federal detention, it had effectively branded his schoolgirl victims prostitutes. In another incredible twist, Acosta, who would later go on to become President Trump's Labor Secretary, agreed not to let the victims know of the court's decision, even though that was illegal according to federal law.

Epstein was found guilty of one charge of soliciting an underage prostitute in 2008 and was sentenced to eighteen months in the Palm Beach County Stockade, instead of the state prison where sex offenders are usually incarcerated. He served just thirteen months of the sentence in a private wing of the prison where his cell door was unlocked. He was allowed out on day release for up to twelve hours a day, six days a week. He was driven to and from his office by his own private driver and was accompanied by Palm Beach police officers whose overtime pay was provided by Epstein himself. Overall, Epstein paid $128,000 to Palm Beach Police for their "services" during this time, which may even have included turning a blind eye while he entertained minors at the small "office" he visited for several hours a day (all records of visitors to the office have been destroyed).

How did Epstein get away with one of the most shockingly open displays of corruption in modern US legal history? The answer came straight from the mouth of Acosta himself. The State Attorney told a Trump team that was interviewing him for the position of Labor Secretary that he was told to "back off" because Epstein "belonged to intelligence" and was "above his paygrade". The answer is clear – something about Epstein's intelligence work was so explosive it could bail him out of even the most serious charges. What was it? The most obvious answer is the dirt he had on some of the most important people in the US from his sexual blackmail operation. Could this have included Bill Clinton? Clinton's wife, Hillary, was in the middle of her first presidential campaign at the time, so it would have been vital to keep any scandals involving her husband covered up, no matter what the cost. And it wasn't as if Bill Clinton didn't have previous form, or that the Clintons were averse to getting their hands dirty, as will be revealed in a later chapter.

Whatever the truth behind the sweetheart deal, it robbed dozens of victims of justice whilst, to add insult to injury, effectively branding them prostitutes and securing their tormentor from future prosecution. It must have seemed like justice would never come. In the event, it would take more than a decade.

After his release, remorse seemed far from Epstein's mind. In fact, he celebrated with a lavish party in his New York mansion. Prince Andrew, Woody Allen and former Clinton advisor George Stephanopoulos were just some of the high-profile guests. Epstein did have the good sense, however, to pivot his intelligence work away from sexual blackmail with minors to a more technologically focused operation.

In 2010, Epstein announced Mindshift, a scientific conference that would host some of the superstars of the scientific world, including Nobel Prize-winning physicist Murray Gell-Mann, AI expert Gerald Jay Sussman and Nobel Prize-winning chemical engineer Frances Arnold among many others. The conference was held on Epstein's private Caribbean island, Little St James, which he had purchased in 1998. It marked the beginning of a decade of collaboration with some of the top scientists and technology entrepreneurs from the US and around the world. Many of them attended lavish dinner parties at the Manhattan mansion, and others flew to Little St James or his 10,000-acre "Zorro" ranch in New Mexico. They included probably the most famous scientist of modern times, Stephen Hawking; Nobel Prize winner and discoverer of the quark, Murray Gell-Mann; theoretical physicist Lawrence Krauss; and cognitive psychologist Steven Pinker to name just a few. In terms of technologists and entrepreneurs, Microsoft co-founder Bill Gates, and Tesla and SpaceX founder Elon Musk, were just two of the figures on his radar.

The New Mexico ranch became something of a hub for Epstein's scientific enterprises. It had its own hospital, which was equipped to perform major surgery, and a mocked-up Wild West-style town where visitors could stay. According to a 2019 *New York Times* article, Epstein intended to use the ranch to seed the human race with his own DNA by impregnating up to twenty women at a time. Jaron Lanier, one of the creators of virtual reality and one of the scientists who Epstein courted, told *The Times* he had the impression that Epstein's many dinner parties – which included many attractive female academics – were in fact being used to screen candidates to bear his children.

Epstein also wanted to have his two most important (to himself) body parts cryogenically frozen so that he could be brought back to life in the future – these were his head and his oddly shaped penis (victim testimonies corroborate that Epstein's penis was egg-shaped). Much of what Epstein was looking into was uncomfortably close to eugenics and should have been as disturbing to his academic guests as his criminal past. However, it just goes to show that, in any field, money and influence can cover a multitude of sins. And there was plenty of money and influence coming from Epstein's direction.

Epstein was involved in or funding some of the most prestigious research and academic bodies in the US, including the Santa Fe Institute, the Theoretical Biology Initiative at the Institute for Advanced Study, the Quantum Gravity Program at the University of Pennsylvania and the Mind Brain Behavior Advisory Committee at Harvard University. Harvard was one of Epstein's biggest beneficiaries, perhaps because he sought validation from it (he was often pictured wearing a Harvard sweatshirt, giving the impression he had attended the university). The prestigious university received tens of millions of dollars in funding from Epstein, as did the Massachusetts Institute of Technology just down the road.

Why was Epstein doing this? Partly, it seems, for his reputation – and his vanity – as a self-styled intellectual heavyweight, but also because the titbits these scientists let slip over dinner could be crucially important to the intelligence agencies he was working for, particularly where they touched upon technology, weapons and surveillance. In terms of the Silicon Valley entrepreneurs he courted, there might be an even more direct intelligence aim – the bugging of new technologies and software for spying purposes, as will be discussed in a later chapter.

By 2019, Epstein appeared to be back on top of the world. However, a few cracks in his apparently unbreakable armour had begun to appear. From 2015 onwards, he faced a number of civil lawsuits from his various victims, all of which were dismissed or settled out of court. In February 2019, a case brought by two of the Florida victims against the US government concerning the legality of the sweetheart deal was judged in their favour. The Department of Justice ruled that the US government had indeed acted illegally, particularly in concealing the non-prosecution agreement from the victims. The way was now open for further prosecutions.

The inevitable came on July 6, 2019. Epstein was arrested at Teterboro Airport in New Jersey as he disembarked, for the last time, from the *Lolita Express*. At the same time, FBI agents stormed his Manhattan town house, seizing hundreds of pieces of incriminating evidence such as pictures and videos of his victims nude or in sex acts with other men.

Epstein was charged with sex trafficking and conspiracy to traffic minors for sex. The State Attorney for the southern District of New York, Geoffrey Berman, made it clear at a press conference that the non-prosecution agreement made in Florida would not be binding in New York. Justice, it seemed, was finally about to catch up with the man who had for so long been untouchable.

In the end, justice *was* visited on Epstein, but not the kind that anyone had expected.

In the early 1990s, was visited by Epstein, but not the kind that anyone had expected.

CHAPTER 5
THE PROCURER:
GHISLAINE MAXWELL

Ghislaine Maxwell's birth was inauspicious. The youngest daughter of Robert and Betty Maxwell was born in 1961, just two days before their eldest son, Michael, was involved in a serious car crash that left him in a coma. Fifteen-year-old Michael died six years later, having never regained consciousness. Betty recalled in her autobiography, *A Mind of My Own*, that the accident had cast a pall across the whole family and left Ghislaine with signs of anorexia even as a toddler.

Nevertheless, the bright and precocious child would go on to become her father's favourite over the six other surviving children: Anne, Philip, Christine, Isabel, Ian and Kevin (another child, Korinne, died at the age of three from leukemia). Intelligent, witty, charismatic and manipulative, Ghislaine would impress people throughout her life with her intelligence, personality and broad range of skills. She was a qualified helicopter pilot, a submarine and underwater ROV operator, and a trained emergency medical technician, and was fluent in four languages. She would come to be known mainly as a socialite, always spotted at the most prestigious events alongside some of the most famous and influential people on the planet. But the frivolous image belied a deeply intelligent, thoughtful and talented personality.

This undoubtedly came from her childhood, growing up under her mother's careful tutelage and her father's strict eye. Family Sunday lunches at Headington Hill Hall, their palatial Oxfordshire mansion, would involve Robert Maxwell grilling the children on geopolitics and current affairs. According to Maxwell biographer Tom Bower, if the children made a mistake, they were beaten in front of the others. "Bob would shout and threaten and rant at the children until they were reduced to pulp," Betty wrote in her memoir.

However, their father's authoritarian manner didn't seem to put off the children, who went on to study at Oxford University and became high achievers. Ghislaine called her father "inspiring" and Christine called him "a great educator". Always ahead of the game, Ghislaine remembered her father teaching her to programme the early computers he'd installed at home in 1973 when she was just twelve, according to British magazine *Tatler*.

Ghislaine was educated at Marlborough and Oxford, where she studied at Balliol College and was friends with future high-fliers such as Hugh Grant. But student life didn't release her from the tyrannical grip of her father. She reportedly avoided being seen in public with her boyfriends for fear of Maxwell senior's reaction. After graduating, Ghislaine became well known in the British social scene, attending all the glitziest events. But she worked as hard as she played, becoming a director of her father's Oxford United Football Club and working for *The European*, one of the many newspapers owned by Robert. When Robert made the crucial purchase of US newspaper the *New York Post*, it was Ghislaine who flew to New York to oversee the transfer. In 1986, the mogul confirmed her status as his favourite by naming his 180-foot super yacht, the *Lady Ghislaine*, after her.

When Robert Maxwell was found dead in the waters near Tenerife in November 1991, it was Ghislaine who was first into his private office aboard the yacht, where she shredded all his most incriminating documents, according to journalist John Jackson, who said he witnessed the scene. It was also Ghislaine who first addressed the press, saying she thought her father had been murdered. She repeated the allegation in several interviews and in her private conversations, according to Maria Farmer. Ghislaine was reportedly heartbroken by her father's death, taking it the hardest of all the children.

Following revelations of Robert Maxwell's £440 million embezzlement of the Mirror Group's pension funds, she became persona non grata in London, so she wisely decided to move to New York. Perhaps unwisely, however, given the delicate nature of the family's reputation, she decided to fly on Concorde. In New York, she rented a $2,000-a-month apartment in Manhattan, according to the *New York Post*, and began to sell real estate to supplement the $100,000-a-year stipend her father had left her.

It was in New York that she supposedly first met and started dating Jeffrey Epstein, who was beginning to make his way as a major financial and social player in the city. However, this narrative is challenged by two inside sources. Steven Hoffenberg, founder and CEO of Towers Financial, the Ponzi scheme that Epstein had helped to run, told the authors of the book, *Epstein: Dead Men Tell No Tales*, that Epstein and Ghislaine's relationship was older, going back to the Eighties. And former Israeli spy, Ari Ben-Menashe, corroborated this, saying that Epstein and Ghislaine Maxwell had met and begun an affair in the Eighties. According to Ben-Menashe, it was through this relationship that Epstein became introduced to a career with Israeli intelligence via her father, Robert Maxwell. Ben-Menashe alleges that after Robert Maxwell's death, Epstein and Ghislaine embarked on a sexual blackmail operation in the US which initially targeted Bill Clinton as well as other leading politicians. This ties in with testimony from Maria Farmer, who claims Ghislaine told her she had been sent to the US for Epstein to look after her, something which couldn't have been possible if they didn't already know each other.

Whatever their background, by 1992 Ghislaine was "officially" working as Epstein's lady of the house, essentially running and organising his day-to-day life. By some accounts, they were also in a romantic relationship, with Ghislaine "desperate" to marry the financial whizz. By other accounts – including Epstein's – they were best friends who had dabbled in romance in the past. However, behind the scenes they were already running a slick child sex-trafficking operation, with Ghislaine acting as a procurer and facilitator for Epstein's sexual abuse of underage girls.

Interestingly, there is a similar discrepancy between reports of when and how Ghislaine first met another high-profile sexual abuser – Prince Andrew. The official story is that they first met when Ghislaine was an undergraduate at Oxford. However, Maria Farmer says Ghislaine showed photos of herself as a child with Andrew and other royals, and claimed to have essentially been brought up around the Royal Family.

Whatever the history of Ghislaine and Andrew's friendship, it clearly became more intense around the turn of the millennium, at about the same time she was said to have introduced the prince to Epstein. An *Evening Standard* article from 2001 documents all the occasions on which the pair had been spotted together over the previous year:

* February 2000: holiday at Mar-a-Lago Club in Palm Beach with Ghislaine, followed by a trip to New York to attend a fashion show with her.

* March: fundraising dinner for London Symphony Orchestra in New York, attended by Ghislaine.

* April: holiday to New York where he socialised with Ghislaine.

* May: official trip to New York then holiday in Florida with Ghislaine.

* June: weekend at Windsor Castle for Queen's party which Ghislaine attended.

* October: official visit to New York and evening partying with Ghislaine.

* December: weekend house party at Sandringham arranged "in honour" of Ghislaine's 39th birthday.

* January: a beach holiday in Thailand with Ghislaine.

In addition, Ghislaine travelled to Britain in September to attend the wedding of Andrew's old flame, Aurelia Cecil. They went together.

Epstein accompanied Ghislaine and Andrew on five of these trips, including the ones to Windsor and Sandringham, leading the report to comment on the trio's "curious symbiotic relationship". It also quoted the concerns of friends and family of the prince, who blamed the relationship for the change in his behaviour, including frequent clubbing and womanising, which was having an impact on his reputation and his relationship with his daughters, princesses Beatrice, twelve, and Eugenie, ten.

Could it be, as some sources have claimed, that Andrew had already been blackmailed by Epstein or, even further, that he had been drawn into Epstein and Maxwell's honeypot scheme, helping them to entrap other big players in their international blackmail operation?

Whatever the truth, Epstein, Ghislaine and Andrew retained close ties until 2010, when Andrew flew to New York to – as he bizarrely claims – sever the relationship in person following the tycoon's release from a Florida prison. Ghislaine continued to work as Epstein's "consultant" following the Florida arrest and her focus shifted, along with Epstein's, to concentrating on forging links with top US technology and science providers, schmoozing some of the top entrepreneurs and scientists at Epstein's New York mansion, New Mexico ranch and on his Caribbean island, Little St James.

In 2012, Ghislaine founded her own TerraMar Project, a non-profit ocean conservation scheme that sought to protect the 64% of the world's oceans that lie outside of national jurisdictions. Ghislaine gave a TED Talk about TerraMar and discussed the project with the United Nations. But the scheme died a death with the arrest of Epstein in 2019. It marked the beginning of the period when Ghislaine went into hiding. Speculation followed her whereabouts around the globe from Paris to London to Israel.

Ultimately, she was found nearer her adopted home of New York, in a hidden-away mountain-top retreat in New Hampshire, aptly named "Tuckedaway".

Ghislaine's life, it seems, has been uncannily like her father's, with much of it lived secretly below the surface. Her trial, if it happens (and she survives to see it), could provide the public with access to secrets they were denied from her father. If so, there is much to come out – who were she and Epstein really working for? What were the roles of Prince Andrew, the Clintons, Leslie Wexner and a host of other big-name players? What was the ultimate goal and how close were they to achieving it? How wide did their dark web of influence extend and how many knew what was really going on? The mystery of Ghislaine Maxwell is far from over. Indeed, the mystery of Robert Maxwell himself abides, not just in Ghislaine but in other members of the family.

It may turn out that Ghislaine wasn't the only child who continued Robert Maxwell's clandestine work. Kevin and Ian took on the legacy of his above-board corporate interests while Anne and Philip stayed largely away from the family business. But twin sisters Christine and Isabel may have continued their father's underground work just as much as Ghislaine.

According to research by investigative journalist Whitney Webb, Christine became the president and CEO of her father's technology company, Information on Demand, which was an early database search engine. This sounds innocent enough, except that Information on Demand was the company Maxwell used to sell the bugged Promis software to the US's Sandia National Laboratories, thus gaining Israel access to America's top nuclear secrets (unlike most of the Promis sales, which had been handled by Maxwell's front company, Degem, the Sandia sale was handled by Information of Demand, as it was a US company). Christine remained president of Information on Demand until her father's death and the unravelling of his empire. Her twin, Isabel, also claimed to work for the company.

According to Webb, after their father's death, Christine and

Isabel set up their own Internet services company called McKinley Group, which included Research on Demand, Christine's successor to Information on Demand. McKinley Group created an indexing and rating system for websites, which later morphed into Magellan, one of the earliest web search engines. In 1995, Isabel negotiated a deal with Bill Gate's MSN to use Magellan as its search engine of choice. Then, in 1996, after falling behind the competition, McKinley Group and Magellan were sold to Excite (later to become Ask Jeeves), netting the sisters a cool $18 million worth of Excite shares.

In 1997, according to Webb, Isabel was approached by an Israeli tech firm, Commtouch, to become its US president. Isabel said she accepted the offer because of its Israeli ties, which were an "affair of the heart" and were "to do with my father and my history". According to Webb, Isabel put the success of Commtouch down to the ties of all of its employees with Israeli military and military intelligence. Isabel's promotion of Commtouch in the US was noted as "almost Messianic", selling its systems to companies like Sun Microsystems and Cisco, and ultimately gaining investment from Microsoft co-founder Paul Allen – all this despite the company remaining an obscure tech provider that had never made a profit. Paul Allen's investment led, unsurprisingly, to a deal to use Commtouch for Microsoft's MSN messaging service and ultimately its email service, Hotmail. During this time, according to Webb, Isabel formed a personal relationship with Gates, and even persuaded him to make a personal investment of several million dollars into Commtouch. Commtouch was ultimately rebranded as Cyren and today, according to Webb, runs in the background of Microsoft, Google, Intel, McAfee and Dell products.

Isabel left Commtouch in 2001 to focus on becoming a liaison between Israeli tech start-ups and US angel investors, creating Maxwell Communications Network in 2006. During this time, according to Webb, Isabel forged many close relationships with high-ranking Israeli politicians and intelligence heads like former Israeli prime minister Shimon Peres, former Mossad deputy director David Kimche, and former head of military intelligence and prime minister Ehud Barak, who was implicated in Epstein's child sex abuse ring.

Could it be that Isabel and Christine were continuing their father's legacy of selling bugged software to the US in order to facilitate Israeli intelligence gathering? Is it possible that programmes run by Microsoft, Google, Intel, McAfee and Dell were fitted with backdoors for Israeli intelligence in deals negotiated by the Maxwell sisters? We may never know but perhaps a hint came from the mouth of Isabel herself.

In a 2000 interview with *The Guardian*, while still president of Commtouch, Isabel told the newspaper that her father would love the Internet if he were still alive, adding: "I'm sure he'd be thrilled to know what I'm doing now." The article noted that, on saying this, Isabel threw her head back and laughed wildly. Not much of a joke, you would think, unless she was making reference to continuing his legacy of spying for Israel. That is a joke her father would very much have enjoyed.

CHAPTER 6
MARIA FARMER'S STORY:
THE ARTIST AND THE
PAEDOPHILE

Before she was legally gagged, I was able to interview the brave Epstein survivor Maria Farmer (whose Twitter handle is @ArtisticBlower). Her account that follows shows the psychopathy and deviousness of the people in Epstein's world:

I first met Jeffrey Epstein in 1995 at an exhibition at the New York Academy of Art. I was twenty-four years old and had just graduated from my course at the Graduate School of Figurative Art. All the graduating students got to display one of their pictures but, being an overachiever, I decided to display three paintings. I was absolutely thrilled, as this was the first time I had ever got to display my pictures in a gallery. Even better, I sold all three paintings that night – the only pictures that were sold in the show. But sadly, my night was about to take a turn for the worse.

One of my paintings was of a young girl reclining on a couch while a man watched her. It was a tribute to Degas's famous painting, *The Rape*, and the model was my fifteen-year-old sister, Annie. I was just celebrating having sold the painting to a German man when the Dean of the Academy, Eileen Guggenheim, found me. When I told her the good news, she wasn't happy at all. She told me I had to give the cheque back because another buyer was interested. I said I wasn't going to do that but she told me I had to do it for the Academy. I was terrified of Eileen. She had manipulated and abused me throughout my time at the Academy so I felt I had no option but to do what she said.

Reluctantly, I handed the cheque back and was introduced to Jeffrey and his partner Ghislaine Maxwell. I had never met either of them before and had no idea who they were, other than powerful benefactors of the Academy that Eileen seemed desperate to please. Jeffrey told me he found my painting both beautiful and compelling, and that it got him thinking. However, he clearly didn't find it compelling enough to pay the full price. He wanted it for a discount – half price to be exact. I remember thinking this guy was incredibly cheap to be asking for a discount from a student, but I did what I was told, took his cheque for $6,000 and went home hoping never to see him again.

It wasn't the first time I'd been controlled against my will by Eileen Guggenheim. While I was a student, she had employed me as a maid and babysitter for her daughter. She paid me minimum wage, which was fine, except sometimes she didn't pay me at all. I often had to walk home so that I had enough money to buy food. But that wasn't the worst thing she did to me, not by far.

In my second year at the Academy, we had a Halloween party. The Academy had just moved to Franklin Street and across the way was the apartment of a famous artist called Christian Vincent. I was dressed as Dorothy from *The Wizard of Oz* and Eileen asked me to go across the street and get Christian because he wasn't answering his phone. So, I went over and rang the doorbell and Christian answered immediately. He asked me if I had a boyfriend and before I could reply he had forced me onto the sofa and was smothering my mouth with his, almost as if he was trying to suffocate me. He tried to rape me but fortunately a phone call interrupted him. He had around seventeen locks on his door and I had to try and open all these locks to escape while he took the call. I told an artist friend of mine about it the next day, and the woman who had sent me over, Barbara Krulak, was fired. But Eileen never had any comeback at all.

On another occasion, Eileen tried to set me up as some kind of concubine to a famous British artist in London. I had to speak to this guy on the phone and he said, "So, Eileen told me you'll come over and be my life partner," and I was like, "No, I will not," and I hung up. That happened on two other occasions as well. Basically, my time at the Academy was one of manipulation and abuse. Not something you would expect from such a prestigious institution but, strangely enough, something I'd been warned about a few years before.

I had been studying at an art school in the South of France as the final year of my undergraduate course at Santa Clara University in Silicon Valley. While I was in France, I saw this beautifully elongated study of a body in red pencil. I said to my roommate how much I'd love to learn to draw like that and mentioned the New York Academy of Art's figurative art school. My roommate said instantly: "You can't go there, it's a paedophile ring." I remember not believing her at the time and thinking she was a bit weird, but the longer I studied at the Academy, the more I realised she wasn't being weird at all.

After the Academy exhibition, I forgot about Jeffrey for a while, but only a few weeks later I got a call from Eileen saying I'd been chosen amongst a select group of students to visit Jeffrey's ranch in Santa Fe, New Mexico. I'd just obtained a position as artist in residence at the Hamptons and I was really happy but Eileen was like: "No, no, no, you're leaving, you're coming here."

Before I knew it, I was on a plane with Eileen, flying to New Mexico. The ranch was still being built then but it was still impressive. It had its own fire station and even its own hospital, where Jeffrey claimed they could do all sorts of surgery. I remember thinking, *Why would you need to do your own surgery?* Jeffrey said it was because a lot of people got bitten by snakes, but it seemed a little over the top for treating snakebites. He also boasted about the Clintons staying there in this old Western village they had built. He tried to paint a picture of a place of learning where scientists, politicians and technology experts from all over the world came to share their knowledge. It has since been reported that it was the place where he planned to seed the human race with his DNA by impregnating twenty women at a time with his sperm, but none of that was mentioned at the time.

The main house hadn't been built yet and instead there was this double-wide trailer. Eileen had instructed me to be complementary about the ranch so I said: "Hey, nice double-wide!" It was meant as a joke but I don't think Eileen found it very funny. Jeffrey thought it was hilarious, though, and said: "You get over here, you're so funny." We got chatting and he was really charming, just super funny and great to talk to. Perhaps Eileen noticed how well we were getting on because, before we went inside, she told me to sit on his lap and flirt with him, which I refused to do.

Inside, things got even weirder. They held a dinner party and when we went to the closet to put our coats inside, there was a skeleton hanging in it. I thought, *Is this ironic or something?* At the party, they asked the students to play a game. We had to wear blindfolds and identify objects they passed around. It turned out the objects were fake breasts. They tried to get us to put them inside our shirts but again I refused. Eileen was laughing, trying to make out like it was all a hilarious game, and I remember thinking, *Wow, this is the dean of the Academy.*

I met Ghislaine for the second time on that trip, too. I had popped outside with Eileen and she came riding up on a white horse in Ralph Lauren tweed. I'd never owned something that expensive in my life and just wanted to touch it. She literally looked like something out of a magazine, sitting there on that horse. Like Jeffrey, Ghislaine was glamourous and charming – she could make you feel like you were the centre of the world. But she had a dark side, too, as I would soon find out.

Back in New York, I was out of grad school and working for Eileen's sister, Barbara. I worked at her house for two weeks, cleaning toilets and helping her pack stuff away because they were moving. Barbara was even more verbally abusive than Eileen, and it all came to a head one day when I had gone to the deli to get some watermelon and I was eating it in one of the empty rooms. Barbara was screaming at me psychotically. It was so abusive that even her husband, a famous lawyer called Bert Fields, said: "You don't need this." So, I was sent away and paid with two expired traveller's cheques and a bag of old junk which Barbara said I could sell at the flea market. I had to walk home because I couldn't afford the subway, and I ditched the junk on the way. When I got back to my apartment in Greenwich Village, I got a call from Jeffrey. He said: "I heard you had to work for that bitch Barbara, and guess what? You're having a real job tomorrow."

So, the next day I went to his office at the Helmsley Palace Hotel because I was desperate for a job. Little did I know I was in for another surreal experience. Jeffrey was sat there with this Cheshire-Cat grin on his face and behind him, perched on the radiator, was the actress Morgan Fairchild. She didn't say a word the whole time, just sat there like this perfect plastic doll. I had this feeling he was trying to make himself look like the Great Gatsby or something – everything was just so different and fabulous and weird.

Also in the office was Katie Ford, then CEO of Ford Models, Inc., and André Balazs, who was the owner of W Hotels. Jeffrey started asking me about my sister Annie and I was telling him how smart she was and how she was going to be Ivy League. Jeffrey kept suggesting that Annie should model for Katie and I was like: "No, she wants to be a doctor." Then, Katie said she would call her friend Harvey – she was talking about Harvey Weinstein – and get her a career in Hollywood. I kept trying to tell them she wasn't interested but they didn't seem to listen.

Alarm bells should have rung but I was young and naïve, and I needed a job. So, the next day I turned up for work at Jeffrey's mansion on 71st Street. It turned out I was going to be a receptionist, signing people in and out. Ghislaine arrived and gave me all the instructions on what to do and how to behave. She also showed me several pinhole cameras that were positioned just behind my head. She seemed really proud of them for some reason. That also struck me as strange – the cameras were so small you wouldn't even notice them unless someone pointed them out.

Right from the start, I saw a lot of young girls going up the stairs into the mansion. There were three to five a day and some-times as many as ten. I asked Ghislaine why so many young girls were coming and going. She told me they were Victoria's Secret models and, at the time, I believed her.

I began to see the dark side of Ghislaine while I worked at the mansion. She would come back from a shopping trip all giddy with happiness because she'd just shopped and then a few hours later she would say: "I'm going out to get the nubiles," and her whole expression and manner would change to what I can only describe as evil. It was so sudden; it was like this Jekyll and Hyde thing. I didn't know what nubiles meant at the time, so I looked it up and found out it meant girls who have just started having their periods. Of course, I thought that was a bit weird, but again Ghislaine said they were getting Victoria's Secret models and they liked to recruit them young. That's when I found out she was working for Leslie Wexner, CEO of L Brands and Victoria's Secret. Ghislaine always made it very clear that she worked for Wexner.

A few times, Ghislaine actually took me with her on these trips to find "nubiles". We would go out in a black limousine with this creepy Hispanic driver, and friends of Ghislaine would often come, too. One who was often in the car was Donald Trump's ex-wife, Ivana Trump. I remember her well because one time she gave me this really tacky plastic bracelet that I think came from her QVC channel.

We would drive around Manhattan in this car and suddenly Ghislaine would shout out "Stop!" and she'd run out and speak to a young girl she'd spotted, often in school uniform. She'd exchange numbers with them and the next day they'd turn up at the mansion for modelling. These girls were twelve, thirteen or fourteen years old maximum. I kept asking her why Victoria's Secret needed such young girls, but she just said they needed nubiles – that was the word she used all the time. A couple of times she slipped up and said she was getting nubiles for Jeffrey. I said, "I thought they were for Victoria's Secret?" and she said, "Oh yeah, Jeffrey authorises it."

It was weird being around Ghislaine. She could be unbelievably charming but then she could suddenly switch and turn into one of the most verbally abusive people I've ever met. The way she spoke to you could just cut you down and make you feel like the smallest person on Earth. She could be physically violent, too. She never was with me, but there were two Filipino maids at the mansion who were lovely and she was sometimes physically abusive to them. Jeffrey could switch suddenly, too. He would accuse someone of looking at Ghislaine funnily, or something like that, and he would constantly be getting rid of people, but he was never as verbally abusive as Ghislaine. I think they were both psychopaths and that was how they controlled the narrative – you were so afraid of them switching from Jekyll to Hyde that you were always trying to keep them happy.

I worked at the 71st Street mansion for several months despite not really knowing what I was doing there. During that time, a number of strange things happened.

One time, I was with Jeffrey in his Helmsley Palace office when he said out of the blue: "Maria, you really don't know how to wear a bra." I was very self-conscious about my body so I felt really embarrassed and didn't know what to say. But Jeffrey didn't seem to care. He sent me over to the Victoria's Secret store, which you could see from his offices. When I arrived, the staff were waiting for me as if Jeffrey had already spoken to them. They had all these bras for me to try on but not one of them fitted me, so I just picked a pair of pyjamas with the credit I had and got out of there.

When I got back to the office, Jeffrey began describing my breasts. It was weird and horrifying – I had some unusual marks and scars, and he described them in perfect detail. He didn't even do it in a sexual way but in this mean, nasty, critical way. I just stood there in a kind of shocked daze. It dawned on me that he must have pinhole cameras in the Victoria's Secret changing rooms that were connected to monitors in his office. He knew that I hadn't bought any bras as well, so he forced me to go back. I just bought a bunch of bras that I never wore and tried to forget about the whole thing.

On another occasion, Ghislaine took me to her apartment and the first thing I noticed was one of my own pictures hanging on the wall. It was the first drawing I had done at the Academy, and I was like: "How do you have that? I didn't give you that." She said: "Oh, I took it. I liked it." It had been in my apartment, which was secured with a police lock and deadbolts, so I have no idea how she got that picture.

Anyway, I tried to forget about the drawing and the next thing I noticed was these glistening objects on her mantelpiece. I asked her what they were and she said they were ancient relics from Peru. They were solid gold and came from the British Museum in London. She told me her dad took them. I was shocked, thinking, *You don't just take things from the British Museum.* That's when I learned that her father was Robert Maxwell, the famous British media tycoon who had stolen millions from his company's pension fund then died mysteriously on his yacht.

I saw all kinds of famous people go up the stairs of the mansion on 71st Street. Bill Clinton was probably the biggest name. He came to the house three times when I was there and each time everyone would have to clear out except the chef, Andy, and the two maids. I was usually the last to leave and Ghislaine would be in a tizzy all day, sending people out to buy stuff and decorating the place with candles and ornaments. Ghislaine boasted about how much Bill Clinton loved her and she wanted the place to be as perfect as possible. No one will ever believe me about this but I've seen the photos of him there and yes, as unbelievable as it sounds, the president of the US used to turn up at Jeffrey's house with no security detail, no announcements or anything – it was all very secretive.

There was clearly something weird going on in New York so I was over the moon when I got a job offer that gave me the chance to escape from Jeffrey and Ghislaine for good. I had received a commission to do some paintings for the movie *As Good as It Gets* by James L. Brooks. I couldn't believe my luck and I was so thrilled to be doing something that was my chosen career at last.

I told Jeffrey I was going to quit but right away he was like: "Oh no, you can't quit." He knew I didn't have enough space to do the paintings at my apartment in Greenwich Village so he offered to put me up at another of his properties in Ohio which was on Leslie Wexner's estate, and I could complete the project there. He tried to make out like they'd already decided to send me there so I could be the Wexners' artist in residence. I didn't really want to move to Ohio but the offer seemed too good to turn down so I decided to go with it.

I had wanted to escape Jeffrey's orbit in New York, but moving to Ohio turned out to be one of the worst decisions of my life. On Wexner's estate, things would get weirder and darker than they had ever been in New York, and from that moment on, I would never feel safe again.

When I first arrived at the Wexner estate in New Albany, Ohio, I was met by a man named Randy Bowie. He told me he was ex-special forces and was Leslie Wexner's right-hand man. He showed me around Jeffrey's house, which was supposedly just a guest house, but it was 26,000 square feet, based on the Rotunda building in Columbus, Ohio. Behind it was the Wexners' main house and surrounding it were 350 acres of land.

I had the entire guest house to myself and I was feeling a little overwhelmed. Then, Randy Bowie told me that I needed to go inside to take a phone call from Abigail Wexner, Leslie Wexner's wife. He said when I'd finished, I shouldn't come outside again without getting permission from Abigail. When I asked why, he told me they had Dobermans and sharpshooters all over the estate so it wasn't safe. I remember feeling my heart sink and thinking, *This is not what I'd hoped, this is really uncomfortable.* Looking back, I guess that was the first clue as to what was coming.

I stayed at the Wexner estate for three months and the whole time I was hungry. I lost twenty pounds and I was already skinny before I arrived. I couldn't eat because I couldn't leave the house. Even though Jeffrey had arranged for me to get a driving license while I was there and he'd left me his SUV so I could pick him up from the airport when he visited, still I couldn't leave. I'd call a hundred times before anyone would pick up and I'd have to ask permission to go outside, and it was all such a rigmarole I ended up only going out four or five times. There was a country club nearby where I was supposed to be able to eat but when I called Ghislaine and asked her about it she said they wouldn't serve me because I wasn't Jewish.

There was only one time I went outside without asking permission and I never did it again because this pack of Dobermans came running towards me, literally flying at me. I had my little Yorkshire Terrier with me and these dogs would have ripped us both to shreds. I didn't leave the house for a month after that.

The other weird thing about the house was the cameras. Just like Jeffrey's mansion in New York, the Ohio place had pinhole cameras in every room and I was being constantly watched. I knew this because if I would go to the restroom or the shower, I'd have Ghislaine shouting at me through a speaker from New York or London or wherever she was, telling me to get out of the shower. One time, I had a friend fly in to visit me. I was dyeing her hair with henna in the main hallway and I accidentally spilled a drop on the carpet. It was so small I didn't think anyone would notice so I just pulled a garbage can over it and walked away. About an hour later, I got a call from Ghislaine screaming at me that Abigail was going to have me thrown out for spilling henna on her carpet.

There was such an uncomfortable feeling of being watched that I ended up doing my painting in the only places I thought didn't have cameras, like the garage and the pool house. There was also an underground level where I used to keep my photos and pictures. It had a huge sauna and a door that was always locked. One day, I asked the maid what was behind the door and she told me it was an underground tunnel that led all the way to Wexner's main house. She told me it led to a giant floor that would raise up into a room in the other building. There was also a huge walk-in safe where Jeffrey said Wexner kept all the recordings from all the cameras. I asked the maid how long she'd worked there and if she'd ever seen Wexner. She said twenty years and no, she'd never seen him once.

The other thing the Ohio property had in common with the New York mansion was that Jeffrey boasted about buying them both off Wexner for just a dollar. I asked how that was possible and he said: "Maria, he adores me. He'd do anything for me. Trust me." I definitely think that Wexner was secretly homosexual and that he had something going on with Jeffrey. Andy, the chef, told me there was definitely something going on between them and I believed him because he'd already worked for Jeffrey for ten years, and before that he worked for Wexner on his super yacht, *Limitless*.

Jeffrey and Ghislaine visited Wexner a few times while I was there. It was on the last of these visits that my life changed forever.

On the last night of their visit, Ghislaine came to my room to tell me Jeffrey wanted a word. She was in a robe and I'd never seen her like that before except when she was having her nails done by her servants. I followed her down the hallway to Jeffrey's bedroom – it was the one room I'd not been allowed in before. I went in and Jeffrey was lying on the four-poster bed. Ghislaine told me to rub his feet and I was like: "I know for a fact that I'm not supposed to rub my employer's feet." Jeffrey said: "Come on, Maria, it's not a big deal, we're all friends."

So, I took off his socks and started massaging his feet. He started moaning in this over-the-top dramatic way, so I pretended that I thought I was hurting him and said: "Let me please stop." He told me to come and sit next to him on the bed. Ghislaine came, too, and started loosening her robe, and I thought, *Oh, I'm going to be raped.* I suddenly just knew.

Jeffrey started touching my chest and kind of twisting it in this weird mechanical way, and Ghislaine mirrored him, doing the same thing, and at the same time they were shaming me about the size of my breasts. At that point, tears started to come out and Ghislaine took my hand and started patting it and kissing it, as if to comfort me. In a strange way, that was the most horrifying moment of all.

While I was being assaulted, several revelations hit me all at once. I realised they were paedophiles – suddenly all of those young girls going into the mansion made sense. All of the pieces fitted together. Then their interest in my sister hit me. Earlier in the summer, they had flown her to the New Mexico ranch for what they said was a college planning session to help her get an Ivy League education. Suddenly, I realised why they had really wanted her there – had they raped her? Was she even alive? She was supposed to be in Thailand doing some programme Jeffrey had sent her on, but was she actually dead? Then another realisation struck me – my photos of Annie. I had several nude and semi-nude pictures of Annie and my youngest sister, who were fifteen and twelve at the time. They were anatomy studies for my drawing class and I kept them in a little plastic safe in the underground level where the sauna and secret tunnel were located. Somehow, I knew that Jeffrey had taken those pictures.

I finally managed to get out of Jeffrey's room. My two little brothers were staying with me at the time so I found them and took them back to my bedroom. I barricaded the doors and stayed there until the next morning. The whole night I kept thinking they were going to kill us all. I kept thinking about my mom and how she would handle the death of three of her children.

The next morning, Jeffrey and Ghislaine had to fly out early. As soon as they had gone, I rushed downstairs to the basement and checked my pictures. The plastic safe had been ripped open and some of the photos removed. I had everything catalogued and stored in envelopes, so I was able to work out exactly which pictures had been taken. One of them was of my youngest sister and the other was of Annie, and they were both totally nude. I called Jeffrey's office in New York and told them my pictures had gone missing and I wanted them back. They hung up on me. Later in the morning, a girl from his office called back and told me the pictures were in Jeffrey's briefcase and he was using them, then she hung up again.

In the meantime, Jeffrey called. He said: "That was just so great last night. I just had so much fun with you." I told him he was sick and that I knew about the missing pictures so I was leaving right away. Jeffrey was like: "Maria, no, no, no. Listen, I will give you anything. What do you want to calm down?"

I hung up and called 911. Unbelievably, 911 then hung up on me. I thought there must have been some mistake so I called them back. The woman at the other end said very clearly: "Listen, the sheriff is at the gate. You're never leaving, okay? We work for Wexner," then she hung up again. That was the New Albany sheriff's department. They basically all worked for Wexner.

Now I was panicking and sure I was going to die, so I called everyone I could think of and told them I was at the Wexner ranch in Ohio and that they were going to kill me. I called Eileen Guggenheim and all she said was, "You must have really done something wrong," and hung up on me. Another girl from graduate school seemed to find it funny and was like: "Oh, they're just swingers."

Meanwhile, the head of security, Randy Bowie, had turned up and he was pacing up and down outside. I have never seen anyone look at me the way he did that morning. There was pure violence in his eyes and he said: "You are never going anywhere. You are never leaving. Do you hear me? Never." In that instant, I felt all the energy in my body drain to my feet. I knew I was going to die.

In desperation, I called my dad and said: "Dad, your sons are going to die." He was like, "What are you talking about?" so I explained everything and begged him to come get us.

About four hours later, my father arrived in his car. I had to get my brothers out of there but they wouldn't let him in and it was a three-mile walk to the front gate. And of course, there were the Dobermans and sharpshooters that Randy Bowie had warned me about. But by now I was so desperate I no longer cared. I thought, *You know what – they can eat me*. So, I walked my two brothers the three miles to the gate. I gave them to my dad and then walked all the way back again. It sounds crazy but all my art, all my pictures, all my worldly possessions were in that house and I wasn't going to leave them.

When I got back, Randy Bowie was waiting for me by the SUV. He promised me again that I would never leave. He tried to get me in the truck to drive somewhere else but I remembered this Oprah show where they said that if ever you're kidnapped, you should never let them take you to the second location, because that's where they will kill you. So, I wrapped my arms around this fake Georgian column and kicked my legs and screamed and made a scene every time he came near me. When I was able to, I went back inside. Because I knew they watched and listened to everything, I called basically everyone I had ever met and said in a very loud voice: "I'm at the estate of Les and Abigail Wexner, and their right-hand man is going to murder me."

I think in the end that's what saved my life – because I had told so many people, they knew there would be no way of getting away with it. So eventually, twelve hours later, Randy Bowie must have got the message to let me go. He stopped pacing but he was still salivating and looking like he wanted to kill me. He said: "You're never coming back and if you do, you won't make it."

I grabbed what I could, got in the SUV and drove out of there. There were other special forces guys at the gate but they didn't try to stop me or threaten me. Finally, I was free. I drove out of there and into a new life, one that would never be the same again.

When I first escaped, all I could think was, *This is the end, I'm going to die, they're going to kill me.* I went to Kentucky at first because my dad was there, so I felt a little safer. One of the first things I did when I arrived was to try to contact Annie in Thailand because I still feared that she was dead. Luckily, she was doing a real programme that Jeffrey had sent her on. Clearly, they were still grooming her before the real abuse began. I spoke to the woman in charge and she put Annie on the phone. It was difficult to communicate well on a payphone to Thailand, but I managed to ascertain that Jeffrey and Ghislaine had sexually assaulted her on her trip to the New Mexico ranch, the trip which, supposedly, was to get career advice for entering an Ivy League college. I was horrified that this had all happened because of me, but at the same time I was relieved because she was still alive.

I spent a month on the couch at my father's before going back to New York. There I had another surprise – Jeffrey had rented out my apartment to his butler's son. This guy had thrown out all my worldly possessions and painted the whole apartment black. I realised that I wouldn't be safe there because they must have my keys and, anyway, I'd already started getting threats. They had threatened to burn all my art and, much worse, Ghislaine threatened my life on several occasions. One time, she said: "Hey, Maria, I know you go running on the West Side highway. You better watch your back, because you can die so many ways there, okay, dearie?" These threats continued until about five years ago. I would change my number, and somehow, she'd find my new one and call me again.

On one of Ghislaine's calls to me, she said: "You're so stupid. Do you even understand what a big mistake you made?" I was like: "What are you talking about?" And she said: "Annie was going to get the privilege of carrying Jeffrey's baby. Do you even understand how amazing that is?" I was so horrified I felt physically sick. Annie was sixteen years old at the time and they were planning on Jeffrey impregnating her. It was almost impossible to take in.

Another thing that happened in New York was that Jeffrey started stalking me. I would be on the subway or in the flea market or somewhere and I'd turn around and there he would be, just smiling at me. Eventually, it got too much and I left New York, but before that I went to the NYPD. I knew a couple of guys from the 6th Precinct department and they believed me, but they told me it was too big for the NYPD and that I needed to call the FBI. So, I called the FBI and told them Jeffrey had abused and trafficked me and my sister, and that he had stolen naked pictures of my younger sisters to use as child pornography. That alone should have been enough to get Jeffrey and Ghislaine put away, but the guy on the other end of the phone didn't seem interested. I told him I even had the envelopes the pictures were stolen from with their fingerprints all over them, but he was like: "No, we don't need that."

I mentioned Wexner as well. I said I thought he was the head of the snake. The funny thing was, as soon as I mentioned Wexner's name, I was handed over to another guy who told me not to mention anything about this to anyone. I put the phone down and waited to hear something back, but that was it – I didn't hear anything for ten years. What makes me so angry is that all the other girls that have been abused – all the girls in Florida and on the plane and the island – all of them could have been saved from that hell, because the FBI had all the information they needed back in 1996. And what did they do with it? Absolutely nothing.

I tried my best to forget Jeffrey and Ghislaine, and to get on with my life, despite the periodic death threats. The next time they really re-entered my life was in 2002. I was contacted by Vicky Ward, a journalist from *Vanity Fair* magazine. She was researching an article on Epstein's sudden rise to wealth and fame, and a mutual friend had tipped her off about me.

Over the space of a year, I told Vicky everything that had happened to me and Annie. She interviewed every member of my family, and my dad even flew in to interview with her. She really got my hopes up that the truth about this monster was finally going to be exposed, but again my hopes were dashed. Jeffrey got wind that Vicky was going to include me in the article. Somehow, he got into the *Vanity Fair* offices one evening and he threatened to curse Vicky Ward, who was pregnant with twins at the time. The editor, Graydon Carter, also started to have dead animals left in his garden and weird stuff like that, and I think everyone got spooked. Jeffrey told Carter to cut me and Annie from the article, and he did. And that was that – Jeffrey was off the hook once again.

But that wasn't the worst thing. Vicky Ward told Ghislaine I had reported them to the FBI, so I got a call from Ghislaine threatening me again. That's when I went on the run and that has been my life for the past eighteen years – constantly moving houses until they track me down and threaten me again.

Unfortunately, it wasn't the last I heard of Vicky Ward, either. She went to work for CNN and it seems she promised them some kind of exclusive on me, because she harassed me and my family continuously about speaking to her, so much so that we had to send a cease-and-desist order. This was the woman who had promised my safety when interviewing me for *Vanity Fair*, then had sold me out to Ghislaine Maxwell. There was no way I was giving her another story, especially because she became friends with these monsters. She was hanging out having drinks with Ghislaine, and she became partners with one of Wexner's friends, who kept her in high style. And all the while, I was hiding out in the woods fearing for my life. She has sat on our story for eighteen years, so as far as I'm concerned Vicky Ward is a co-conspirator in these hideous crimes.

I said the FBI did nothing with the information I gave them, and indeed it wasn't until 2006 that I next heard from them. I was on the run still, hiding out in a gated community in the woods in North Carolina, when one day two FBI agents turned up at my door. I was so shocked that I thought they were there for my unpaid student loans. But in fact, they wanted to speak to me about Jeffrey. This agent, Nesbitt Kuyrkendall, had actually been working on the case for years. She was a mother and you could tell she really cared. She really wanted to get this guy.

Nesbitt told me about the Florida case where reports had been coming out about Jeffrey abusing high school girls at his mansion in Palm Beach. She wanted me and Annie to testify but she said the FBI couldn't offer us witness protection. I thought that was a pretty rough deal but I didn't care. I wanted to get Jeffrey and so did Annie, so we both agreed.

The trial happened two years later and me and Annie were waiting to testify, but we never got the call. It wasn't until seven years later – about five years ago – that we actually found out what had happened. Jeffrey had got a sweetheart deal and been sent down on a prostitution charge instead of his real crimes of trafficking and sexually abusing children. The unbelievably slack deal sentenced him to thirteen months in a state jail during which he was allowed to leave the prison for up to twelve hours a day. He spent most of his time in his office and it's even been reported that he was meeting young girls there.

Not only did the deal let Jeffrey off the hook, but it gave immunity to all his co-conspirators like Ghislaine, rendering them effectively untouchable. In terms of the victims, not only were we in effect branded prostitutes by the ruling, we weren't even given the dignity of being told about the verdict. This was why Annie and myself were still waiting to testify seven years later – no one had bothered to tell us.

I remember Nesbitt calling me around that time, but she was so distraught and in such floods of tears that I couldn't work out what she was talking about. As for her – the only good FBI agent I have ever come across – she is now completely incommunicado. Our lawyers have tried to reach out to her but, although she's supposedly still in the FBI, it seems she is under some kind of witness protection scheme. It's all very mysterious. Each time our lawyers have tracked her down, they've found out from her neighbours that she left suddenly in the middle of the night. Who knows what kind of danger she has brought down on herself by daring to go against the likes of Wexner and the upper echelons of her own organisation?

My experience with Jeffrey and Ghislaine was a long time before the Florida victims, but I had visited the Palm Beach mansion a few times with Jeffrey and Ghislaine. I had been struck immediately by the pictures on the walls – there were lots of pictures of naked children and also of Ghislaine naked. Another thing I remember was Ghislaine taking me to this room and there were these leather straps attached to the wall. I asked, "What are those?" and she said: "I put my feet in and I hang upside down like a bat for forty-five minutes. It keeps me young."

There was another contraption I asked about and she said: "Oh, that's a sex swing, dearie." She seemed to find it hilarious that I didn't know what a sex swing was. There were various other sexual devices in the room and also a massage table. I thought it was weird at the time but now I can't even bring myself to think of what might have happened in there. One of the other things I noticed in that place – and all Jeffrey's properties – was occult symbolism. Jeffrey had this statue of a creature with a goat's head that was called Baphomet but which was basically a symbol of Satan. And at various places they had these weird symbols inscribed on the walls which I have since found out are occult.

Another thing I remember clearly at the Palm Beach mansion was on a few occasions being told to go for a jog because Jeffrey was having a massage, so even back then it was clearly happening.

After the sweetheart deal, Jeffrey and Ghislaine became less a part of my life, thank God – even the death threats began to dry up. However, my experiences left their own scars which came back to haunt me. I was diagnosed with a rare brain tumour and when I asked the doctor how long it had been growing, he said over twenty years. When he said that, I knew exactly when it had started – the moment Randy Bowie had told me I was never leaving the Ohio estate. It was so traumatic that even at the time it was like I could feel my brain chemistry changing – that feeling of, *Oh my God, I'm going to die.* They also found a second form of cancer, a kind of lymphoma on my heart. The brain tumour had become so bad they told me I was just two weeks away from permanently losing my voice. That was doubly bad timing, because Jeffrey was now being investigated again, this time by the NYPD. Fortunately, I had surgery just in time to save my voice and file my affidavit.

In July 2019, Jeffrey Epstein was arrested on charges of child sex trafficking – the same charges he should have received ten years before. Annie and I felt a sense of elation like we hadn't for many years. However, it was to be short-lived. Only a month later, he was found dead in his cell having apparently hanged himself.

The circumstances around his death were suspicious to say the least – failed CCTV cameras, sleeping guards, broken bones in the neck that only come from violent strangulation, and a bunk bed too low to hang himself from, to name but a few.

I can add my own testimony to the list of reasons why Jeffrey's death was not suicide – I knew that man very well. He was a narcissist and never in a million years could he have taken his own life. Right to the very end, he would have thought he was too important to be bumped off or left to rot in a prison cell. He would have been too confident in his own position to ever imagine he wouldn't get out of there lightly.

Unfortunately for Jeffrey, everyone's luck runs out some time, and he had obviously made himself too much of a liability to save even his own valuable skin. Probably rumours of him ratting out other conspirators to cut a plea deal was the last straw and meant he had to go. Some of these players – like the Wexners and the Clintons – are on another level and Jeffrey simply had to be shut up. I just feel bad that the victims never got the chance to see justice done and Jeffrey answer for a lifetime of the most terrible crimes.

As for Ghislaine, people speculate as to whether the same thing will happen to her. I don't believe it will because I believe she has protection from the highest-possible levels – the Rothschilds, no less. I know this because she used to speak about them all the time. She called the Rothschilds "the great protectors of my family". She used to brag about how they owned everything and she could get them to do whatever she asked, particularly when she was making death threats over the phone.

The relationship with the Rothschilds went back to Ghislaine's father, Robert Maxwell. She made it very clear that he worked for Israeli intelligence. She used to make me look at all these photos of him while she cried over them. She was constantly grieving for her dad. He had died a few years before in 1991 and some of these pictures were of his lavish Israeli state funeral. I asked how he had died and she said: "Those cunts pushed him off the

Lady Ghislaine." At the time, I didn't understand what she meant, but the *Lady Ghislaine* was his yacht and Israeli intelligence had pushed him off the boat.

There was definitely an attitude of racism and what you might call Jewish supremacy around Jeffrey and Ghislaine and all that circle. The way they spoke about African Americans was horrible, it made me sick to my stomach. And they weren't much better about white people. They made it quite clear that you were inferior to them. I remember one time hearing Eileen Guggenheim's daughter, Isabelle, saying: "Mummy, why do you call Maria a nobody?" And Eileen replied: "Honey, Maria is not a Jew. She *is* a nobody."

I wasn't sure about Ghislaine's relationship with Israeli intelligence since they'd killed her father, but she told me they had given her to Jeffrey to take care of. I didn't really know if by "them" she meant the Rothschilds or Israeli intelligence, but that's what she kept saying, that Jeffrey had been assigned as her protector after her father's death. She certainly had some hidden source of power and influence, that was very clear. Like when she showed me her passports. She had a French passport, an English passport, an Israeli passport, an American passport and one other that I can't remember. I remember thinking, *Isn't it only legal to have two passports? How does anyone manage to get five?*

And then of course there was her connection with the British Royal Family. I saw a lot of them at the New York Academy of Arts – Prince Andrew, Prince Charles, Sarah Ferguson – they were always hanging around the Academy. But Ghislaine also showed me pictures of her growing up and these pictures were all full of royals. She basically grew up with the Royal Family, and she was great friends with Prince Andrew and Fergie. The weirdest thing about seeing those photos was Princess Diana. This was back in 1996 when Diana was still alive, and she showed me this photo of Diana in tears and Ghislaine was like: "Look, we made her cry. We hate Diana." That made me feel sick because I idolised Diana. I had grown up basically wanting to be her. That was another occasion where I saw the evil side of Ghislaine just kind of take over.

Now that Jeffrey is gone and Ghislaine is in jail, life feels a bit more normal, but after what was done to me, nothing will ever be truly normal again. I gave up painting for twenty years because of it. I had been painting from pictures of my younger sisters and after what happened, I found it so disturbing I just couldn't pick up a brush. I've started painting again now, but it will never quite be the same.

And I consider myself lucky. At least I was an adult when it happened. What about all those young girls – fourteen, fifteen, sixteen years old – who had their innocence taken away? I can't even imagine what they've been through. And what about all the other girls? Only thirty women came forward to testify against Jeffrey. But I saw up to ten girls a day going into that mansion on 71st Street. And that was just New York – what about Florida, Ohio, New Mexico, the island and his private jet? There must be literally thousands of women out there who have been abused by Jeffrey Epstein. Where are they? Are they even alive? The scale of this thing feels almost too large to comprehend sometimes.

As my journey with Jeffrey began with Eileen Guggenheim, it seems fitting to end it with her, too. The last time I saw Eileen, I went to visit her daughter, Isabelle, at their New York home. I'd lived there as an au pair while I was studying at the Academy and I'd gotten to know Isabelle very well – I'd practically raised her during the time I was there. Isabelle had just gotten into a really great high school, so I was visiting to congratulate her and see how she was doing.

As I was leaving, I spotted something shiny on the counter and wandered over to have a look. It was a gilded invitation to a benefit function in the UK hosted by the Royal Family. The invitation was from Ghislaine. I looked at Eileen and said: "Are you kidding me?" And she said: "No, I'm not kidding you."

After all I'd been through with Jeffrey and Ghislaine, because of her basically pimping me out to them, Eileen was still in touch with them, still friends. I walked out of there and never spoke to her again. A week later, I found out that Ghislaine had gotten Eileen a job as Prince Charles's press secretary in the US.

Since first meeting Eileen, Jeffrey and Ghislaine, I have had many moments in my life where I felt kind of dizzy, like I was living in some kind of surrealist movie. This was one of those times. People often tell me my story is too far-fetched to believe – with the Wexners, the Clintons, the Rothschilds, Israeli intelligence, you name it – like it's just one huge conspiracy theory. Sometimes it almost feels like that to me, too, but then I remind myself – it's not a conspiracy when you've actually lived it.

CHAPTER 7
ARI BEN-MENASHE:
THE SPY WHO TOLD ALL

From 1977 to 1987, Ari Ben-Menashe moved in the highest circles of international espionage. The mysterious Iranian-born Israeli businessman worked for Israeli military intelligence, including being the handler for Robert Maxwell. In 1989, he was arrested in America for arms dealing, but was acquitted in 1990 after a jury believed that he was acting on behalf of Israel. The Israeli government tried to distance itself from him and statements were issued that he never had anything to do with intelligence, but the book, *The Assassination of Robert Maxwell*, details Ari's involvement. He also wrote a book exposing the arms trade: *Profits of War: Inside the Secret U.S.-Israeli Arms Network*.

Ari claimed that Epstein and Maxwell were running a honeytrap, providing girls to powerful people to gain leverage over them and to obtain information for the Israelis. Interviewing Ari, I found him to be extremely guarded, yet he provided valuable snippets into the intelligence agency operation, and he gave the history of Epstein's relationship with the Maxwells, which mainstream media has failed to report.

Here's an edited version of his interview:

Shaun: There are so many videos online about the Epstein case by researchers and journalists, and these videos, a lot of them are great information, but these are published by people looking into a goldfish bowl of the intelligence community. Now anyone who's worth their salt, who's been researching Epstein, would try and find one of the goldfish that are in the bowl to interview. And

I'm blown away today by having Ari on the podcast. Ari was at the top of the Iran-Contra fiasco. He was dealing with Robert Maxwell, he met Epstein, and he's got a lot more to say than those in the mainstream media. Ari, thank you for coming on. Would you like to just tell the people who you are and how you got into intelligence?

Ari: I worked for Israeli military intelligence after spending some time in Israeli military. And as such I met Robert Maxwell because he worked for us as well.

Ari first joined Israeli intelligence during his three years of compulsory military service (1974–77), working in a code-breaking unit deciphering Iranian communications. Ari had grown up in Tehran, the son of Iraqi Jewish immigrants. At fourteen, he moved with his mother to Israel where, on completing his education, he lived in a kibbutz before doing his military service. His fluent Farsi – as well as Arabic, English, French, Spanish and Hebrew – made him a perfect fit for the role. During this time, he found a way of cracking the code the Iranians used and also had a hands-on role in Operation Entebbe in 1976 – freeing Jewish hostages from a hijacked Air France flight in Kenya.

After his military service, Ari moved, as a civilian, to Israel's prestigious External Relations Department, its premier overseas intelligence operation. There, he monitored the overthrow of the Shah and the rise to power of Ayatollah Khomeini in Iran, had a key role in freeing the fifty-two American hostages in the US Embassy in Tehran, worked with the Sandinistas in Nicaragua, and was involved in the Iran-Contra affair. He also helped broker arms deals with the Soviet Bloc in return for banking Israeli intelligence money behind the Iron Curtain. It was also where he met Robert Maxwell.

Shaun: What year did you first meet Robert Maxwell?

Ari: I started with him in 1977.

Shaun: What year did you meet Epstein?

Ari: It was probably in the early Eighties in Maxwell's office.

Shaun: And how early did Epstein establish a relationship with Maxwell?

Ari: Quite early, I'm not sure. I'm not sure how they met, but Epstein was a young man about my age at the time. I was working for Israeli intelligence and he was working or had some sort of connection with Robert Maxwell, and he spent a lot of time in Maxwell's office at the time, at the *Daily Mirror*.

Shaun: So, the mainstream media is reporting that Ghislaine Maxwell went to America in the Nineties and then got in this relationship with Epstein. Is that bunk? Were there prior relationships to what's being reported?

Ari: Well, there was a prior relationship between them in London, and then she goes off to America to join Epstein. There was a prior relationship. Actually, Daddy helped create that relationship. Epstein at the time was a young, good-looking guy, Jewish boy from New York. And that was a nice little thing to have the daughter meet.

Shaun: And his motivation behind that was an intelligence motivation, or there was going to be some romance there?

Ari: He thought he was putting his daughter together with some sort of relationship, for some sort of personal relationship.

Shaun: So, it's like the emperor's built power by marrying the kids off to other powerful people, that kind of thing?

Ari: That's right.

Shaun: How high up in intelligence were you back then?

Ari: At the time I was working for military intelligence. Everybody mistakes it for the Mossad. I was not working for the Mossad. I was actually a civilian, working for military intelligence, and they were in charge of the Iran project. We were working through an independent committee that was running the Israeli policy towards Iran. So, we had a lot of connections and power up there.

In 1980, Ari was appointed to the Joint Committee, a small, select group of high-ranking personnel from military intelligence and the Mossad that oversaw Iran-Israel relations. The prime objective of the Joint Committee at the time was to supply arms to Iran to fight Saddam Hussein's Iraqi regime in the Iran-Iraq War. This led to his involvement in the Iran-Contra affair.

Shaun: There are a lot of young people watching this and they're not familiar with Iran-Contra. Could you just explain what Iran-Contra was and your role in that?

Ari: Yeah, the Israelis started to—we call it the Iran-Contra because of me, I'll explain. The Israelis were running a policy of arming the Iranian military to fight Iraq and Saddam Hussein, because at the time the Israelis saw Saddam as a threat and they had an ongoing alliance with Iran, first with the Shah, and then for another ten years with the Khomeini regime. And we were pretty close to the Iranians at the time, and they were arming the Iranians against Saddam. Saddam had invaded Iran's southern province, Khuzestan, wanted it because it was oil rich and so on.

But Israel helped the Iranians throw Saddam's army out of Iran. It was a scandal because it was a secret that Israel had a relationship with the Khomeini regime. The Iran-Contra scandal centred around the clandestine sale of US arms to Iran in the Eighties under the Reagan administration. Although officially there was an arms embargo on Iran, the US were secretly selling weapons to Israel, which was passing them on to Iran at a profit. In return, Iran promised to secure the release of American hostages held in Lebanon by Hezbollah.

The Nicaraguan Contra rebels later became involved when Lieutenant Colonel Oliver North of the US National Security Council began secretly diverting some of the profits from the Iranian arms sales to the right-wing Contra insurgents who were fighting against Nicaragua's socialist Sandinista government.

Shaun: And you were involved with Robert Maxwell around this time. Also, he had a big role in distributing Promis software. Could you explain to people what that project was about?

Ari: Promis software had the back door at the time, and the Israelis would have it sold through Robert Maxwell, and then we'd be able to follow or see what other intelligence services were doing through the computers.

Promis was a software programme developed by communications expert William Hamilton, for the US National Security Agency (NSA) in the 1970s. Hamilton then further developed the software through a non-profit organisation, Inslaw, before it was reclaimed by US intelligence. The software was able to track the movements of vast numbers of people and was seen as a way of keeping tabs on dissidents and terrorists. When Israeli intelligence got their hands on the programme, they quickly realised the software could be fitted with a backdoor and sold on to other intelligence agencies, giving Israel access to government secrets around the world.

To achieve this, Israeli intelligence needed a company to sell the bugged software. They turned to British media mogul Robert Maxwell, who they had already worked with – Maxwell had been laundering Israeli money made through the arms sales to Iran. Through Maxwell's front company, Degem, Promis was sold to a number of regimes around the world, including Guatemala, where it led to the capture and disappearance of 20,000 government opponents, and South Africa, where it helped round up, disappear or maim almost 12,000 black activists.

Bugged Promis software was sold by the US to a number of governments, including Britain, Australia, South Korea, Iraq, Canada and even the USSR.

Shaun: And this is all described in the book, *The Assassination of Robert Maxwell*, which quotes you extensively. How accurate is that book and how do you think Maxwell died?

Ari: I'm not commenting about the book, but I believe Maxwell died because he was about to be arrested by the British government over the pension scandal. As you may know, he stole the pension funds from the *Mirror*, yes. And the Israelis did not want him to sing. So, I believe the Israelis took care of him.

Shaun: Well, that's a very relevant answer and I was hoping you would say something like that, because I believe that people didn't want Epstein to sing and he met his untimely demise. Do you think that—

Ari: Maxwell and Epstein probably had a similar end.

Shaun: Now, in the book they are pointing at Israeli intelligence taking Maxwell out. To take someone out in a federal US prison, would that have to have been a concerted effort between multiple intelligence agencies?

Ari: I would assume so. If you read my book, I spent time in MCC in that exact same facility. Almost impossible to commit suicide in those cells. It would have had to be some coordination between different agencies, yes.

As mentioned earlier, MCC is the Metropolitan Correctional Center, a detention centre in New York where Jeffrey Epstein was held and where he allegedly committed suicide in August 2019.

Shaun: Because Epstein was six-foot tall, to hang off the top bunk his feet would still be on the ground, and you can commit suicide by leaning forward, but that wouldn't fracture those bones in your neck.

Ari: All I'm saying is it was probably impossible. You could probably commit suicide outside the cell, but not in the cell.

Shaun: I've looked at the unredacted black book and I've seen the names in there, and people often speculate as to who gave the order for him to have to go. Do you have any theories yourself?

Ari: Well, he had to go for various reasons, lots of reasons. And I believe that the Israelis wanted him to go because he might have started singing about what type of material he had, or had given, the Israelis.

Shaun: Now, after his first arrest, he got the sweetheart deal. How was that arranged and why later on was he not protected in a similar way?

Ari: Initially, he got the sweetheart deal because the Israelis felt that this could be under control and they could still work with him. But then later on, they felt that he had to go, it was too much.

Shaun: How did they feel about his co-conspirators? Ghislaine Maxwell, Jean-Luc Brunel, Leslie Wexner, just to name a few.

Ari: If I were them, his co-conspirators, I'd go into hiding, I'd just disappear.

Shaun: What do you believe that the role of the Clintons was in all this?

Ari: Well, one of Epstein's main targets at the time, going back to 1992, was Bill Clinton. The Israelis feared him, they thought he was going to be another Jimmy Carter to force them to give concessions to the Palestinians or to the Arabs as Carter did. So, Epstein had a role in compromising President Clinton.

Shaun: If Wexner gave Epstein this mansion for free, the mansion was already camera-ed up, and I just recently listened to a victim – Maria Farmer, I believe her name is – who was assaulted at a Wexner property. The cops were called out and they basically worked for Wexner. And her impression was that Wexner, in the intelligence agency operation, was Epstein's boss in America. Do you concur with that?

Ari: Possibly. At different stages, he may have had different bosses.

Shaun: And what do you believe Prince Andrew's role in all this was?

Ari: Prince Andrew made Epstein a very valuable asset of Israeli intelligence due to the fact that he was a royal in Britain. And he could attract certain personalities to play golf with him and maybe have fun with them in the evening with girls provided by Mr Epstein and then they would be compromised. Certain personalities were compromised by Prince Andrew, by bringing them into this trap. Now, Prince Andrew – the way I see it or the Israelis saw it – he was doing it for fun. It was just a decadent royal doing it for fun.

Shaun: Yeah. The impression I get is that he was a useful idiot with a big name.

Ari: Very useful idiot with a big name, very bored, decadent. He's having fun doing this.

Shaun: Epstein got the sweetheart deal when Obama and Hillary Clinton were in power, and now Trump is in power. Do you think that makes any difference? Like, will people be brought to justice in this case or will there just be a continuation of coverups?

Ari: Personally, I think there will probably be a cover-up, probably an attempted cover-up. But who knows? There are lots of people that got hurt by Mr Epstein and this operation. So, you never know. You never know.

Shaun: If Epstein was only a mid-level manager of the operation, is the operation continuing right now in a way that people aren't aware of?

Ari: The Israelis continue operating. They don't stop.

Shaun: Is every intelligence agency, then, is it like an arms race where you have to become more devious and diabolical and they're all engaged in the honeytrap schemes?

Ari: No, no, no. I wouldn't say every intelligence agency does these things. Intelligence agencies do collect information, I think. But this, the Israelis always took it to an extreme, and they always claim we're in danger, the Arabs are about to destroy us so we need an intelligence agency that does certain things.

Shaun: Earlier on, you said that a sweetheart deal came about because of Israeli intelligence. How much pull does Israeli intelligence have in America?

Ari: There is an Israel lobby in the United States that has lots of pull, I don't need to get into it. And when they're told to do something by the Israeli government, they will do it.

Shaun: So, it seems that people in these operations, including yourself, when your usefulness is over, you are sacrificed one way or another, either killed, incarcerated, criminalised, so that you can't speak in court. What happened in your situation?

Ari: In my situation, I believe that what really happened was that I was into the peace deal with the Palestinians, and they had to get rid of me at the time. I went to see, as the advisor to Prime Minister Shamir at the time, I went and saw Arafat and we started the Oslo process. People in Israel were not very happy about it, so they tried to set me up with the Iran deal, which I was part of. But to everybody's surprise, I did not plead guilty and ask for a pardon, then I went to trial, and I got acquitted. Very unusual situation, but it happened and the whole thing blew up because I got acquitted and I testified in Congress. The whole story's written in my book.

In 1989, Ari was working as a personal intelligence advisor to Israeli prime minister Yitzhak Shamir. He became involved in secret talks between Israeli intelligence and the Palestinian Liberation Organisation (PLO). At the time, Shamir was involved in clandestine plans with PLO leader Yasser Arafat to organise a Palestinian uprising against King Hussein's regime in Jordan. The intention was to create a Palestinian homeland within Jordan, thus relieving tension around the West Bank and Gaza Strip in Israel, and ultimately leading to peace between Israelis and Palestinians.

As part of the talks between Israel and the PLO, Ari was sent to Sri Lanka to meet a PLO representative and organise the transfer of cash via arms sold to local Tamil freedom fighters. This had the two-fold objective of bringing Israel closer to the PLO and helping to free three Israeli soldiers held hostage in Lebanon.

However, the PLO talks were leaked and there was a backlash against Shamir for doing deals with Israel's sworn enemies. Ari believes he was used as a scapegoat for the regime. Lured to America on the pretence of meeting an acquaintance, Ari was arrested in Los Angeles in 1989 and charged with conspiracy to sell three US C-130 aircraft to Iran in contravention of the US Arms Export Control Act. The charge was a fit up and was discredited in court by Ari's lawyer during the subsequent trial, leading to his acquittal. Ari later testified about the Iran-Contra affair to the US Congress. He has been unable to return to Israel ever since.

Shaun: During the Iran-Contra period, who were the highest people in the American government you were liaising with? Did you have access to Bush, Reagan, Oliver North, Felix?

Ari: Well, we had the access, the Israeli government had access to the highest levels. But as for us, we had access to the higher levels of the CIA. I mean the National Security Council in the White House and so on. Pretty high up.

In 1986, Ari personally briefed then-Vice President George Bush Senior about arms sales to Iran, during Bush's visit to Jerusalem.

Shaun: Would you say that Reagan was just a figurehead at that point and George H. W. Bush perhaps had more power?

Ari: Over intelligence matters, yes. Because George H. W. Bush was CIA and worked for the CIA. He was head of the CIA earlier on. So yeah, I would say so.

Shaun: I've written a book about Barry Seal, *American Made*, who was flying the cocaine in as part of Iran-Contra. Do you think that some of Epstein's money came from laundering drugs?

Ari: The Israelis weren't into drugs so much, they were into guns. So, I would believe that Epstein's funds actually came from Israel more than from the drugs that were sold to Central America. And why I claim, by the way, that Iran-Contra was named after me, it was because after the Iranian project was sort of over, I was Israel's point man in Central America for a while, working at the Israeli consulate in New York, flying back and forth.

Shaun: So, on the weapons story, what was Maxwell's relationship with Khashoggi and Epstein's relationship with Khashoggi?

Ari: Well, weapons. I don't think Epstein had a serious role in the weapons trade; everybody seems to connect him with that, but I don't believe that for a minute. [Robert] Maxwell was laundering funds for the Israeli government, money that was being received from Iran for the weapons they were transferring to the Iranian government, that was Maxwell's role. We had a relationship with him for quite a long time. But again, once he got into trouble financially, the Israelis did not want him to sing. He was about to be arrested by the British authorities over the *Mirror* scam.

Shaun: During Iran-Contra, we had the cocaine coming into Arkansas and then getting distributed throughout America; Oliver North was supposedly in charge of that under George H. W. Bush, and Bill Clinton was providing the security – the state police – which was protecting that. Do you agree with those statements?

Ari: Probably there was drug dealing back and forth, yes. We as Israelis knew about it, but the details I'm not sure about; the Israelis weren't part of that.

Shaun: How does the president, like George H. W. Bush, do a photo with a big seizure of cocaine? How does he get away with actually coordinating bringing cocaine into the country at the same time?

Ari: I have no answer to that. I mean, it is what it is. How does Prince Andrew get away with messing around with young underage girls for such a long time? And some people believe that George H. W. Bush lost the presidency to Clinton because of the testimonies that were going on in Congress in 1991 and '92 over the Iran-Contra affair. And one of the people that testified was myself in the Senate and in the House of Representatives. And if you remember, they were controlled by Democrats, the two houses, while the Republican was president. But before that, he was still doing very well. He had a very high popularity rating.

Shaun: When you're called to testify like that, what kind of questions do they ask you?

Ari: Everything. Very detailed. Some of it was closed.

Shaun: Okay. Who's more likely to get extradited to America? Julian Assange or Prince Andrew?

Ari: Probably Julian Assange.

Shaun: And why is he so dangerous to them?

Ari: He knows a lot, put out a lot, and, quote unquote, we have to teach people a lesson. You cannot put out this information. If you do, you're going to pay for it.

Shaun: So, do you find that when you put out your own information, there's a line you have to draw?

Ari: Of course you have to draw a line. And at the time, I was real lucky that Mr Clinton became president, because I testified against George Bush, and if he would have been president, I would probably have been dead meat.

Shaun: Have you had threats on your life over the years?

Ari: At the time, yes. I was almost killed in Washington driving together with a very well-known journalist, and also a friend, called Robert Parry. He died of cancer recently, but we were about to be killed when I flew from Australia to Washington to testify in the senate.

Shaun: Wow. What attracts you then to this kind of work if you know there's a risk?

Ari: Now we're doing political consultancy work. We have a company in Canada that does the political consultancy. I say we have privatised diplomacy. We help different governments or different personalities politically, and getting them into the right position. We're pretty well known. We just recently helped the Sudanese government.

Shaun: Would you say that when you first joined military intelligence you were idealistic?

Ari: Yes. I never became cynical, but you start seeing the real thing.

Shaun: What was the first event that caused you to start seeing the real thing?

Ari: The attitude of the Israelis towards the Palestinians. Things like Epstein. [Robert] Maxwell wanted Epstein to join our team, but we refused. So, Maxwell goes to his friend over our heads at Israel who was head of military intelligence, Ehud Barak, and gets Epstein to join.

Shaun: And what was your impression of Epstein then? Did you think he was this super villain, super-intelligent?

Ari: No, no, no, my impression was just another useful idiot.

Shaun: Ghislaine Maxwell speaks four languages. She can pilot submarines and underwater robots, and she's been described as quite an intelligent villainous character. Do you agree with that?

Ari: She is an intelligent person. Yeah, sure.

Shaun: Do you think that she was bringing these kids into Epstein's orbit to impress him because she loved him?

Ari: She was working with him.

Shaun: But there was a romantic relationship at some point?

Ari: Well, there was a relationship at some point, because you have to also understand that it turned out that Mr Epstein did not like women.

Shaun: He wanted kids. And do you think that when she was rebuffed and she found that out and she was in love with him, she continued in this conspiracy to try and be around him?

Ari: Yeah, that's right.

Shaun: What was your impression of her when you first met her then?

Ari: Well – a smart, well-schooled young lady at the time; she was pretty young.

Shaun: Do you think this will blow over or will it be an unsolved mystery like the Kennedy assassination where there's still speculation?

Ari: Epstein is not as important as Kennedy, let's not give him too much credit. But, there's a but here. I believe when all the nasty stories about Israeli intelligence or the Israeli state start coming to the surface, and they might, the story will probably continue.

Shaun: From my research, I've asked you the questions at the top of my mind, is there anything that you feel I've left out that you would like to tell people?

Ari: Yeah. And again, Prince Andrew was a prize for the Israelis. Epstein was able to trap real-important people and compromise them. And this is why the Royal Family really were upset when they found out about this stuff. Again, a useful idiot.

Shaun: And then for Andrew to go back after the conviction and be the guest of honour at Epstein's coming-out-of-prison party. That is what flabbergasts people a lot, especially in this country.

Ari: Again, useful idiot. He was having fun and he didn't want to – little girls, he liked little girls – he didn't want to give it up, did he? Until the very end.

CHAPTER 8
ROBERT MAXWELL:
"THE BOUNCING CZECH"

Robert Maxwell was not always Robert Maxwell. Born Abraham Leib Hoch on June 10, 1923 in the Czech village of Slatinské Doly, his name was changed to Jan Abraham Ludvik to make it sound less Jewish on the birth register. It was the first of several name changes in his life before he finally settled on the very British-sounding Ian Robert Maxwell.

His mother, Hannah, was a survivor of anti-Jewish pogroms in Poland. Her family had fled until they settled in what would later become Czechoslovakia. His father, Mechel, was also an immigrant Jew whose family had traded cattle and horses for the few generations they had lived in Slatinské Doly, after arriving from some unknown origin in the east. Maxwell inherited his physique from his father – who was tall and broad-shouldered – and his mind from his mother. Hannah was a quick-witted woman with a passion for social justice and a Palestinian home for the Jews. Maxwell would later say she had intended for him to be a rabbi who would take the family to Palestine where they could live in the dignity denied them in Slatinské Doly.

Life was indeed harsh in the village. Winters were severe and two of Maxwell's six siblings died of pneumonia in childhood. The rest shared a single bed, ate a staple of potatoes with an occasional piece of smoked fish, and shared a single pair of shoes which they stuffed with paper to adjust the size.

It was no place for someone with Maxwell's burning ambition. As he grew, his mother encouraged him to move away to avoid the cloying poverty and the growing anti-Semitism that was emanating from Nazi Germany.

In 1939, Hitler annexed Czechoslovakia. Maxwell, aged sixteen, left his village and family behind and joined the Czech army. He later claimed to have fought the Nazis in Eastern Europe, retreating to the Black Sea and finally making his way to southern France via Bulgaria and Greece. In Marseille, he joined the Second Regiment of the Czech Legion and sailed with them to Liverpool. Stationed just outside Dover, the man – now calling himself Jan Hoch and speaking almost no English – requested to join the British Army. He was transferred to the Pioneer Corps stationed near Birmingham, where in his downtime he began to learn the English language and the finer points of English etiquette from a local woman who he may also have been having an affair with.

By 1943, he had adopted the speech and mannerisms of an English gentleman. He applied for a post with the North Staffordshire Regiment and was enlisted in its 17th Infantry Brigade under the new name of Leslie du Maurier, the moniker inspired by the popular brand of Du Maurier cigarettes. In 1944, he rejoined the war as part of the second wave to storm the Normandy beaches on D-Day. In France, Maxwell fought with distinction, receiving the Military Cross for bravery under fire and receiving a commission as an officer. He also changed his name again to Leslie Jones and, finally, to Ian Robert Maxwell on the advice of his commanding officer, who said the name sounded more fitting for an officer in the Staffs. France was also the place where Maxwell met his future wife.

A French protestant from a middle-class background, Elizabeth Maynard first met Maxwell in the newly liberated Paris of 1944. Working in the offices of the Paris Welcome Committee, she was supposed to introduce him to Parisians who wanted to meet and entertain Allied servicemen. At the sight of the big charismatic man in his officer's uniform, Betty found herself becoming faint. Maxwell, playing the part of the dashing officer, caught her in his arms. It was love at first sight. In just a few months, the couple were married – a marriage that was to last more than fifty years, not all of them as happy as the first.

When the war was over, Maxwell continued his military service in Berlin where, as an intelligence officer, he was responsible for interrogating high-ranking Nazi officials. It was a time when the political map of Europe was being redrawn. New ties were being forged and new partnerships formed, and much of it was happening in Berlin. Maxwell met a lot of interesting and important people, particularly from the intelligence and business worlds.

It was through one of these contacts that Maxwell's long career in publishing began. He started working with Ferdinand Springer, a German publisher of scientific books, and became the British and US distributor for his company, Springer Verlab. In 1951, Maxwell merged the German publisher with a British rival, Butterworth Press, and renamed it Pergamon Press. It was the first in a long line of publishing and media companies that Maxwell would have a hand in.

Back in the UK, Maxwell was not content just as a businessman. He began a political career and, following his mother's socialist leanings, became a Labour Party candidate in 1959. In 1964, he won a seat as Labour MP for Buckingham, which he kept until 1970. In the meantime, he continued to consolidate a corporate power base and build his ties with the intelligence world. Maxwell's post-war scientific publishing empire had extended from Germany and Britain into Eastern Europe and the Soviet Bloc. He had built ties with the KGB and at some point he had begun working for Israel's most famous – or infamous – intelligence agency, Mossad. Although throughout his life Maxwell would be linked to the intelligence services of Britain, the Soviet Bloc and Israel, it was to the latter that his true and ultimate loyalty would be bound. He would never forget the religion or culture of his family upbringing, and he described Jerusalem as the only place he was ever truly happy. Nor would he forget the ultimate fate of his family – the mother, father and siblings he had left behind in Slatinské Doly, most of whom had been killed during the Nazi occupation.

Perhaps this was one of the reasons Maxwell used his ties with the KGB to help arrange the transit of Soviet Jews to Israel, a task which, according to Maxwell biographers Gordon Thomas and Matt Dillon, earned him the reputation of a modern-day Moses. According to Thomas and Dillon's book, *Robert Maxwell, Israel's Superspy*, he also laundered money and bought and sold arms for Israel, and he used his scientific publishing interests to sell technological secrets to the burgeoning state. But it would be through a piece of computer software that Maxwell would make his biggest and most successful contribution to Israeli intelligence.

Promis was a programme developed by US intelligence services and was, at the time, being used by the US Department of Justice to track criminals. The software was capable of tracing the movements of vast numbers of people and, as such, could be invaluable for the purposes of spying. Israeli intelligence had covertly obtained a copy of the software, redesigned it and fitted it with a trapdoor. This meant it could be sold on to foreign governments and organisations, who would unwittingly be sending all the information back to Israel.

In order to market and sell the bugged software without the fingerprints of Israel's spy agencies, a cover organisation was needed – a corporation with global reach and international influence. Israel turned to Maxwell, who marketed the software through his computer company, Degem.

In 1984, Maxwell, who was still celebrating his acquisition of Mirror Group Newspapers, went to work on the project, and quickly secured the first customer for Promis – Robert Mugabe's Zimbabwe. South Africa's apartheid regime quickly followed along with Guatemala, Colombia and Nicaragua. All these regimes used the software to round up, incarcerate or disappear thousands of political dissidents. Maxwell even installed the software in the shadowy world of Swiss banking, selling the product to Credit Suisse. This enabled the security services to identify Israeli millionaires who had illegally opened overseas accounts. It also led them to secret money-laundering operations by the CIA and the American mafia, who were rinsing up to £300 million a day through Credit Suisse. The software gave Israel the numbers of every one of these top-secret accounts.

Promis, either through Degem, or the US's own version, went on to serve many of the prime intelligence agencies in the world, including those of France, Germany, the UK, the Netherlands and even China. Maxwell alone would make £500 million from sales of the software, all while providing a steady stream of information back to the Mossad. But perhaps the tycoon's greatest coup was to sell the software to Sandia National Laboratories, the home of the US's ongoing nuclear weapons research programme. Maxwell secured the deal via a Republican senator, John Tower, who was a powerful voice in Washington and a close ally of then-Vice President, George H. W. Bush. Tower, who was being paid by Maxwell using Mossad funds, effected an introduction to the Sandia officials, and Maxwell completed the sale. It was an intelligence coup of staggering proportions, one that would enable Israel to steal nuclear secrets from the world's foremost nuclear weapons research lab and stay one step ahead of its competitors in the arms race.

It wasn't the only clandestine nuclear weapons operation that Maxwell was part of. In September 1986, he received a worrying call from his foreign editor at the *Mirror* (and by many accounts fellow Israeli spy), Nick Davies. Davies had been approached by a Colombian-born journalist from Australia called Oscar Guerrero, claiming he had proof that Israel was manufacturing nuclear weapons. Guerrero had made friends with an Israeli citizen travelling in Australia who claimed to have worked at a top-secret Israeli base in the Negev desert, where nuclear devices were being developed. This whistle-blower, Mordecai Vanunu, was said to have photographic proof of his claims and was thought to be in hiding in London, where he was selling his story to *The Sunday Times*.

Maxwell immediately called Nahum Admoni, director general of the Mossad, with the news. The well-oiled gears of the intelligence agency went immediately into action and Maxwell's *Sunday Mirror* published a story ridiculing Guerrero and Vanunu's claims. In the meantime, Israeli agents were scouring every hotel in London for the whereabouts of Vanunu. Towards the end of September, they finally located him and an elaborate honeytrap was set up to capture the traitor. A beautiful female approached Vanunu in Leicester Square and got chatting to him. The woman, posing as an American called Cindy, was actually a Mossad agent called Cheryl Ben-Tov. Ben-Tov seduced Vanunu and persuaded him to accompany her on a trip to Rome.

The spy flew with Vanunu to the Italian capital and accompanied him to an apartment where three more Mossad agents were waiting. They overpowered Vanunu and injected him with a paralysing drug. Later, they escorted him in an ambulance out of the city and down to the coast, where a speedboat was waiting. The speedboat rendezvoused with a freighter off the coast and three days later, Vanunu was in Israel, where he was to spend the next eighteen years in solitary confinement. Maxwell's part in the affair had been brief but crucial. It was another in a growing list of services to his spiritual homeland.

For every idealistic motive, Maxwell seemed to have a baser counterpart. Through his KGB connections, he had long been laundering money through the Bank of Bulgaria. In the late Eighties, with the onset of Mikhail Gorbachev's Perestroika and the loosening of the Iron Curtain, Maxwell saw an opportunity to make lots of money through the impoverished Eastern European country. Maxwell made a deal with Bulgaria's president, Todor Zhivkov, to help fund and oversee the wholesale theft of technology from Western companies and its resale in the Soviet Bloc. To accomplish this, Maxwell was effectively given the keys to Bulgaria's secret service to help run the operation.

Not only did the scheme, dubbed Neva, go on to succeed – stealing technological secrets from every major Western nation and reselling them in the East – but it led to the creation of perhaps the world's first globalised criminal network. Through the Russian and Bulgarian contacts Maxwell made via Neva, he began to construct a criminal web that would encompass US mafia, South American drug cartels, the Triads, the Yakuza and the Russian mafia. This criminal octopus traded in prostitution, money laundering, drug trafficking, pornography, contract killings and human trafficking of every kind. It was a global criminal syndicate worth billions and it all transpired under the umbrella of an intricate web of shell companies that Maxwell had set up. It made Maxwell what one FBI executive called: "The man who set in motion a true coalition of global criminals."

Yet it still didn't seem to satisfy Maxwell's insatiable greed. Nor, incredibly, did it provide him with financial security. Despite the huge money-laundering operations and increasingly seedy business deals, Maxwell was edging closer and closer to the brink of financial ruin. His acquisitive nature was beginning to get the better of him and he couldn't keep up with the interest on loans that had financed the buying of his latest assets, such as the publishing company Macmillan. On top of this, falling share prices in his above-board companies like Mirror Group Newspapers (MGN) and Maxwell Communication Corporation (MCC) had led him to increasingly desperate measures. Maxwell had been secretly buying shares in his own companies to prop up their prices. To accelerate the downward spiral, this money was being drawn from funds which were already being used as collateral for other bank loans. When his financial situation became desperate, Maxwell did the previously unthinkable. He began to plunder the pension funds of his employees at MGN.

It didn't stop the rot. By the time his bank repayments had reached £415 million a year, Maxwell was resorting to evermore desperate measures. He persuaded his bankers at Goldman Sachs to buy shares in MCC to boost market confidence, saying he would then buy them back. The problem was he needed to borrow the money to do so from other banks. To break the vicious cycle, he resorted to serious fraud, fictitiously claiming he had sold two of his companies for £120 million in order to set the share prices rising. It worked, for a while. But by now it was just postponing the inevitable.

His personal life was also falling apart. His marriage to Betty had long been a sham. His affairs had started early – his first serious one, lasting several years, had been in 1974 – but by now they numbered perhaps in the dozens. He had usually kept his assignations in the penthouse suite at Maxwell House or on his super yacht, the *Lady Ghislaine*. But by now, he was even bringing them back to the family house at Headington Hill Hall, where they masqueraded as personal assistants or secretaries. Whenever he arrived in Bulgaria or Israel on a business trip, he expected to have one of his favourite prostitutes waiting at the hotel room. Aside from the physical cheating, he had become emotionally distant from Betty, sharing none of his thoughts or concerns, indeed hardly seeing or speaking to her at all. His visits home were increasingly fleeting and his manner cold. The inevitable came shortly after her seventieth birthday – Maxwell said he wanted a divorce. When Betty presented him with her list of financial settlements, he agreed to only one – eight days a year aboard the *Lady Ghislaine*.

Maxwell's increasingly rogue financial activities hadn't escaped his Israeli backers. The new director general of the Mossad, Shabtai Shavit, was openly distrustful of the supposed superspy. Maxwell's increasing financial indiscretions and his involvement in organised crime were beginning to make him more of a liability than an asset. Perhaps sensing this, Maxwell was beginning to become paranoid for his safety. He hired the services of Jules Kroll, one of the world's most accomplished private detectives, to investigate what Maxwell called his "business enemies", who he thought were conspiring to destroy him. His personal behaviour became more erratic – cancelling engagements, switching travel plans at the last moment, and spending hours alone listening to tapes of his employees' conversations at Maxwell House, which he'd had bugged.

His paranoia was not necessarily irrational. A fellow Israeli spy and close friend, Amiram Nir, who had been embroiled in the Iran-Contra scandal, had recently met with a mysterious end in a plane crash over Mexico. When John Tower – Maxwell's backdoor into the White House – was also killed in a plane crash, Maxwell's obsessive tendencies went through the roof.

In the meantime, he was fending off groups of enraged bankers left, right and centre, repaying loans with other loans and using shares as collateral that had already been promised elsewhere. Somehow, he managed to keep all the plates spinning – just. But in his desperation, he began to pester the Mossad for financial help. It may have been the last straw. Maxwell had recently been outed as an Israeli spy in Seymour Hersh's book, *The Samson Option*, about Israel's nuclear programme. Coupled with this unwanted publicity was Maxwell's increasingly worrying involvement in Russian politics. The tycoon had suggested holding a meeting between KGB head, Vladimir Kryuchkov, and Mossad chiefs over engineering a possible coup in Moscow in exchange for the transportation to Israel of Russian Jews. The suggestion of getting Israel directly involved in the attempted overthrow of a super-power regime must have only confirmed the Mossad's appraisal of Maxwell – that he had lost his judgement and become a liability.

In November 1991, everything came to a head. On November 4, Maxwell had missed a meeting with the Bank of England about his default on £50 million worth of unpaid loans. On the following day, he was reported missing in the seas of the Atlantic just off the Canary Islands, where he had been cruising aboard the *Lady Ghislaine*.

Later that day, his body was found. The autopsy uncovered no injuries and an inquest ruled death by accidental drowning caused probably by a heart attack. Suicide could not be ruled out – Maxwell clearly had a lot on his plate and it was beginning to catch up with him. But Maxwell's daughter, Ghislaine, would claim something very different. She said her father had been murdered. Two former Israeli intelligence officers, Victor Ostrovsky and Ari Ben-Menashe, agreed with this conclusion. Ben-Menashe described how a Mossad hit team had drawn up alongside the *Lady Ghislaine* in the early hours of the morning, boarded the boat using rubber grappling hooks and injected Maxwell in the back of the neck with a lethal nerve agent before dumping his body over the side and making their escape.

Maxwell, according to Ben-Menashe, had finally become too much of a liability. The possibility of his arrest and trial for financial crimes could spell the leakage of some very uncomfortable state secrets. Maxwell was always a wild card but he had, in the end, become too unpredictable. He simply had to go.

Israel had always been Maxwell's spiritual home and it was there that he found his final resting place. His funeral was a lavish state affair conducted on the Mount of Olives, where he was buried amongst the heroes and statesmen of the modern state of Israel. Prime Minister Yitzhak Shamir, President Chaim Herzog, and no fewer than six serving and former heads of Israeli intelligence attended the ceremony.

The glowing testimonials to one of the world's most powerful businessmen were soon followed by the fallout from his collapsing empire. Banks from around the world were frantically calling in loans. Maxwell's sons, Kevin and Ian, desperately tried to hold the sinking ship together but it was too far gone. They were declared bankrupt with debts of £400 million. Maxwell's theft of his Mirror Group pension funds soon came to light and in 1996 Kevin, Ian and two other former directors went on trial for conspiracy to defraud. They were all acquitted. The pension funds were partially replenished by the British taxpayer; however, the company's employees ultimately only received half of what they were due.

Maxwell's legacy was ultimately one of lies and deceit. Characterised in the British media as "Cap'n Bob" and "the bouncing Czech", he had become something of a joke. However, the legacy he left the state of Israel was something altogether different: thousands of Soviet Jews repatriated; millions, perhaps billions of dollars laundered and stored through his banking networks;

the sale of bugged Promis software to some of the most powerful countries in the world; and a major hand in the theft of US nuclear secrets. Liar, fraudster, bully, philanderer, criminal, cheat – whatever else he had been, Maxwell was an unswervingly loyal servant to his spiritual homeland.

And then of course there was the protégé he left to the world – Jeffrey Epstein.

CHAPTER 9
LESLIE WEXNER:
"THE HEAD OF THE SNAKE"

On March 6, 1985 in Columbus, Ohio, lawyer Arthur L. Shapiro bolted suddenly from his parked car. The forty-three-year-old attorney sprinted across a cemetery, chased by a man with a gun. Shapiro made it as far as the door to an apartment before the gunman caught up with him, firing two bullets into Shapiro's head at point-blank range as the victim hammered desperately on the door, killing him instantly.

The murder of Arthur Shapiro would never be solved. But, ten years later, an unexpected clue turned up, shedding light on who might have been behind the mob-style hit. It was a leaked copy of a document thought to have been destroyed in 1985 by then-Columbus police chief James Jackson. The incriminating document pointed the finger at a famous Ohio billionaire who had an otherwise pristine reputation, at least on the surface.

The man was Leslie Wexner, an Ohio born-and-bred businessman whose life story read like a template for the American dream. Born on September 8, 1937 in Dayton, Ohio, Wexner's parents were both Russian Jews. The family owned a clothing store named 'Leslie' after their son in which Wexner got his first retail experience after graduating from Ohio State University with a degree in business administration. Wexner said in a report for CNN that he was tasked with running the family store while his parents took a much-needed vacation. While they were away, Wexner analysed the profit and loss margins and discovered that the less high-end items such as blouses and skirts were more profitable than the expensive clothing such as jackets. This led to the inspiration behind his own clothing retail store, The Limited, which he set up in 1963 with a $5,000 loan from his aunt. As the name suggested, The Limited ran a reduced selection of moderately priced clothes with a high turnover and good profit margin.

Wexner opened a second store a year after the first, and by 1969 the company had gone public. By 1976, The Limited had 100 stores across the United States and Wexner was buying up other companies to expand his empire. In 1982, Victoria's Secret joined the list – the women's lingerie brand that Epstein would use as a cover for his sexual abuse and trafficking. By the time of the Shapiro murder, Wexner was already a household name across America and a fixture in every shopping mall. He was also giving lots of money to Jewish causes with his Wexner Foundation, set up to educate Jewish communal leaders in Jewish history and culture. Nobody could have been less likely to be involved in a mob-style murder.

Perhaps that's why Columbus police chief James Jackson ordered the destruction of the report linking Wexner to the crime. According to a later investigation into Jackson's potential corruption, he had destroyed the report by one of his detectives because he thought it could have been libellous. The report linked Wexner and a number of other millionaire Ohio businessmen as being potentially connected to the murder of Shapiro. According to local journalist, Bob Fitrakis, who was sent a leaked copy of the report, the document revealed that Shapiro was due to appear in court the day after his murder. The partner in Columbus law firm, Schwartz, Shapiro, Kelm & Warren, had apparently failed to file income tax returns for the previous seven years. The report stated that Shapiro was the lawyer who represented The Limited, and speculated that the hit had been organised by Wexner and his colleagues to stop incriminating information coming out in Shapiro's testimony.

Irrespective of whether Wexner was actually involved in Shapiro's murder, the Columbus police report is interesting because it exposed links between Wexner and organised crime. The report, written by Elizabeth Leupp – an analyst with Columbus police's Organized Crime Bureau – noted that The Limited used a haulage firm called Walsh Trucking Company and was owner Francis Walsh's "single biggest customer". Walsh, according to the report, even used The Limited's headquarters as his mailing address. Nothing suspicious about this except that Walsh had known ties to the Genovese crime family, and was charged in 1988 with making illegal pay offs to reported mob figures. Interestingly, the indictment against Walsh mentioned unindicted co-conspirators as legendary mafia figures Anthony "Fat Tony" Salerno and Matthew "Matty the Horse" Ianniello.

Despite the legitimate nature of Wexner's public profile, it seemed shadier things were going on beneath the surface. But it wasn't just ties to organised crime, like Epstein and the Maxwells; Wexner was moving in even deeper circles, circles that involved intelligence networks like the CIA and the Mossad. As we have seen, by the mid-Eighties Wexner was already working with Epstein, who himself was deeply tied to intelligence. Then, in 1991 Wexner founded an organisation called the Study Group or Mega Group, along with partner Charles Bronfman. Ostensibly, the Mega Group was made up of rich businessmen with an interest in promoting Jewish interests in the United States. However, many of its members had links to Israeli intelligence and organised crime, according to an article by independent journalist Whitney Webb.

Charles Bronfman was a business partner of Israeli "superspy" Robert Maxwell, having partnered with him in a bid to buy *The Jerusalem Post* in 1989. Charles's brother, Edgar Bronfman – another Mega Group member – was, as has already been noted, Epstein's client at Bear Stearns, where an SEC investigation into financial irregularities with Bronfman's company, Seagram, was the possible reason for Epstein's dismissal. The Bronfman family as a whole had a history of organised crime, as Webb shows, with their father, Samuel Bronfman, one of the main importers of illegal alcohol to the US during the prohibition era. As such, the Bronfmans built up extensive ties with various mafia leaders, including Charles "Lucky" Luciano, Moe Dalitz, Abner "Longy" Zwillman and Meyer Lansky. The family, according to Webb, was also tied to sex-trafficking rings and the use of underage honey-trap victims to blackmail key figures.

It seems unlikely that the children of such a mob-connected man as Samuel Bronfman would entirely dissociate from the criminal underworld, and indeed Webb shows that many prominent members of Seagram's dynasty were connected to major Canadian crime figures throughout the Sixties and Seventies. Fast forward to the present and Edgar Bronfman's daughters, Clare and Sara, are heads of the infamous NXIVM sex-trafficking cult, with Clare Bronfman pleading guilty to sex-trafficking offences in 2019. Some things, it seems, just run in the family.

Other prominent Mega Group members have ties with organised crime, intelligence and senior figures in the Israeli government. One of these is Ronald Lauder, the heir to the Estee Lauder cosmetics dynasty and president of the World Jewish Congress. Lauder served as US Deputy Assistant Secretary of Defence, and during his time at the Pentagon had become a friend and ally of then-Israeli representative to the United Nations, Benjamin Netanyahu. Lauder became an instrumental player in Netanyahu's rise to Israeli prime minister in 1996 and was a major donor to Netanyahu's party, Likud. According to Webb, Lauder also has ties to Israeli intelligence via his funding of Israel's IDC Herzliya, a university closely associated with the recruitment of intelligence agents.

Even more interesting, in 1986 Lauder became the US ambassador to Austria. As was revealed earlier, Epstein had an Austrian passport that was discovered when his New York mansion was raided by police. Given that Epstein's lawyers claimed this was given to him in the Eighties by "a friend", Webb makes the credible assertion that this friend was likely to have been Lauder. As the US ambassador in Austria, he was in a unique position to obtain such a document. Another prominent Mega Group member, hedge fund manager Michael Steinhardt, admitted to his own links to organised crime in his autobiography, where he wrote that his father worked directly for mob boss Meyer Lansky. Indeed, Wexner's own mentor and fellow Mega Group member, Max Fisher, is alleged to have worked with an organised crime group called the Purple Gang, smuggling illegal Bronfman liquor from Canada to the US during the prohibition. Another member, and founder of CBS News, Laurence Tisch, worked for the Office of Strategic Services (OSS), the precursor to the CIA.

But it wasn't just his colleagues in the Mega Group that had ties to Israeli intelligence, Wexner had enough of his own. The Wexner Foundation paid $2.3 million to former Israeli prime minister and head of military intelligence, Ehud Barak, for two studies – one of which was not even finished – according to *The Times of Israel*. It was Barak who, according to Ari Ben-Menashe, signed Epstein up to Israeli intelligence in the Eighties. In 2015, Barak co-founded a company with Epstein which is now called Carbyne 911 and will be discussed further in a later chapter. Barak has flown on more than one occasion on the *Lolita Express* and also visited Epstein's New York mansion several times. He has also been spotted in several instances entering the building owned by Epstein's brother, Mark, on Manhattan's East 66th Street, where models from the Epstein-funded modelling agency, MC2, were housed. The huge apartment building was purchased from none other than Leslie Wexner.

If there were any doubts remaining about Wexner's high-level influence on geopolitical events concerning Israel, a document uncovered by Ohio journalist Bob Fitrakis should dispel them. The leaked report, entitled "Wexner Analysis: Israeli Communication Priorities 2003", outlines a political PR campaign to keep American interests tied to those of Israel using propaganda concerning the Iraq War. The report recommends the use of the words 'Saddam Hussein' as much as possible as a fear-instilling bogeyman and to constantly link Arab terrorism against America to Israel's "ongoing efforts to eradicate terrorism on and within its borders". Fitrakis noted that the PR campaign was part of "a systematic campaign to identify Israeli national security interests with U.S. military and security interests". And Wexner and the Mega Group, it seems, were at the heart of it.

Could it be that Wexner, co-founder of the Mega Group, was the head of both an overt and covert Israeli operation to tie America's interests inseparably to those of Israel? Was part of the covert operation a honeytrap scheme involving underage girls to entrap prominent political figures that he ran in conjunction with Epstein? Ex-Israeli intelligence agents like Ari Ben-Menashe and Victor Ostrovsky certainly think so. And independent researcher Ryan Dawson, who has been studying Epstein for thirteen years, has come to the same conclusion – that Epstein and Ghislaine Maxwell were the frontmen for the operation, with Wexner the shadowy sponsor. It certainly fits the evidence of all the properties which Wexner kitted out with cameras then essentially gifted to Epstein. And Epstein victim Maria Farmer claims that Ghislaine Maxwell always made it clear that she worked for Wexner, not Epstein. According to Farmer, Wexner was "the head of the snake" in the US. And it was on Wexner's Ohio estate that Farmer was abused by Epstein and Maxwell. When Farmer called 911, she was told, she claims, that Wexner owned the local police, so there was no chance she would escape from the billionaire's estate with her life.

Wexner himself always claimed that Epstein had pulled the wool over his eyes, alleging Epstein had misappropriated millions of dollars from his funds. Was Wexner really the naïve victim he claimed to be? It certainly doesn't fit with the evidence. Limited staff had reportedly told Wexner that Epstein was using Victoria's Secret as a front to abuse underage girls as early as the Nineties, and yet Wexner did nothing to stop it.

Wexner formally ended his relationship with Epstein in 2007, distancing himself from the Florida sexual abuse case. And in 2020, Wexner stepped down as CEO of his L Brands empire, following bad press connecting him to Epstein. However, Wexner's involvement in the story may not stop there. Former Epstein lawyer, Alan Dershowitz, has brought the shadowy billionaire back into the spotlight thanks to his ongoing legal battle with Epstein victim Virginia Giuffre. Giuffre has claimed she was forced by Epstein to have sex with Dershowitz, and Dershowitz is counter-suing Giuffre for defamation.

In the ongoing battle, Dershowitz has claimed that Giuffre tried to extort money from Wexner by making similar claims that the Ohio businessman had raped her. Dershowitz is seeking to subpoena Wexner to testify in his case. This must be embarrassing for Wexner because this is the first time this information has come to light and he clearly wanted to keep any dealings with Giuffre secret. Even worse for Wexner, Dershowitz, who seems less inclined to keep his mouth shut, claimed in an interview with Turkish news channel TNT World that Wexner had been accused of raping Epstein victims on no less than seven separate occasions.

And there has been further bad publicity. Yair Netanyahu, son of Israeli prime minister, Benjamin Netanyahu, is in court for claiming that several top Israeli officials are part of a Wex-ner-funded "paedophile cult". The officials are all alumni of Harvard University's Kennedy School, where they were beneficiaries of Israeli fellowships funded by the Wexner Foundation. It is unclear why Netanyahu is claiming the school is a paedophile cult, but given the ties between Wexner, Epstein and Harvard, and Netanyahu's possible insider information, it is certainly not a claim to be dismissed out of hand.

It is unclear yet whether the Ohio billionaire will be dragged into the ongoing Ghislaine Maxwell investigation, but it seems more information is bound to come to light one way or another. For a man who has kept his private life largely under lock and key and his reputation intact, Leslie Wexner may soon be forced to step out of the shadows. The secrets he brings with him could be more shocking even than Epstein's or Maxwell's, and perhaps more egregious. Nevertheless, come out they must. Light, as they say, is the best disinfectant.

CHAPTER 10
EPSTEIN AND CLINTON:
"HE OWED HIM FAVOURS"

On January 26, 1998, in a televised address to the nation, US President Bill Clinton uttered the famous line: "I did not have sexual relations with that woman, Miss Lewinsky." Monica Lewinsky was a twenty-one-year-old unpaid intern working for Clinton's chief of staff, Leon Panetta. In secretly taped conversations with her friend, Linda Tripp, Lewinsky admitted to nine separate occasions of sexual contact with the president at the White House. She had also kept a blue dress with Clinton's semen stains on it.

Clinton was later forced to testify in court and admitted to having "inappropriate intimate contact" with Lewinsky. Later the same day, a shocked nation watched his televised speech as he admitted: "Indeed, I did have a relationship with Miss Lewinsky that was not appropriate." The man who many had thought would be the new JFK hadn't quite turned out how the nation had expected. Instead, he had abused his position to take advantage of a young girl.

Talk about the tip of the iceberg ...

Looking into all the scandals and cover-ups in Bill Clinton and wife Hillary's personal and political careers would require several volumes. I have documented some of them in my books, *Clinton Bush and CIA Conspiracies* and *American Made*. For this chapter, we will concentrate solely on his links to Epstein and the crime and intelligence circles he moved in.

Clinton's connections to Epstein are clear and well documented. He flew at least twenty-six times on the *Lolita Express* and Epstein had more than twenty different contact numbers for him in the infamous black book (which contains contacts thought to be mostly Maxwell's). According to official sources, there was also one meeting between the pair in Clinton's Harlem office and one trip to Epstein's New York mansion with his full security detail. In addition, *New York Magazine* reports that in 2003 Epstein threw a dinner party at his house in Clinton's honour. Although Clinton himself didn't turn up, other notable attendees were Donald Trump, magician David Blaine and Clinton's closest advisor, Doug Band.

As we shall see, this is just scratching the surface and the two had a friendship which spanned at least the late Nineties to the late Noughties. Clinton has vehemently denied ever visiting Little St James island but Virginia Giuffre, in her legal testimony, recounts Clinton spending an evening at the island in which he had dinner with Epstein and Maxwell before retiring to bed with two young girls from New York. And Clinton's aide, Doug Band, admitted in an interview with *Vanity Fair* that Clinton had visited the island in January 2003. Band said it was one of the few presidential trips he declined to go on as he had smelled a rat on an earlier 2002 *Lolita Express* trip to Africa, accompanied by Kevin Spacey and Chris Tucker, in which Band claimed Epstein had made a series of ridiculous claims, including that he had invented the derivatives market. Band said he hadn't known about Epstein's sexual improprieties but that he "got enough bad vibes" that he "advised Clinton to end the relationship".

One thing that has not come to light from Clinton's relationship with Epstein (so far anyway) is any sexual relations between Clinton and minors. Epstein's masseuse and sex slave, Chauntae Davies, who was pictured giving Clinton a shoulder massage on the 2002 Africa trip, told the press that he had acted like a "perfect gentleman" the whole time. In Virginia Giuffre's account of Clinton's trip to the island, she makes no mention of the two girls accompanying him as looking underage, and indeed Epstein himself — when questioned in prison in 2019 as to whether

Clinton had a predilection for underage girls – told fellow inmate William Mersey: "No, he liked them mature."

However, to say Clinton was a womaniser would be an understatement, and he was no stranger to sexual misconduct. He has been accused of rape or sexual assault by four women: Juanita Broaddrick accused Clinton of raping her in 1978; Leslie Millwee accused him of sexually assaulting her in 1980; Paula Jones accused him of sexually harassing and exposing himself to her in 1991; and Kathleen Willey accused him of groping her without her consent in 1993. Aside from this, Clinton has publicly admitted to two extra-marital affairs, one with Monica Lewinsky and the other with singer, model and actress Gennifer Flowers. One can only imagine the number of affairs and flings he has not admitted to.

One of those affairs might even have been with Ghislaine Maxwell herself. We have testimony from Maria Farmer about an occasion when Clinton came to dinner at Epstein's New York mansion. Farmer describes Maxwell in a state of extreme nervous excitement as she rushed about the place making sure everything was perfect, ready for the president's visit. Before Clinton arrived, everyone was banished from the property except for two house-maids and the chef, according to Farmer. There are also pictures of Clinton and Maxwell posing outside the Lolita Express looking very close. And in 2014, when Clinton visited LA, Maxwell was invited to an intimate dinner with him, as reported by *The Daily Beast*. This was three years after Maxwell had been exposed as having taken part in Epstein's abuse of minors by the *Daily Mail*. According to the *Beast*, Clinton's aides argued over the decision to invite Maxwell, and to this day still apportion blame over the move.

There was also a strong connection between Clinton's daughter, Chelsea, and Maxwell. *Vanity Fair* journalist, Gabriel Sherman, told of how Clinton's advisor, Doug Band, showed him a picture of Bill and Chelsea posing with Epstein and Maxwell at the king of Morocco's wedding. According to Band, Chelsea and Maxwell remained friends well after Epstein's exposure as a paedophile. Chelsea took a yacht trip with Maxwell in 2009 and in 2010 she invited Maxwell to her wedding to Marc Mezvinsky in New York.

But what was the nature of the connection between Clinton and Epstein, assuming Clinton wasn't interested in young girls, as Epstein averred? According to one source, there was one clear reason – Epstein had a plane and, after his presidency, Clinton needed transport to fulfil all his philanthropic goals around the world. Similarly, he was after money and we know that Epstein donated $25,000 to the Clinton Foundation in 2006. In Clinton's own words to *New York Magazine* in 2002: "Jeffrey is both a highly successful financier and a committed philanthropist with a keen sense of global markets and an in-depth knowledge of twenty-first-century science. I especially appreciated his insights and generosity during the recent trip to Africa to work on democratization, empowering the poor, citizen service and combating H.I.V./AIDS." Epstein's typically cold view of the friendship was: "I invest in people – be it politics or science. It's what I do."

According to Virginia Giuffre's testimony, when Clinton visited the island, she asked what he was doing there and Epstein answered that Clinton "owed him some favors". It seems likely then that Epstein did have something over Clinton that he could blackmail him with. Whether that was connected with underage girls or something else remains to be discovered. The assumption is supported by the strange painting of Clinton that hung in the 71st Street mansion. The large painting shows Bill Clinton draped over a chair wearing a blue dress and pointing to the viewer. The dress, which could be a reference to Monica Lewinsky's blue semen-stained dress, or a similar dress worn by Hillary Clinton, is clearly a humorous hint that Epstein had dirt on the ex-president.

Whatever that dirt was, it might have come from their numerous trips together on the *Lolita Express* or it may have originated from long before. According to the official narrative, the financier and the president first met at a White House charity event in the Nineties. However, like so many of Epstein's associations, the relationship may have gone back far longer.

To appreciate the full extent of the ties between the two, we need to go back to the Eighties, when Clinton was the governor of Arkansas. As I revealed in my books, Clinton was no stranger to political corruption right from the beginning of his career. Throughout the early Eighties, the CIA, with the full collusion of then-vice president George H. W. Bush, were trafficking millions of tonnes of cocaine from Central and South America into the United States as part of the deal to supply arms to the Nicaraguan Contra rebels. The CIA were then off-loading these drugs to dealers around the States and raking in the profits.

Arkansas was the base of operations from which cocaine was smuggled into the US, with much of it coming into the airport in Mena or being dropped off at designated points to be picked up by agents on the ground. Clinton was the governor of Arkansas throughout the Eighties, and despite claiming he knew nothing about the operation, it is clear that he was deeply involved. As I show in *Clinton Bush and CIA Conspiracies*, Clinton's Arkansas state troopers acted as security and protection at the drop sites and for the agents carrying out the operation. Clinton's cronies were also used to murder witnesses to the drug-smuggling operation, including sixteen-year-old Don Henry and seventeen-year-old Kevin Ives, otherwise known as the "boys on the tracks". Henry and Ives were run over by a cargo train in Alexander, Arkansas at around 4 a.m., as they lay on the rail tracks covered, according to witnesses on the train, by a green tarp. According to the official investigation, the boys had fallen asleep on the tracks after smoking too much marijuana (somehow covering themselves with a green tarp before doing so). The ridiculous nature of the conclusions led Kevin Ives's mother to push for a second autopsy, which found that Henry's shirt had evidence of a stab wound to the back and that Ives's skull had been crushed prior to the train collision.

As I show in *Clinton, Bush and CIA Conspiracies*, it is likely that the boys, who were out hunting with flashlights, had stumbled over one of the CIA cocaine drops and had been murdered by agents at the scene.

The ridiculous ruling of accidental death in the boys on the tracks case was just one of many hallucinogenically bizarre verdicts by Clinton-owned state medical examiner, Dr Fahmy Malak. Just some of his weirder rulings included the case of Raymond P. Allbright, who was found shot dead outside his house in Mountain Home. Malak ruled the death as suicide despite the fact that he had been shot five times in the chest. Another case was that of Gregory Stephens who, according to witnesses, had been shot outside his home from 40 feet away in the street. In court, Malak testified that Stephens had been shot at point-blank range. Several other pathologists were brought in and confirmed that Stephens was not in fact shot at point-blank range, and subsequent DNA analysis found that Malak had been studying tissue samples from a different corpse.

Malak was also instrumental in helping Bill Clinton's mother, Virginia Kelley, avoid scrutiny for the death of one of her patients. Kelley, who was a nurse anaesthetist, had been involved in the death of a patient from lack of oxygen during a fairly routine dental operation because Kelley had been unable to intubate her correctly. Malak, however, ruled that the woman had died from the original incident – a piece of concrete thrown at her during an altercation, that hit her in the mouth and knocked out several teeth. Despite a string of such "mistakes" and complaints about his performance, Clinton refused to get rid of Malak, instead giving him a raise. Indeed, despite the many victims of Malak's corruption coming together to form a pressure group called, brilliantly, Victims of Malak's Incredible Testimony (VOMIT), Malak survived most of Clinton's tenure as governor, only resigning his post when Clinton announced he would be running for president. He quickly found a new job at federal level, however, as a consultant for the Health Department.

Not only was the corruption surrounding the murder of witnesses ludicrously obvious, but Clinton himself was directly profiting from the CIA drug-smuggling operation. As I document in *Clinton, Bush and CIA Conspiracies*, a Clinton employee called Larry Nichols blew the whistle on Clinton's Arkansas drug operation. Nichols, who worked his way up to become director of marketing for Clinton's Arkansas Development Finance Authority (ADFA) – supposedly founded to create jobs and assist churches – soon became so suspicious of the money pouring into the organisation that he began studying its accounts. He discovered that ADFA, among other things, was acting as a massive money-laundering operation for the CIA's cocaine-smuggling activities. According to Nichols: "There was a hundred million a month in cocaine coming in and out of Mena, Arkansas."

There is a lot of evidence that Clinton himself was a heavy cocaine user at this time. Numerous witnesses have attested to seeing Clinton using it at parties, including one party attendee, Sharlene Wilson, who said Clinton used her "one-hitter" cocaine snorting device and took so much cocaine "he slid down the wall into a garbage can and just sat there like a complete idiot". Such was the extent of Clinton's cocaine abuse that his half-brother, Roger Clinton, said on record: "He's got a nose like a vacuum cleaner." And Roger Clinton was himself arrested for dealing cocaine when he tried to sell some to an undercover police officer.

The common thread between Clinton's governorship of Arkansas, the CIA's cocaine-smuggling operation and Jeffrey Epstein is the cargo airline, Southern Air Transport (SAT). SAT was a front company for the CIA and was used to transport weapons to the Nicaraguan Contras and to import cocaine during the Iran-Contra scandal. In 1994, SAT transferred its operation from Miami, Florida to Columbus, Ohio, where it was predominantly used to transport clothing from Hong Kong. Its premier customer? None other than Leslie Wexner.

Could there have been more to the SAT transfer than met the eye? As investigator and author Charlie Robinson pointed out in one of our many interviews: "Why do you need a CIA plane to run a cargo for your Limited brand operation?" Robinson went on: "Could that be a cover story? Absolutely, you're damn right. It could be 90% women's lingerie for Victoria's Secret and pants for

Limited and shirts from Express and all that stuff. And it could have been 10% filled with heroin, or guns, or kids, or whatever."

From what we know about the large number of underage foreign girls Epstein was taking into the US and his links with Wexner, it is not at all far-fetched to suggest that the pair were using SAT planes to smuggle children into the country. Indeed, Robinson goes further and suggests that Epstein may have had direct links with the Clinton Foundation in smuggling children out of Haiti in the aftermath of the devastating 2010 earthquake. Robinson refers to the New Life Children's Refuge case, where ten US missionaries led by Laura Silsby were caught illegally smuggling thirty-three children from Haiti to the Dominican Republic. Although the group were supposedly orphans, it soon became clear that most of them in fact had living parents. Despite being arrested by Haitian authorities, nine of the ten missionaries were released, with only Silsby facing trial and six months in a Haitian prison. This leniency was due to direct intervention by Bill Clinton.

It turned out that this wasn't Silsby's first attempt to smuggle children out of Haiti. According to a CNN report, Haitian police had previously intercepted her at the border trying to remove forty children from the country. According to a WikiLeaks exposure in 2013, Silsby's former legal advisor, Jorge Puello Torres, was arrested in the Dominican Republic by Interpol, who were looking for him "after El Salvador officials said they suspected him of being involved in running a human trafficking ring that recruited Central American and Caribbean women and girls and forced them to work as prostitutes".

After her return to the US, Silsby married and changed her name to Gayler. She was then appointed VP of Marketing for a company called AlertSense, which works with the US government on its Amber Alert system, triggering alerts when children go missing. What an astonishing role for a woman with a history of kidnapping and child trafficking.

Robinson suggests that there were heavy links between what

Silsby was doing and the Clinton Foundation, which was deeply involved in Haiti after the earthquake, and that these links may have extended to include Epstein's child trafficking operation. As Robinson said in one of his interviews:

When reporters had gone to the US Virgin Islands to talk to the people at the airport, they had asked them: "When Jeffrey Epstein was coming and going all these years, did you ever see kids?" And they said: "Yeah, yeah, yeah, we saw a lot of kids." And they said: "Well, where were the kids from?" They said: "Well, a lot of the kids were from Puerto Rico and the Dominican Republic and Haiti." And so you have to wonder, and it's speculation, but I think it's a logical step to make, was Laura Silsby taking kids out of Haiti through the Clinton Foundation and taking them to Epstein somehow? The Island is not that far from Haiti. If you look at it geographically on a map, it's not that far, it's a quick plane ride or a boat ride.

Given the mystery of how Epstein was smuggling such vast numbers of underage girls into the US, together with Epstein's close links to Clinton, the evident ties between Clinton and Silsby, and Silsby's connection with child trafficking, it doesn't seem at all beyond the realms of possibility that these seemingly disparate actors were all in fact linked in a massive Caribbean-based child-trafficking operation.

CHAPTER 11
WHITNEY WEBB

Whitney Webb is an independent journalist and researcher who has dived deep into the background of the Epstein case. She is the author of *One Nation Under Blackmail: The Sordid Union Between Intelligence and Crime that Gave Rise to Jeffrey Epstein*. (Her Twitter handle is @_whitneywebb). Here's an edited version of her interview:

Shaun: Could you say how you came into the Epstein case, please?

Whitney: I have been writing with MintPress News for about three years. And that is where this series ended up being published. I got into writing about the Epstein scandal quite by accident and I only really had decided to investigate it for myself when it came out that Alex Acosta – who used to work in the Trump administration – when being interviewed by the Trump transition team, stated that his reason for signing off on Epstein's sweetheart deal in 2008 was because Epstein had belonged to intelligence. So, when that came out, I was really interested in seeing if I could find out which intelligence agency that was and the nature of how that relationship began and things like that.

And what I found is that this is something that did not really start with Epstein but that goes much farther back. And there's a lot of ties between Epstein to previous sexual blackmail operations that really date back to the prohibition era. Because this is a tactic that was really perfected in the US by the American mafia, who later got into bed with intelligence. And that nexus is essentially what gave rise to Jeffrey Epstein, which is probably like the shortest summary I can give of the whole series I did, which was a four-part series with a couple of spin-offs.

Shaun: Shall we start with the relationship between Bloomberg and Epstein and his associates?

Whitney: That is my most recent Epstein-related article and I think it's really relevant because Michael Bloomberg, of course, is seeking the presidency now as part of the Democratic Party, and oddly enough, even though he has pictures with Ghislaine Maxwell, and he was in Epstein's book of contacts where Epstein had at least five different numbers and a couple of addresses for Bloomberg, there has been no questioning of Bloomberg on those ties, which I think is really troubling, and a very damaging indictment of mainstream media. Especially because, when the Epstein scandal first broke, there was lots of – even in the mainstream and alternative media as well – speculation about his ties to the Clintons, his ties to Trump, and really anyone that was seen as having very close ties with Epstein, they automatically almost became radioactive as it were.

After Epstein was arrested in July, 2019, Bloomberg announced his candidacy on November 24 of that year. There has been no interest, apparently, in American mainstream media in asking Bloomberg about those ties, oddly enough; and rival campaigns for the presidency in the US that have sought to throw shade on Bloomberg and have criticised him for various things, they have also declined to pursue this, which I think is quite troubling. Another of those ties that I think is also significant is Bloomberg's ties to Leslie Wexner, who of course was a very close associate and the source of a large amount – if not the majority – of Epstein's so-called fortune. Bloomberg was known to socialise and attended parties at Wexner's homes on more than one occasion.

We know from Epstein accusers that Wexner's homes on occasion were used by Epstein for his nefarious ends. And, of course, there's been no interest in that. And also, Wexner was one of these figures that was pressured in the wake of the Epstein scandal to recuse himself from public life, not unlike what happened to Prince Andrew and some other close Epstein associates. And that is why Wexner was pushing really to sell and leave his position as CEO of his company, The Limited or Limited Brands. And it was actually a Bloomberg-backed private equity firm that took over that company recently. Sycamore Partners bought the controlling stake from Wexner, allowing him to step out of his role in the company with a hefty payout. I forget the exact sum, but it has over $100 million dollars of Bloomberg's money in it.

So, I think that connection was also glossed over and that's why Bloomberg is attending Democratic debates and is very much a relevant figure in US politics, but he hasn't been questioned on those ties at all. Which I think is really significant. And I also in the article go over a couple of other ties that Bloomberg has to people that were also connected to Jeffrey Epstein in various forms, including Mort Zuckerman, a media executive who bought, for example, the *New York Daily News* after Robert Maxwell's death. Maxwell was the previous owner and also had close ties with Jeffrey Epstein, who I believe was a former business partner of his and also attended dinners at his home and is a long-time supporter and backer of Michael Bloomberg – who, not unlike Mort Zuckerman, is also a New York media executive.

Shaun: So, in the eyes of the public, the tabloids, there is a trafficking conspiracy that has Epstein at the top, and then there's Ghislaine Maxwell, Jean-Luc Brunel, etc. But you've said that what Epstein was doing was part of a much bigger picture of intelligence agency honeytraps, which have been going on for decades. So, is the grand conspiracy bigger than the tabloid conspiracy? Where does Wexner fit into that? Was he above Epstein?

Whitney: Oh yeah, I definitely think so. I think Epstein was really more of a frontman for interests that Wexner is closely associated with and represents. But going back into the history – I'm trying to think of where is the best place to start with Wexner – basically, we know that Wexner had ties with organised crime by the early 1980s and his relationship with Epstein … it's not exactly clear when it began because both Wexner and Epstein, when they were asked over the years about the day that they had met, both gave different responses, each one of them saying – depending on who was interviewing them – a different year at any given time. The range goes from 1985 to 1989, with 1987 also being thrown out there. So, it's not exactly clear when they met. But it appears—my guess would be that it was 1985, based on my research and some of the sources that I've cited in my series and subsequent articles, and this is because in 1985, Leslie Wexner was implicated in the murder of his lawyer, Arthur Shapiro, and a police report from that time period directly linked Leslie Wexner to organised crime interests, specifically the Genovese crime family, which is one of the main factions of the National Crime Syndicate to which numerous other families in the so-called Mega Group that Wexner co-founded with Charles Bronfman … they all have ties to the same National Crime Syndicate either through their families or through their own business relations.

Wexner is one of those individuals to have co-founded the Mega Group, but before then he and Epstein were involved together in a lot of shady real-estate deals in New York. This was also at the time when Epstein had met and began to associate publicly with other figures in the New York real-estate circle, I guess you could say. This included Donald Trump, this included Thomas Barrack of Colony Capital, who was and continues to be a close associate of Trump. And going forward, by the time the Nineties had really begun, Wexner and Epstein were incredibly close. Epstein exercised an incredible amount of control over Wexner's finances, had power of attorney, had the right to hire and fire people at Wexner enterprises. And it was at that point that Wexner and Epstein together oversaw the relocation of the CIA front company, Southern Air Transport, that was involved in the Iran-Contra scandal from its previous base in Miami, Florida to Columbus, Ohio, presumably to run cargo for The Limited, which at the time was the nation's largest retailer.

But of course, there were figures in Ohio's government that speculated about Epstein and Wexner, because this was well known to the public actually to be a CIA front company because of reporting on the Iran-Contra scandal. These officials speculated and had apparently strong reason to believe that Epstein and Wexner were both working with the CIA in some capacity, and were smuggling for interests that related to both the CIA and organised crime, leading Ohio's inspector general at the time to refer to that cargo run for The Limited that Southern Air Transport relocated to do as the "Meyer Lansky run", a reference to the famous Jewish-American mobster who was really the head of the National Crime Syndicate that I just mentioned. So, this National Crime Syndicate has close ties both to US intelligence and Israeli intelligence in a sort of, I would call, a transnational crime syndicate.

And I think honestly that Epstein, even though he had ties to both intelligence agencies, was really working more for them because they have transnational interests that at times thrive better with perhaps Israel's current government than the US's current government. But these billionaires that are behind this group have their own agenda and occasionally the governments to which they're closely tied will deviate from that, at which point someone like Epstein could use blackmail to keep them in line with the so-called Mega Group's agenda. So, that's my personal take on it, though substantial evidence has grown or come out, since I published my series in August, that the sexual blackmail operation in particular was most closely tied to Israeli military intelligence.

This comes from a couple of sources, including a person who most recently came out and said this – Steven Hoffenberg, who was Epstein's former business partner at Towers Financial, which was this huge Ponzi scheme, basically, that they started together in

1987 and which collapsed in 1993. Only Hoffenberg was charged, even though Epstein was the architect of the scheme, because his name was later dropped from the case, not unlike what happened with his sweetheart deal. So, he clearly had friends in high places way back then. The sexual blackmail operation is believed to have begun somewhere around 1993 and 1995, but well before then, as I just sort of laid out, there were ties to intelligence that were ongoing, and even during later in his life, Epstein would claim that during the 1980s he worked directly with the CIA. He had ties to people or was working on behalf of people like Adnan Khashoggi, the infamous Saudi arms dealer who had ties to Saudi, US and Israeli intelligence.

So, I think Epstein, honestly, was more like a mercenary, I guess you could say in the world of intelligence, doing things like sexual blackmail, financial crimes and things of that nature. And was really a frontman for the sort of mafia-type enterprise, the Mega Group, that hides behind this mask of philanthropy; they call themselves philanthropists, but they all have deep ties to organised crime.

Shaun: So, you've mentioned about Southern Air Transport. So, I wrote a book on Barry Seal and he was flying loads of cocaine into America for the CIA, weapons out, financing the war, going down to Nicaragua. And through that research it brought me to the Clinton crime family. And I learned there's a place where organised crime and the intelligence agencies and the political mafia co-exist. It seems like we've been on separate journeys, but we've reached the same destination. You've mentioned the Mega Group several times. For people who are not familiar with all this terminology, could you just expand on what the Mega Group is?

Whitney: The Mega Group is this group of so-called philanthropist billionaires which was founded by Leslie Wexner and Charles Bronfman in 1991. Its membership roster isn't public, but there was a *Wall Street Journal* article that was the first public reveal, I guess you could say, of the group's existence. That was published, I believe, in either 1998 or 1999. The group was founded in 1991 and they were referred to as the Mega Group or the Study Group. They had a couple of different nicknames, but I guess Mega Group is the name that stuck, because they are these so-called mega-billionaires. And what these guys all have in common is that they are nominally American, but they also all have an extreme support for the state of Israel. And nearly all of them have direct ties to organised crime, either through their families or by virtue of their actions and business interests.

I mentioned Leslie Wexner being named by the Ohio police as an affiliate to the National Crime Syndicate. The Bronfman family has its ties to the National Crime Syndicate going back to when that crime syndicate was founded – actually, it predates the founding of that crime syndicate. Anyway, the Bronfman family's ties, it goes back to the prohibition era in Canada, which preceded the US on prohibition. You have other figures like Michael Steinhardt, who is also very close to Michael Bloomberg who we were just talking about. And Michael Steinhardt's father was actually Meyer Lansky's jewel fence and was a major player in the New York criminal underworld and was actually the person that jump-started his son's Wall Street career. Michael Steinhardt is a well-known hedge fund manager and has recently made headlines because of the numerous amounts of women accusing him of sexual harassment and very deplorable behaviour. Another figure that's tied to organised crime would be Max Fisher, who is not alive anymore but used to be a major political operative and advisor to Henry Kissinger and Nixon.

And he was also, I believe, the founder of the Republican Jewish Coalition, which is basically one of the main funding sources for neoconservative uplift candidates. Today, it's dominated by Sheldon Adelson [Adelson died on January 11, 2021] and Paul Singer, but Leslie Wexner used to be a major player there as well as some other members of the Mega Group. Max Fisher used to associate with the Detroit Purple Gang, which was another sort of faction of the National Crime Syndicate of the Jewish-American mob based in the area where he grew up in Detroit, Michigan. And there's several more. Even Steven Spielberg, for example, who's part of this Mega Group, he's a protégé of Lew Wasserman, who was a protégé himself of Moe Dalitz, who was this well-known Jewish-American mobster based in Ohio who was named by the FBI and the precursor to the DEA of being basically second in command or the number two-type ranking figure in Meyer Lansky's criminal empire, which really is the National Crime Syndicate.

The National Crime Syndicate, which I've mentioned a lot, that was founded by Charles Luciano and Meyer Lansky in the 1920s, and sort of brought the Jewish mob and American mob together. But at a certain point during World War Two, when that syndicate first got in bed with US intelligence, Luciano was deported to Italy and basically Lansky took over the whole operation and dominated it. So, Lansky is a really key figure in how this developed. And, of course, these figures themselves were very involved in sexual blackmail operations well preceding their union with US intelligence, and they actually helped the CIA or the precursor to the CIA, the OSS, blackmail the long-time director of the FBI, J. Edgar Hoover, among numerous other politicians and military officials.

But basically, the Mega Group is sort of an outgrowth of that same syndicate that has long-standing ties to US and Israeli intelligence. But they're also major political donors, as I mentioned; the Republican Jewish Coalition, they're major political donors, not just in the US but also in the state of Israel. A lot of members of the Mega Group, including Ronald Lauder, who's a close friend of Trump and was also a close friend of his mentor, Roy Cohn … he was one of the main backers of the Likud party and oversaw Netanyahu's first victorious campaign as a prime minister of Israel in 1996 and was largely credited with that campaign being successful, which was really—Netanyahu was the underdog there and Lauder through his large financial backing of that campaign and also connecting him with Arthur Finkelstein, this Republican political operative in the US who's quite controversial, that was basically credited with Netanyahu winning that campaign. So, they have close ties to both governments and both intelligence agencies. And that's sort of where—the more you look at this group, that starts to really seem like the centre point of this whole web that Epstein was a part of.

Shaun: A lot of people were baffled when it came out that Epstein was courting all these heads of technology, and reading what you've been researching and writing about, the power is in tech and the intelligence agencies are permeating themselves in the fields of tech to get that power. You mentioned in a recent article about Twitter and how, in particular, Israel is putting people in these positions, in these technology companies to get that information and get that power. Could you expand on that, please?

Whitney: Yeah, sure. So, this is something that both US and Israeli intelligence had been doing for several decades. A good place to start would be the 1980s with the Promis software scandal, which involved both US and Israeli intelligence, the installing of a backdoor into the software that was stolen from the company that created it and then was basically marketed all over the world by people, including by Robert Maxwell. And then that allowed both the US and Israeli intelligence through separate backdoors to have access to all the databases where that software was installed. Promis was just the first of many such companies that have been doing that for a very long time. There was recently an exposé, I believe published in *The Washington Post*, about how a cryptography company based in Switzerland, that was very widely used and respected, was actually secretly owned by the CIA.

And a lot of that same software had a trapdoor, not unlike what had taken place several years prior with the Promis software. But increasingly, even though both the US and Israel in the past, like in Promis, had collaborated to do that type of activity, there are also situations where Israel has done—Israeli intelligence has basically used that same approach, but in targeting the US rather aggressively. Leaked NSA documents have revealed that the NSA considered Israel to be the third-most aggressive spy agency targeting the US behind Russia and China; that would put Israel ahead of countries like Iran and North Korea, which is quite significant. So, anyway, after September 11, there were a series of reports on Fox News by Carl Cameron, who basically revealed that there were several companies – Israeli companies, software companies, tech companies and telecommunications companies – that were very involved in basically providing back-doors to sensitive US communications to Israel's government.

And we also know that one of those companies was involved in basically the wiretapping of the White House, which is how Netanyahu acquired tapes of Bill Clinton and Monica Lewinsky basically having phone sex and attempted to use it as leverage over Clinton. And that apparently was a factor in Clinton deciding to pardon Mark Rich, who is the founder of Glencore and was a fugitive for a very long time, and a controversial part in Clinton's last days in office. So, this same operation – there's Promis and there's all this going on in the Nineties up until after 9/11. And in the post-9/11 era, this I would say, exploded because in the era of post-9/11 America, there's been a push to sort of digitise counter-terrorism efforts. A lot of those software, the software used for that, have had ties to the Maxwell family, including one that was used by the FBI and several other agencies after 9/11.

And this continues up until today. There's a company that I wrote about recently called Cybereason, that is basically run by the former head of offensive nation state hacking operations for Israeli military intelligence, who viewed his work at Cybereason, he said himself, as a continuation of his work at Israeli military intelligence, and they have been installed, their software has been installed – it's an antivirus software – it's basically been installed on networks for the DISA, the CIA, the NSA and several other sensitive networks for the US Army and the US Navy. And technology experts quoted in numerous articles have noted that antivirus specifically gets access to end points of the entire system – not just the computer itself, but the networks its connected to – in order to protect the software, and is the "ultimate back door", one of them said, into these networks.

So, this type of stuff continues. A lot of it is pushed through really actively by the Israel lobby, which includes organisations funded by these Mega Group donors and also other lobby groups. And it has really been to the benefit of the state of Israel, all of that. Epstein was even involved in one of these companies. He was funding one called Carbyne 911, which is basically an Israeli military intelligence-linked company that gets installed in all the emergency-call software or the infrastructure for 911 emergency calls in the United States. And then what that software does is that when you call 911 from your phone, it gets access to literally everything on your phone and then stores it, and then uses algorithms to predict your future behaviour and future crime and precrime, and all this other Orwellian stuff.

And of course, this company, not only did Epstein invest in it, Peter Thiel of PayPal and Palantir, who's very close to the Trump administration, and also has ties to Israel, also invested in that. And the chairman of the board, one of the other main investors, is Ehud Barak, who we know had very close ties to Jeffrey Epstein. He's not just the former prime minister of Israel, but the former head of Israeli military intelligence at the time that Epstein was allegedly recruited to work for them in the 1980s. So, that's pretty significant. He was a frequent visitor, not only to Epstein's island, but also spent the night at apartments where Epstein kept a lot of his sex slaves basically. That was owned by Epstein's brother, Mark Epstein. And Ehud Barak has somehow evaded – not unlike many other figures connected to the scandal – a lot of political scrutiny. He sort of got some mud thrown at him by Netanyahu when he tried to run in the recent Israeli election. And then he stepped back and decided not to run. But beyond that, there hasn't been any push for accountability from Ehud Barak and this company that I just mentioned that was funded by people like Epstein directly and backed by Ehud Barak, who's chairman of its board.

They're still installing phones with the 911 software in several counties in the US, with plans to expand. So, that's where that is at this current point in time. The fact that Epstein would be interested in backing something like this is significant, but it's part of a broader policy push with Israel's government and some of these Mega Group-linked or other pro-Israel billionaires in the US to basically outsource or make US tech dependent on Israeli tech with the ostensible purpose of preventing boycotts of Israel at any point in the future, which has sort of been a push of the Israel lobby within the United States where you can't even criticise Israel in US universities or at public institutions or things of that nature due to legislation that's gone forward. And I think that that broader push is part of why we see someone like Epstein, after his sexual blackmail operation was exposed, begin to cultivate really close ties with the tech industry, cultivating ties with people like Elon Musk of Tesla, and appearing at dinners with people like Reid Hoffman of LinkedIn, meeting with people like Mark Zuckerberg of Facebook and really trying to rebrand himself – before his most recent arrest – as a tech investor. A lot of those interviews where he was trying to promote himself as such ended up not being published after his arrest, but there were several outlets that came out and said they'd interviewed Epstein from that perspective of sort of painting him as this investor in tech, in the US technology sector.

Shaun: You've raised Bill Clinton's name, and a lot of people have asked where did Epstein's money come from? So, there's this mind-boggling amount of money in circulation because of these deals that the intelligence agencies are running. Do you think that some of Epstein's money came from that or was he laundering proceeds from such deals?

Whitney: I definitely think he was super-involved in money laundering. And I think, if you look at Epstein's history, he left Bear Stearns in 1981. I think he had ties to the BCCI, the Bank of Credit and Commerce International, which was very involved with the Iran-Contra scandal, because we know that some of Epstein's clients during that time – like Adnan Khashoggi – relied heavily on that bank, and that that bank was heavily connected to intelligence at a time when Epstein claimed at one point that he was working for intelligence. I think that there are definitely connections there. As to the laundering that the Clintons set up in Arkansas while Bill Clinton was governor, I don't know if Epstein had direct ties to that one in particular, but that was just one of many money-laundering operations that were being supervised and run at the behest of the CIA during that period of time.

But I think Epstein, because during the 1980s he was not really in the US that much, he spent a lot of time in London and traveling around, as evidenced by this mysterious Austrian passport that sort of came to light after his recent arrest. He was going all over the world, but it appeared that he wasn't spending any amount of time or long periods of time in the US specifically. I also think it's interesting – and which hasn't really gotten enough coverage, in my opinion – in terms of the BCCI scandal, that BCCI was also involved in the sex trafficking of minors as an attempt to blackmail and basically bribe officials in different governments to get them to go along with or rather to not prosecute and look the other way when it came to the BCCI's criminal activity, money laundering among other things.

And we know for a fact that this happened because it's in the US Senate report or Senate investigation of the BCCI and its activities. So, it's pretty much on the record that this happened. And what you mentioned earlier about how you and I … you went sort of the drug investigation route and I sort of went the sexual blackmail operation route. You know, this is really arms trafficking, drug trafficking, the sexual blackmail and the trafficking of minors. All of this stuff is done by the same group, I guess you could call them, or the syndicate. They're involved in all of these activities and they have used all of these activities for years for different purposes and have gotten away with it because there's been no accountability. They've been doing this, as I mentioned, for decades, probably like around a century now, and they just have so much influence and power, it seems, in a lot of public institutions that normally we would presume would hold these people accountable.

But as far as Epstein's money laundering goes, he also laundered a lot of money through New York real estate. Real-estate deals or shady real-estate deals, especially if they are cash-only transactions, which are frequently used for money laundering. I think that, as I mentioned earlier, Epstein and Wexner were involved in a lot of real-estate deals in the 1980s that were basically flipping all these properties around for cash-only deals to shell companies they also owned and all this other shady activity.

And at this time, as I mentioned, Epstein was personal friends with people like Trump and Thomas Barrack, and people like that who also have been accused of using their real-estate empires for the purpose of money laundering. That's the way I think the Epstein-Trump connections didn't really get as much coverage perhaps as the Clinton ones, because the Clinton ones have much more direct ties with the sexual blackmail operation than the Trump one does. But I think that's because the ties of Trump to Epstein are related more to the sort of criminal activity that has taken place for a long time in the New York real-estate market. And also the fact that one of Donald Trump's mentors, Roy Cohn – who I talk about in my series quite a bit – was also very involved in a sexual blackmail operation.

So, if your mentor is someone involved in that, they will tell you how not to be ensnared. And by all indications, we know that Trump knew what Epstein was doing because several years before Epstein was even arrested, Trump talked about how he was always surrounded by women "on the younger side" and things of that nature. And we also had recently the widow of Senator John

McCain in the US go out in public and say: "We all knew what Epstein was doing." Which I think didn't really get any coverage at all. So, it's pretty much [common knowledge] that this was known to be going on.

I dug up a bunch of reports about Epstein and Ghislaine Maxwell that were scrubbed from the Internet after his first arrest in 2007, but I still found quite a bit of them and a lot of those also revealed – if you read them – that it was very clear it was going on. There were reports as early as the Nineties about Ghislaine Maxwell taking groups of young teenage girls and training them in sex techniques and things like that. It's very obvious. If that was even able to make it into mainstream journalism at the time, it's very obvious that this was known to the people that ran in these social circles with these individuals.

Shaun: This level of information that you have, does it worry you at all?

Whitney: What do you mean, in what way?

Shaun: Last year you were doxed and hacked and everything was upside down for like a month.

Whitney: I had a guy trying to harass my father in my hometown where I haven't lived since I left to go to college, and put pictures of him online and threatened to go and interview him on his YouTube channel and just a lot of other stuff like that. And I've gotten some weird messages, but I don't really let it bother me. I don't live in the United States. I'm not really that worried about a lot of pushback from this, especially because the mainstream media ignores it so much. A lot of this has, unfortunately, in the months since the scandal really broke, has sort of faded from the public interest. I think the mainstream media is a major factor in that, not just because they basically ignored and don't touch the story anymore, but even when they did, they just focused on the salacious details of the case and sort of sensationalised it and made it tabloid coverage and totally ignored the intelligence angle and the government involvement in all of this stuff. But basically, what that does in the public mind is sort of degrade this down to a tabloid salacious story and not what it should be, a huge scandal about the fact that there are governments and intelligence agencies who are using taxpayer money to finance the abuse of children for the purpose of blackmail, which in any other sane world would be a massive story and lead to some accountability for those involved, and there's really been nothing except that some people have been forced to retire from public life. Oh, poor them. You know, I don't really have a lot of pity for people like Wexner and Prince Andrew who no longer feel comfortable showing themselves, showing their faces at public events. I mean, I honestly think they belong in prison for what they did.

Shaun: What do you think about Prince Andrew's sixtieth birthday party getting cancelled?

Whitney: Well, I didn't even know it was cancelled. But, as I was saying, I don't feel bad at all for those people. A lot of times when this sort of stuff happens and a birthday gets cancelled, mainstream media will make it sound horrible and omit the fact that these people are criminals. So, I don't really have any sympathy at all. Actually, when it comes to Prince Andrew, those scrubbed media reports that I was referencing, most of them were in the UK media and a lot of them had to do with either a controversy about Ghislaine Maxwell herself because her father was very much hated for a rather long period of time in the UK for his embezzlement of worker pension funds and things like that. So, she would get some coverage there. But Prince Andrew as well, there were reports of him going on vacation numerous times in the year 2000 with Maxwell and Epstein, and that he would bring along with him his own personal massage table so he could receive massages from the girls that surrounded Epstein and Maxwell at the time, and this didn't get any mainstream media coverage.

A lot of them took it at face value: Prince Andrew's claims that he was innocent. But of course, even though it came out in the court case itself, that massage and massage tables and all of this, this was the way they hid these sexual activities that were codenamed as being massages when really it was forcing these girls to have sex with these people. And so, the fact that he would take his massage table around and would frequently get massages from people on vacation with Ghislaine Maxwell and Epstein, this was going on during numerous vacations that Prince Andrew took with the two of them in the year 2000. Let's remember, too, that Prince Andrew's only accuser that has kind of gone to public, Virginia Roberts is her original name, she said that she first encountered Prince Andrew in March of 2001. So, the fact that this was going on before then, his involvement in this is much more significant.

It's not surprising why more girls don't come forward to accuse Prince Andrew when we know now that the reason ABC News, which apparently had this story before the scandal broke for a second time after Epstein's second arrest, more recently largely killed it due to pressure from Buckingham Palace and from the Royal Family itself, which freaked ABC News out. So, imagine being a girl that was abused like this. And then you have no money, no connections, and you have the Royal Family come after you. You know, it makes sense why there aren't more accusers personally. There is definitely a lot of evidence that suggests that Prince Andrew abused lots of girls, much more than just Virginia as part of this operation. He was very involved in it for a very long time. And the fact that he's been forced to recuse himself from public life. I mean, I don't really care. I feel sad for anyone that actually does care and sees him as a sympathetic figure in all of this.

Shaun: So, do you think Prince Andrew has become a useful distraction then for bigger players? Because the media in this country, on this case, that's all they've been focused on day after day after day: Prince Andrew.

Whitney: I think people like Prince Andrew and Bill Clinton were some of the biggest prizes of the blackmail operation that Epstein was running. And I think that the focus on them has allowed attention on who Epstein was working for to be evaded. And I think that is the key there. Not that I want to paint people like Prince Andrew and people like Bill Clinton as victims, I certainly don't feel that way, but the fact is they were pretty clearly sort of entrapped in this. And you know what I was talking about with those scrapped media reports? There's quotes up there of Epstein saying that Ghislaine Maxwell sort of arranged that relationship between Epstein and Andrew, and that Epstein considered Andrew to be one of his biggest prizes.

And this was before any of this about blackmail came out or anything like that. So, I think the focus on them keeps attention away from the intelligence agencies that were tied to this. And to an extent Wexner has gotten some of the flack as well and been forced to recuse from public life. But Wexner's connection to the Mega Group or to politics in the US and Israel or intelligence or organised crime, none of that was covered, just "Oh, he got money from Epstein" or "He helped Epstein get money" and stuff like that. But Wexner, when all this came out last year, claimed that Epstein had actually embezzled a bunch of money from him, but never provided any evidence. And actually, it shows the opposite is true, that when Epstein was going to prison for the first time, the amount of money that Wexner claimed Epstein had embezzled, Epstein had actually transferred to Wexner right before he went to prison. So, the evidence suggests just the opposite, but mainstream media reported Wexner's claims at face value and didn't even look at the obvious evidence, how the evidence contradicts what he was saying, so it's ridiculous.

Shaun: So, I've almost finished reading *The Assassination of Robert Maxwell* and it's just blown me away that this guy could sit down with Bush, sit down with Gorbachev, launder money for criminal organisations from the Russian mafia to the cartels. He was feeding intelligence to all of the various agencies. And do you think that Maxwell brought Epstein into that world?

Whitney: Well, that's what I've been told. I did an interview with someone, a former member of Israeli military intelligence who worked with Maxwell during the 1980s, and he said that he personally saw Epstein at Maxwell's offices on several occasions, was introduced to Epstein by Maxwell, and that Maxwell said that Epstein had been approved by the higher-ups and was going to start working with them and things of that nature. And that this had been facilitated due to the fact that prior to that, Epstein and Ghislaine Maxwell had already started to date. And, of course, the official story holds that they didn't meet until 1991. This would obviously contradict that fact in that Robert Maxwell saw Epstein, as you know, as a potential future son-in-law or something and wanted to get him and his daughter sort of set up in the family business of doing all this shadowy activity on behalf of intelligence.

Shaun: So, Robert Maxwell was riding high for years, and according to this book, he – because he was in such desperate need for money – he started to put pressure on Israel to come up with almost half a billion pounds, which is more than half a billion dollars, at the present translation rate. So, when they weren't forthcoming, he started to threaten certain things. So, they said: "All right, we will be forthcoming – get on the yacht, get on the *Lady Ghislaine*, you need to meet these people at this location." And he goes off to the Canary Islands, where he's later found dead in the water without any clothes on. If he had had a heart attack, he would have just crumpled and been found dead on the yacht.

Whitney: Without his clothes on, right?

Shaun: Yeah. So, nothing makes any sense. They took him out. Do you think Epstein was taken out by the same people? And for what reasons do you think he was taken out?

Whitney: So, going back to [Robert] Maxwell first, from what I understand, it had to do with the fact that, like you said, Maxwell was involved with a lot of different intelligence agencies and that a lot of the money that he had pilfered out of his businesses in the UK had for a long time been going to finance Mossad activity in Europe. And at some point he had given some of the money – that was intended for the Mossad or to be paid back to people that had lent money to the Mossad or Israeli businessmen linked to the Mossad – that he had given that money instead to Mikhail Gorbachev of the Soviet Union, and then was unable to make those payments. And that's sort of where that whole debacle ended up coming from and he started threatening Israel over money and all of this stuff.

But anyway, in terms of Epstein, we were talking about sort of like the media attention, a lot of it is just focused on his death specifically. And so, I think a lot of the focus on his death and like the exact circumstances of it and exactly who was behind it also sort of detracts from the accountability in the media pressure on the people that were behind Epstein and financed his operation, what he was meant to do. In terms of what actually happened to Epstein, if you want to look at it super-objectively and just look at the facts, there's a lot—we know so little about what actually happened, there's been no camera footage, the FBI investigation has been a total farce and just gone away, basically. They were going to charge the prison guards for a while – who were found asleep and forging stuff, and one of them wasn't actually a prison guard and all this stuff. I mean, the whole thing was honestly just so ridiculous.

So, when you take into consideration the intelligence-agency angle, that raises a lot of different possibilities as to what could happen. It's very possible that what happened to Robert Maxwell could have happened to Epstein before he died. He was alleged to have said that he was afraid for his life. He was allegedly willing to cooperate with the authorities and naming names and things of that nature. If that's true – I mean, I don't want to necessarily put all of my trust in what Epstein was saying, either, because he's obviously not a trustworthy individual, but it's certainly very possible. Intelligence agencies—when someone – even if they're a long-time agent and a long-time asset – if they become a liability, just like Robert Maxwell, they get taken out.

I don't really want to rule out other possibilities. Some people have raised that he may have been whisked away somewhere. When you get involved with intelligence agencies, they do all sorts of stuff like that. And I think it would be—I don't really want to underestimate that they're capable of that. I mean, I don't really want to commit myself to any specific theory. It seems likely, just given the precedent with Robert Maxwell, that he would be killed off. But there's been a lot of speculation about the coroners involved and claiming he was dead or he was murdered and all of that, like the independent coroner that was hired by Epstein's brother, Mark Epstein, is a very shady individual who was involved in the Kennedy assassination cover-up and the Martin Luther King Jr assassination cover-up, which involved intelligence and governments and all of that stuff.

So, it's really hard for me to marry myself to one possibility, but at the same time, I really want to urge people not to focus so much on the circumstances of his death, but on the people who are still with us and who should be held accountable for their role. This of course includes Ghislaine Maxwell, this includes people like Leslie Wexner who at least are known to the public to be directly associated with this operation. But I think more broadly, the intelligence agencies, if they were paying someone like Epstein to do this, they were likely paying other people at the time to do the same. Historically with a lot of the sexual blackmail operations, intelligence agencies use underage boys. Epstein was known to only really exploit underage girls. So, presumably at the same time that Epstein was involved with his activity, there was someone also doing the same to underage boys that we don't know about. So, I think until intelligence has been held accountable, we'll never really know how many of these, how many Epsteins, are out there and how many kids they're exploiting and taking from schools and homes and forcing them into this work. You know, as long as it has state protection and an infinite source of financing through black budgets or taxpayer funds, this type of stuff will continue. So, focusing all the attention just on Epstein specifically and Epstein's death and things of that nature sort of prevents us from eradicating the problem.

CHAPTER 12
THE PRINCE AND THE CAR CRASH INTERVIEW

Quickly regarded as the most spectacular car crash interview of the century, Prince Andrew's appearance on the BBC's *Newsnight* programme was supposed to be a candid response to the allegations of Epstein survivor Virginia Giuffre that she had been forced to have sex with the prince on three occasions. It was meant to show the man behind the title for whom he really was – honourable, trustworthy and ultimately well-meaning, perhaps even naïve enough to be fooled by a less salubrious character like Jeffrey Epstein.

Instead, the whole conversation came across as awkward, confusing and downright bizarre. The denials were vague and lacklustre, the alibis frankly weird. Slammed as a PR disaster of monumental proportions, it was so bad that rather than having the intended effect of clearing his reputation, the opposite occurred, and Andrew was forced to step down from royal duties. Commentators were torn about the prince's motives. Some claimed he was so assured of never being brought to trial that he was sticking two fingers up at the media. Others just said he was a bit thick. Whatever the reasons, the Duke of York's excuses were almost all either demonstrably false or seriously contentious, as we shall see in this chapter.

The lies started almost as immediately as the interview with BBC journalist Emily Maitlis began. After just a few minutes, Maitlis asked how Andrew and Epstein had first met. Andrew answered that they had done so back in 1999, through their mutual friend Ghislaine Maxwell. The prince went on to add about his friendship with Epstein: "I suppose I saw him once or twice a year, perhaps maybe a maximum of three times a year ..."

But as Maitlis pointed out later in the interview, Epstein's Florida housekeeper testified under oath that Andrew had visited Epstein's Palm Beach home alone four times a year, not including visits to other Epstein properties or meetings with Epstein outside his homes. And the *Evening Standard* article from 2001, which we have already looked at, found that Andrew and Epstein had made no less than five trips together in the year 2000 alone.

Andrew went on to say: "But it would be a considerable stretch to say that he was a very, very close friend." The prince claimed that his relationship with Epstein was only ever as Maxwell's "plus-one" and that it was more about Epstein's "extraordinary ability to bring extraordinary people together". However, one trip documented in the *Evening Standard* article was a holiday in Phuket, Thailand where the two men were photographed lounging aboard a yacht surrounded by topless women. Hardly the arm's length professional relationship Andrew was alluding to.

Maitlis next asked Andrew about his title as the "party prince" and wondered if that was in connection to his relationship with Epstein. To which he responded: "Well, I think that's also a bit of a stretch. I don't know why I've collected that title because I don't ... I never have really partied. I was single for quite a long time in the early Eighties but then after I got married, I was very happy and I've never really felt the need to go and party and certainly going to Jeffrey's was not about partying, absolutely not."

Yet a former lap dancer told UK newspaper the *Daily Mirror* that she saw Andrew at parties held by Epstein at least twice a year in Epstein's New York mansion. So, he clearly did party and definitely with Epstein. The stripper added that she was paid by Epstein to provide other strippers for the parties and that some of them had to be curvy in order to suit the prince's sexual tastes. She also said that Andrew had blown a raspberry between her breasts and told her that she should be in a magazine for big-breasted women. The ex-stripper also claimed there were underage girls at the parties who were kept in rooms upstairs and that guests were constantly disappearing into other rooms for sex.

Perhaps the odd fling in New York might be excused, but what if the partying was closer to home? What about in Buckingham Palace itself? In my interview with ex-royal protection officer, Paul Page, who used to work security at Buckingham Palace, he said that women would often turn up asking to see the prince and that security was instructed to let them in without taking their names or details, or following any of the strict security procedures surrounding admissions to the palace.

Page even spoke of a time when security were convinced that two prostitutes had turned up to visit Andrew. Page described an evening when two women wearing short skirts, low-cut tops and heavy make-up arrived at the palace in a taxi, asking for Andrew. Security was ordered to let them through in the usual way and they went straight to Andrew's private quarters, where they spent exactly one hour before leaving. Much to the officers' distress – because they had all come down to look at the girls as they left – Andrew was actually accompanying the women outside, so security officers had to hastily conceal themselves behind parked cars and in bushes while the prince hailed the women a taxi. Apart from the amusing scene, it only confirmed Page's suspicion that the women were high-class escorts, as Andrew always arranged for his female visitors to be taken home by security officers and never hailed them a cab from outside the palace.

In the BBC interview, Andrew claimed he had never seen anything suspicious at any of his visits to Epstein's properties. We have already seen that Andrew attended Epstein's sex parties in New York where underage girls were kept in rooms upstairs – is it possible that the prince had no idea at all that this was happening? Perhaps. However, the BBC's *Panorama* show found that five of Epstein's victims had testified that Andrew had witnessed young girls giving massages at Epstein properties and that in all five cases Andrew had been subpoenaed to testify about his knowledge, so again it seems that Andrew knew more about what was going on than he wants to let on.

The untruths now started coming thick and fast. Maitlis questioned the prince about his December 2010 visit to Epstein in New York, following the paedophile's Florida prison release earlier that year. Andrew had attended a party to celebrate Epstein's release and stayed four nights at his Manhattan mansion. Andrew claimed he had received advice both for and against the trip but decided ultimately that it was the right thing to do and that it would show "leadership" to end the relationship in person. Apart from questions as to why it would take four nights stay at someone's house to end a friendship, there is a clear contradiction here with Andrew's previous statements. Either he was not a close friend of Epstein's, as he had claimed earlier in the interview – in which case there was no friendship that needed to be terminated either in person or remotely – or he was a close-enough friend to feel the need to fly 3,000 miles to end the relationship in person. The two claims cannot both be true.

Next, Andrew asserted that he had never attended a "party" on the visit, just a sober dinner occasion with eight to ten guests. What he failed to mention is that the dinner *was* the party – a dinner party to celebrate Epstein's release from jail at which Andrew was the guest of honour. There is also evidence that what the prince was getting up to on that visit was a lot less sober than he would have us believe. On December 6, Andrew was photographed peeping round the doorway of Epstein's Manhattan mansion waving goodbye to a young, dark-haired woman before disappearing surreptitiously back inside. An hour earlier, Epstein had been captured leaving the house with a young, shivering blonde girl.

Andrew admitted to regretting the trip but put the mistake down to his own better nature, saying: "I mean, I've gone through this in my mind so many times. At the end of the day, with a benefit of all the hindsight that one can have, it was definitely the wrong thing to do. But at the time I felt it was the honourable and right thing to do, and I admit fully that my judgement was probably coloured by my tendency to be too honourable, but that's just the way it is."

Leaving aside questions of how honourable it is to attend the prison-leaving party of a convicted paedophile, let's look at Andrew's self-promoted "honourable" character. In my interview with royal protection officer, Paul Page, the security man paints a picture of the prince that is far from noble. Page tells of an occasion when one of Andrew's frequent female visitors turned up at Buckingham Palace. As usual, the visit was unannounced and the woman's name wasn't to be put in the book. However, on this occasion, the protection team couldn't get hold of Andrew's footman to check whether the woman was expected so, deciding to err on the side of caution, they opted not to let her in.

Paul Page picks up the story: "So, rather than let this person in, then we were there to say: 'Look, sorry, we can't let you in.' So, she said: 'Oh, well, I'll tell you what, I'll ring him on his mobile.' So, she proceeded to ring Prince Andrew, who was in his room. His apartments face the front of the palace, so he clearly could look down and see us. And so, she just said to him: 'Well, it's me, the officers won't let me in because I'm not expected, apparently.' We could hear him on the phone. He said: 'Put one of the officers on the phone.' So, my colleague picked the phone up and he basically said to him: 'Listen to me, you fat-arsed cunt, let my guest in now or I'll come down there immediately.' And so, we all heard it, even the female guest went bright red. So, my colleague, unfortunately, he was quite a plump boy, so [the prince was] obviously looking out the window, he could see that my colleague was a bit plump, that's why he called him fat. [My colleague] gave the phone back to the female and we just let her go, just let her go straight into the palace."

Honourable?

Perhaps we could excuse his Highness the one slip but unfortunately, according to Page, it wasn't the only time Andrew was rude to staff. Page recalls another occasion when he and other security went to investigate an unidentified person roaming around the corridors of the palace. According to Page: "The security cameras couldn't work out who it was wandering around. So, obviously I sent myself and two officers and a sergeant to go and investigate to just ask the person who it was. So, service went, I ran the corridor, and service went the other way in order to come over and, as we got closer, it was Prince Andrew just dressed scruffily. And the sergeant approached him and said: 'I'm really sorry, your Highness, we got called because no one could recognise who it was on camera, and we were just coming to make sure that it wasn't an intruder.' And [the prince] said: 'Hey, listen to me, this is my house and I'll go where I want, now fuck off.'"

Oh dear.

Perhaps understandably, according to Page, Andrew was unpopular with the staff, who thought of him as rude and obnoxious. Even the prince's closest personal servant wasn't a fan. According to Page: "His private personal valet of twenty-five years, I used to know him quite well, I used to see him at night, he used to take Prince Andrew's Jack Russell for a walk. He used to wake him up, Prince Andrew would press his royal button and the poor valet would have to come out and take the dog and take him out into the back garden for a walk, and I used to speak to him on a regular basis, and even he didn't like Prince Andrew. In fact, on one occasion Prince Andrew was going skiing and the valet said: 'At least he'll be gone for a week, I hope he skis off a fucking cliff.'"

Moving along from Andrew's "honourable" nature, the lies began to concentrate on the night when Virginia Giuffre claims she was forced to have sex with the prince in Ghislaine Maxwell's Belgravia townhouse in London. That night – March 10, 2001 – began at Tramp nightclub, Mayfair's prestigious members-only venue that has hosted A-list celebrities from Sean Connery and Roger Moore to Drake and Rihanna. Giuffre claims she was taken along by Maxwell and Epstein to act as a kind of escort for the prince. She says she danced with Andrew at the club where he was, according to Giuffre: "Sweating all over me."

In his *Newsnight* interview, Andrew denied ever being at the nightclub or meeting Virginia Giuffre. He claimed he was at home at Buckingham Palace that night and could clearly recall because he had visited a Pizza Express in Woking earlier in the day to attend a birthday party of one of Princess Beatrice's friends – an event sufficiently unusual to make the evening stand out in his memory. According to Page, there should be security paperwork documenting the prince's trip to Pizza Express, as well as his presence at the palace that night. So, if Andrew is so sure about his whereabouts – and his innocence – why doesn't he just provide the documentation that proves where he was?

As to his claim that he never met Giuffre, the BBC uncovered emails between the prince and Maxwell discussing how to handle Giuffre's accusations. Shortly afterwards, Maxwell sent Epstein's lawyer, Alan Dershowitz, a list of supposed inconsistencies in articles about Giuffre. However, in the note to Dershowitz, Maxwell consistently mentions that the night at Tramp included Giuffre. If Prince Andrew had never met Giuffre, why wouldn't Maxwell simply have said this, instead of including her in the narrative? It directly contradicts the prince's claim never to have met the young victim.

Another problem with Andrew's story is that an independent witness claims to have seen the prince with Giuffre at Tramp in March 2001. Epstein victims' lawyer, Lisa Bloom, told British press how her client, Shukri Walker, had witnessed the pair dancing together on the Tramp dancefloor. Bloom, who has passed Walker's information to the FBI, claims her client vividly remembers the occasion because seeing a member of the Royal Family was "such a very big thing to her". According to Bloom, Walker was herself a victim of sex trafficking and noticed on the night that "Prince Andrew was happy, smiling and dancing, and Virginia did not look happy".

Not content with bending the reality of his whereabouts that night, Andrew then went on full psychedelic mode by refuting the claim that he was sweating all over Giuffre on the dancefloor. In his own words: "There's a slight problem with the sweating because I have a peculiar medical condition which is that I don't sweat or I didn't sweat at the time and that was … was it … yes, I didn't sweat at the time because I had suffered what I would describe as an overdose of adrenaline in the Falklands War when I was shot at and I simply … it was almost impossible for me to sweat. And it's only because I have done a number of things in the recent past that I am starting to be able to do that again. So, I'm afraid to say that there's a medical condition that says that I didn't do it, so therefore …"

The problem with this mind-bending distortion of reality is, well, reality. There are a number of photos from around the time which clearly show the prince sweating, one of which is mentioned in the same *Evening Standard* article we looked at earlier, written in 2001. The article mentions that Andrew was pictured in October 2000 "sweating profusely outside the West End nightspot China White".

Paul Page also corroborates this. He worked as a royal protection officer from 1998 until the mid-Noughties, and clearly recalls a time he saw the prince sweating. According to Page:

"He would come out in the garden and play golf; he hit golf balls up the garden. Which on one occasion, it was an occasion where I needed to be on the phone and I couldn't because he'd come out to the garden entrance with his protection officer, who was carrying his golf bag, which I had a particular issue with, because I thought, *You're not a fucking caddy, you're a police officer. What are you doing?* But this is what I'm trying to explain to you, he had that sort of purpose about him. If he's asking a protection officer to pick his golf bag up, [the officer is] going to do it, because otherwise he'd be off the protection squad, probably. And so, Prince Andrew, it was a really hot day that day and he was whacking golf balls up the end of the garden and he was sweating profusely, you know? And the reason I noticed that is because I wanted him to go back inside because I needed to use the post phone urgently."

As the night in question developed, Andrew's touch with

reality seemed to lessen. According to Giuffre, the four of them went back to Maxwell's townhouse in Belgravia. On the taxi ride home, Giuffre claims Maxwell told her she would have to do the same for Andrew that she did for Jeffrey, in other words a massage that would lead to some kind of sexual activity. Giuffre told BBC's *Panorama* programme that this made her "feel sick. I just didn't expect it from royalty." Giuffre says she asked Epstein to take a photo of her with the prince upstairs in Maxwell's house, then proceeded to take a bath with Andrew and then have sex in the bedroom. The whole process, according to Giuffre, "didn't last very long, the whole entire procedure. It was disgusting. He wasn't mean or anything, but he got up and he said thanks and walked out. And I sat there in bed just horrified and ashamed and felt dirty."

Andrew denies ever being in Maxwell's house on that night and claims he has no recollection of the photo being taken, intimating that it is a fake. In the *Newsnight* interview, he claimed that it was "a photograph of a photograph of a photograph", so it was impossible to tell if it was a fake, but he intimated that someone had doctored another picture of him so that it looked like he had his arm around Giuffre.

Panorama contacted the photographer who copied the original picture back in 2011. The man said he had no doubt the photograph was genuine. And the programme received further corroboration in the form of a sworn affidavit of a man who was dating Giuffre in 2001, who said he saw the picture back then. According to Giuffre, the original picture had the date it was printed – March 13, 2001 – stamped on the back. This photograph is currently with the FBI.

Apart from the potentially faked photo, Andrew offered several corroborating reasons why he could never have been in the picture: that he had never been upstairs in Maxwell's house, where the photo was taken; that he was not given to "public displays of affection"; and that he never wore the kinds of casual clothes he was pictured in when going out in London. I recently paid a visit to Maxwell's Belgravia townhouse and knocked on the door. It was answered by a house cleaner and I was able to get a quick peek up the hallway and caught a clear glimpse of the white bannister on the landing pictured in the photograph. As to the prince's aversion to public displays of affection, a quick Google search turns up dozens of images of him with his arms around women, many of them also with him clearly sweating.

And as for the claim that he always wore a suit when going out in London, here's Paul Page again: "He is talking rubbish. He used to sometimes come back in his shirt and chinos, a shirt without a tie with like a jumper on. He would come back casually dressed on quite a few occasions. He would only go out dressed in shirt and tie if it was a sort of official engagement, but a lot of the times I'd see him in like a polo shirt and what have you."

From there, the *Newsnight* interview wound down, ending with Andrew desperately trying to talk about moving forward with various charity projects. However, by that point the damage had been done and, unbeknownst to the prince at the time, who – incredibly – looked quite happy with his performance, his fate was sealed. Not long after the interview was broadcast, the Queen and the rest of the Royal Family distanced themselves from his actions and Andrew was forced to step down from further royal duties.

Whether Andrew will face tougher and more serious consequences for his actions remains to be seen. Paul Page doesn't think so. "He would have had a legal team around him and if they thought there was a possibility of an indictment coming his way, they would have shut down the idea of him being interviewed then. So, he must've had some guarantees that this isn't going anywhere for him to speak publicly."

Since the allegations against Andrew surfaced, the FBI has repeatedly requested to speak to him. But despite the prince's claims that he is helping the investigation, no such meeting has yet taken place. It seems that for royalty, justice works differently than for the rest of us.

CHAPTER 13
VIRGINIA GIUFFRE:
BRAVE SURVIVOR OF
JET-SET SEX SLAVERY

The following account is taken from Virginia Giuffre's legal testimony, including her memoir of the events that took place during her time with Epstein. (Her twitter handle is @VRSVirginia).

High on a cocktail of pharmaceuticals and alcohol, the girl wished herself a happy fifteenth birthday, then climbed onto the balcony railing of the apartment she shared with her sixty-five-year-old abuser and pimp. Looking down at the street far below, the girl thought back on a brief life filled with sexual abuse and suffering, and set her mind on the only path she felt left open to her – jumping. Such was the fifteenth birthday of Virginia Roberts (now Giuffre).

In many ways, she was the type Epstein preyed upon. Her past of suffering and abuse made her an easy target for further manipulation. As Maria Farmer observed, Epstein and Maxwell would specifically seek out girls with troubled pasts, questioning them on their relationships with their parents and pouncing on the ones who had suffered abuse. In Virginia, they found their perfect prey.

The childhood that led up to that balcony railing was one of pitfall after pitfall. At eleven years old, Virginia was sexually abused by a family friend. By twelve, she was smoking pot. At thirteen, she had run away from home and was in and out of the care system, and by fourteen, she was living on the streets. It was on one of those nights, hungry and alone and crying to herself on a street near Miami Beach, that she was picked up by

Ron Eppinger. The sixty-five-year-old pulled up in a black stretch limousine and offered her a ride. Sitting with him in the back was a beautiful Czech girl in her late teens wearing a skimpy red mini-dress. Eppinger said he was the owner of a modelling agency called Perfect 10. He told Virginia a sob story about how his own teenage daughter had died in a car crash seven years earlier and how he had never gotten over it. He presented her with a bizarre offer – that he would take her in and she would become his "new baby forever".

Dazzled and confused, Virginia got in. Eppinger took her for dinner at a local restaurant, then clothes shopping, buying her outfits that should have immediately rung alarm bells – cut-off shorts that revealed the curve of her buttocks, skimpy tops and G-strings. After shopping, he took her back to his apartment, a plush property overlooking the sea. The bedroom had a raised circular bed under a mirrored ceiling. Told she would be sharing this room with Eppinger himself, she was then introduced to five beautiful girls, all in their late teens and all from the Czech Republic. The girls shared a room at the other end of the apartment and were all lounging around naked or wearing just G-strings.

If the penny hadn't already dropped, it did now. She found out that Eppinger's "model agency" was really an international sex-trafficking ring and high-end escort agency. The girls were hired out to rich clients for more than $1,000 per hour and trained to satisfy every possible sexual desire. They pretended to enjoy the lifestyle and regaled Virginia with stories of their exploits with rich clients while they combed and styled her hair and nicknamed her "baby". Soon, Eppinger reappeared and took Virginia to the bathroom, where he gave her two blue pills which he said would help her relax. He then took her clothes off and sexually assaulted her for the first of many times.

Virginia was quickly introduced to the lifestyle – lazing around with the girls in the day, having laser hair removal treatments, waxes and tanning sessions, then at night attending lavish parties where the girls would flirt with potential clients before accompanying them home. Eppinger always kept Virginia for his own use, but she was forced to partake in orgies with the other girls as a kind of training where she would learn sexual techniques to keep men happy. Eppinger would drive her around topless in his open-top convertible, carelessly showing off the fourteen-year-old as his latest possession.

Several weeks of this lifestyle took its toll and by her fifteenth birthday, Virginia found herself on the balcony of Eppinger's apartment, balancing on the rail and looking down toward the potential release of death.

But it wasn't to be. As she contemplated the drop, the door slammed open and Eppinger grabbed her, pulling her back into the apartment. He gave her three pink pills to swallow and she sank quickly into unconsciousness.

The routine of abuse continued but Eppinger's carelessness was beginning to expose him. Someone seeing him parading Virginia around topless had reported him to the police. In a panic, he cleared out of the Miami apartment and fled with all the girls to a remote ranch in the Florida countryside. Here, Virginia began to enjoy life a little again, spending time on her own, writing in her journal, painting and spending time with the horses – her favourite pastime since early childhood.

Feeling increasingly isolated, she began using one of the ranch phones to call her childhood friend and first crush, Tony Figueroa. Tony told her how worried her parents were and that they had hired a private investigator to search for her. Although it was risky, she began to call Tony regularly, creeping into the same unused guest room to whisper furtively down the line and listen eagerly to news from home.

It was a mistake. Eppinger soon found out. He was tipped off by the housekeeper that Virginia had been using one of the guest bedrooms regularly, but that the sheets were never messed up. Eppinger checked the telephone bill and found the same number was being called regularly from the room.

Furious, he gave her five minutes to pack her few possessions before she was kicked out. A driver arrived precisely five minutes later. She was being taken away, Eppinger shouted, to another man, another owner who, he promised, was not as "nice" as himself. She threw a few clothes into a bag and hid some hundred-dollar bills she had been saving inside her scrunchy, then she was inside the car and speeding away toward the next nightmare.

Charlie had an apartment in downtown Miami. He was a forty-something businessman who owned a restaurant-nightclub in Fort Lauderdale. The first night Virginia stayed with him, he took her out drinking and dancing at his club. Afterwards at his apartment, he sexually abused and raped her. Over the next few weeks, he kept her by his side day and night so that she had no chance to call Tony even if she had found the courage to do so.

Fortunately, she was soon rescued from the stifling grip of her new abuser and it was Tony she could thank. One morning, she was woken by the sound of the door being smashed open. FBI agents in black military outfits burst into the room and arrested the still-naked Charlie, dragging him off in handcuffs while he screamed threats to Virginia to stay quiet.

Taken to the local police station, she was informed that Tony had told her parents about his phone calls with Virginia. They had informed the police and the FBI had been tapping Eppinger's phones ever since. They had followed her from his countryside ranch and been keeping tabs on her until the raid. Unfortunately, Eppinger himself got news of Charlie's arrest and fled the country to Eastern Europe, where he managed to live a few more years of freedom before being arrested and extradited back to the US. He was sentenced to a hefty prison term but, being then in his mid-seventies, he died just one year into his sentence.

Virginia was met at the police station by her father. He said her mother wouldn't allow her back to the family home so she'd have to return to the care facility she had escaped from before. Her father promised to find her someone to stay with and a place back in school, but Virginia didn't trust him. She gave him one week to make good on his offer, after which she promised to escape again and this time for good.

A week came and went in the facility with no word from her father so, true to her promise, she escaped, slipping the grip of her inexperienced driver on a trip for a routine drugs test. She bought herself some new clothes to disguise her identity, then called her father from a payphone. He assured her that he had found a suitable family for her and that he was just trying to convince her mother to sign the papers to let her out. He persuaded her to come home to speak to her mother and she reluctantly agreed.

Back at the house in Palm Beach County, there was an emotional reunion with her mother that began with anger and ended in tears. With the air cleared, her mother asked her to rejoin the family and Virginia agreed. She would go back to school and in the meantime get a summer job working at Donald Trump's luxury resort, Mar-a-Lago, in Palm Beach, where her father worked as an engineer. She would study and work hard, with the ultimate goal of becoming a qualified massage therapist, her dream job. Perhaps, Virginia dreamed, even after everything she had been through, she could go back to the normal life of a teenager. Little did she know that the job at Mar-a-Lago would be the steppingstone to her worst nightmare yet.

She began working as a locker room attendant at the Mar-a-Lago spa. One afternoon, she was enjoying a break from work, sitting on the lawn under the summer sun, reading a book about anatomy, when she was approached by a slim, elegant-looking woman with short dark hair. In a perfect English accent, the woman introduced herself as Ghislaine Maxwell and politely enquired about Virginia's reading material. Virginia said she hoped to become a massage therapist and Maxwell offered to introduce her to the wealthy businessman she worked for. Virginia at first declined, saying she didn't have any experience or training, but Maxwell said if he liked her, her boss would get her the best training money could buy. Excited, Virginia agreed to come meet the businessman at his mansion in Palm Beach. Her slide into Epstein's orbit had begun.

The next afternoon, her dad drove her to Epstein's mansion on

El Brillo Way, one of Palm Beach's most sought-after addresses. Maxwell met them at the entrance and escorted Virginia upstairs, leaving her father to drive home. Maxwell led Virginia through the opulence of the Palm Beach mansion, past crystal chandeliers and dozens of pictures of nude and semi-nude young women. At the top of the stairs, Maxwell took her through a bedroom with a king-size bed and into the massage room, which compared to the Mar-a-Lago spa in its lavishness, with marble walls and a glass-enclosed shower cubicle. In the middle of the room, lying on his front, was a naked man. Virginia felt a stab of unease but told herself this was what she would have to get used to if she were to become a professional masseuse.

Epstein angled his head around and introduced himself, smiling knowingly to Maxwell, who proceeded to instruct Virginia on how to massage him. Taking a foot each, Virginia mirrored Maxwell's movements, pushing the blood up his calves and into his legs, as the two asked questions about her life. Virginia told them the truth about her unfortunate past but, to her surprise, instead of responding with horror as most people did, they probed her as much as possible on all the terrible experiences she had undergone, even seeming to be entertained by the stories.

Epstein called her a "naughty girl", smiling wryly.

Virginia responded: "No, I'm not. I'm really a good girl, just always in the wrong places."

"It's okay," said Epstein, turning over to expose his erect penis, "I like naughty girls."

Virginia tried to hide her shock by concentrating on the massage, but now Maxwell was behind her with her top off. She quickly began unbuttoning Virginia's top and took off her bra, cupping her bare breasts and licking her nipples. She then undressed Virginia completely, pausing only to share a laugh with Epstein about Virginia's young, girlish panties. Still in a whirl of shock, Virginia was instructed to lick Epstein's nipples, then to give him oral sex. All the time an oppressive feeling was settling on her – that this was what was meant for her in life, that there was no escape from this kind of sexual abuse and she might as well just accept her fate. Her fears were confirmed as Maxwell instructed her to finish the massage by straddling Epstein's penis.

When it was all over, she went to the sauna with Epstein, where he told her about his past and his meteoric rise from high school teacher to millionaire financier while Virginia listened politely. She was quickly learning to play the role of student to his wise and knowledgeable teacher in order to massage his ego as well as his body.

Afterwards, they took a shower together, but rather than being an intimate occasion, Virginia was shocked to be asked to wash his feet and body, and to even shampoo his hair. After towelling him dry, she was accompanied downstairs, where Maxwell was waiting. The older woman complimented her on her performance and asked her to come back at the same time the following day. Epstein then opened a bag stuffed with hundred-dollar bills and handed two to Virginia, joking that this was nearly her whole week's wages at Mar-a-Lago. With that, the "interview" was over and Virginia was driven home, where she took another shower and tried – unsuccessfully – to scrub the memories from her body.

The next day, Virginia went to work at Mar-a-Lago as usual. All day, she worried about the evening ahead, but she managed to convince herself that this was her life now and that she had to "grow up" from a naïve teenager to a mature young woman if she wanted to achieve her goals. When the workday ended, she found herself standing before the large double doors of Epstein's mansion again. He was waiting for her as before and events proceeded in much the same way, with Maxwell instructing her until Epstein could control himself no longer and the "massage" turned into a threesome. The next day was the same routine again except Virginia was expected to satisfy Epstein on her own without Maxwell's instructions.

It seemed that she had made the cut and passed Epstein's sordid work trial. The next week, she was expected at the mansion every evening after work and soon found herself exhausted yet unable to sleep, each night going over in her mind the sickening images from just hours earlier. Sometimes the sessions would only involve Virginia and Epstein, while other times Maxwell would join in and sometimes Maxwell's assistant, Emmy, would also be involved.

Emmy was a young, attractive English woman with blonde hair and striking eyes. The women would be expected to perform lesbian acts on each other to get Epstein aroused before satisfying his desires in whatever manner he chose. After it was over, everyone would get dressed and go about their business like a normal day. Before one session, Virginia was invited onto a balcony for a smoke with Maxwell and Emmy. She found herself having a nice chat and a laugh with the two older women. It was like an everyday cigarette break at any workplace around the world, except for the task they were about to get back to.

Virginia's compliance to Epstein's whims had clearly gone down well because it wasn't long before he asked her to quit Mar-a-Lago and work full time for him. She would be paid $200 per massage, of which there might be as many as three a day, and would accompany him on his private jet to his many residences both at home and around the world. She accepted, knowing what the job would really entail but still telling herself the lie that this was the fast track to the life she always wanted.

The next day, instead of Mar-a-Lago, her father dropped her off at Epstein's mansion. She hugged her dad goodbye and felt the last of her innocence wash down the drain as she turned to enter the house. Later that same day, she found herself with the pilot in the cockpit of Epstein's private 727, rushing with adrenaline as she watched the jet take off and head north towards New York. Minutes later, she was brought back down to earth as she was ushered into the back to give Epstein a massage. This contrast of jet-set glamour and sordid slavery would characterise the rest of her time with Epstein and Maxwell.

Virginia was suitably wowed by the East 71st Street mansion in New York, with its opulent, eccentric décor, its mediaeval tapestries, dark corridors and hidden stairways. She noticed the many pictures of naked and half-naked young women, some photos of Epstein with famous celebrities and politicians – even one of the financier with his arm around the Dalai Lama – and a statue of the horny goat god, Pan, which Virginia thought particularly appropriate. It was soon down to business, though, and she was escorted via an elaborately styled lift downstairs into the black-marbled darkness of the steam room and massage area that she would later come to call the "dungeon". The massage ended in the predictable way and afterwards Virginia was directed to her room, a plush loft space with a king-size bed and more mediaeval tapestries decorating the walls. Virginia hardly had time to take in her surroundings and test the bed before being summoned on the intercom to Epstein's office. She was surprised to be told she could spend the day shopping and sightseeing, and was given several hundred dollars to entertain herself.

She bought a disposable camera and spent the rest of the day taking snaps of the various sights. When she returned to the mansion, she was reprimanded by Maxwell for staying out too long. The next day, Maxwell bought her a cellphone so she could keep tabs on her and summon her home to satisfy Epstein at a moment's notice. Virginia kept her trips into the city shorter but they remained the highlight of her day.

It was now that the job took on a new twist. Epstein told her he would pay her double if she began recruiting women off the street to join her in massages. Virginia reluctantly agreed, feeling she had to go along with anything asked of her. Epstein explained that she should use her charm to get chatting to the kind of girl he liked (young, blonde, blue eyes, uniquely gorgeous – but no African Americans) before using his money and contacts in the acting and modelling world to entice them back to the mansion. She complied, but already the strains of the role were beginning to tell on her. When they flew back to Palm Beach, she saw a doctor and got a prescription for an anti-anxiety medication called Xanax. She took the pills before encounters with Epstein or his friends in order to get her through the degrading experiences she was forced to suffer.

Her seventeenth birthday was spent on Epstein's Caribbean island of Little St James. As a present, she was given a new set of designer make-up. When she blew the seventeen candles out on her cake, Maxwell joked that she'd soon be too old for Epstein's tastes.

A few days later, a beautiful young woman named Sarah Kellen arrived on the island. A few years Virginia's senior with ash-blonde hair and large brown eyes, it was clear she had been Epstein's toy in the past. She was now living in LA, trying to start up an acting career with Epstein's help, and had flown to the island for a short break. Sarah lounged naked around the pool and would tease Epstein for sex. Epstein told Virginia that Sarah was one of the best he'd ever had for procuring young girls. And when it came time to entertain Epstein in tandem with Sarah, it became clear her expertise extended to all areas of the role.

On Sarah's last night, they all took a stroll on neighbouring St James island. As the evening progressed, Epstein suggested that Sarah and Virginia go to a local nightclub to see if they could procure any girls. Suddenly it dawned on Virginia the nature of Sarah's trip to the island – she was there to instruct Virginia in her new role as procurer. That night, they didn't find any suitable candidates, but Virginia learned much about the dark arts of her new job by the cool, confident way that Sarah approached girls and flitted from group to group.

Despite her qualms, Virginia soon became accustomed to the new role and began introducing girls to Epstein. Just as had happened with her, she would lure them to the house with the promise of easy money and then instruct them how to massage. At some point, Epstein would tell them to get undressed, and if the girl complied, Epstein knew he could get away with whatever else he wanted, which might include lesbian acts between the girl and Virginia, and manual, oral or full penetrative sex. The girl would receive $200 and Virginia $400. To mark her upgraded status, Epstein now rented apartments for Virginia in Palm Beach and New York. Virginia began to increase her intake of Xanax and added Ecstasy and LSD to her growing list of recreational drugs. She was partying hard in her downtime and even recruiting some of her friends to help satisfy Epstein's needs. Her life was spiralling out of control. She needed some form of stability and the chance came with the return of her one-time rescuer and childhood crush.

Tony knocked on the door of her Palm Beach apartment one day, saying he'd found her address from mutual friends and had been knocking randomly on her door ever since. The two quickly fell into a relationship and Tony moved secretly into the apartment with her. Feeling guilty about the deception, Virginia tentatively raised the subject of Tony with Epstein during a massage. She was surprised at his reaction – no jealousy or rage, just amusement that she would even think that he'd be bothered. "No one in this world is monogamous," said Epstein, laughing. "Why would I expect you to be?"

Epstein started providing her with massage training from professional therapists and Virginia soaked up the knowledge, daring to think again that her career goals would be achieved through Epstein. But her hopes were smashed when the real reason for the extra training became clear – Epstein intended to farm her out to other clients.

The call came direct to her Palm Beach apartment – Epstein wanted her to visit the exclusive Breaker Hotel that night to massage his two friends, a married couple called Glenn Dubin and Eva Andersson-Dubin. Eva was an ex-girlfriend of Epstein's, a doctor and former Miss Sweden. Glenn was a billionaire hedge fund manager. Virginia was worried to hear that Eva was heavily pregnant, as her training didn't qualify her for that; however, Epstein encouraged her to just make Eva comfortable and do what she asked, as the real client was going to be Glenn. That's when it dawned on her what the visit was really all about.

She entered the hotel with a heavy heart and found the

couple's apartment. She was escorted to the bedroom, where she was asked to massage Eva. She did so to the best of her ability, even massaging the woman's swollen breasts to help ease their soreness. When Eva was relaxed enough to sleep, Virginia turned out the light and went to find her next client – the husband.

Glenn was in the lounge waiting with the lights dimmed. Her worst fears were confirmed when he undressed and laid on the floor on his back, exposing his penis. Hoping to delay the inevitable, Virginia instructed him to turn over and began going about the task of a regular massage. After a couple of hours of hard work, Dubin asked her to remove her top. She complied. Soon, she was completely naked and responding to more of his requests. Finally, he had sex with her while his pregnant wife slept in the other room. When it was done, he coolly got dressed and tipped Virginia before sending her off into the night feeling more like a prostitute than she ever had before.

Two days later, Virginia flew with Epstein to his "El Zorro" ranch in New Mexico. With its indoor pool and gym, its fake Western town and thousands of acres of land to explore on horseback or quad bike, this was Virginia's favourite property. She flew in with Epstein, Maxwell and Emmy, and the four went on a sightseeing and shopping trip in nearby Santa Fe. Returning home, she was required to give Epstein a massage, then the dysfunctional family watched a film together in the movie room while Virginia and Emmy massaged Epstein's feet. The night's entertainment concluded with a foursome before bedtime. Virginia retreated to her room to call Tony for some comfort, only to find he was off his head as usual with a group of friends at her apartment, no doubt trashing the place. Since moving in, Tony had refused to get a job and had sponged off Virginia's earnings from Epstein, using them to fund his ever-increasing drug habit.

The next day, Virginia flew alone with Epstein to Carmel in California, while Maxwell and Emmy headed back to New York. Epstein gave Virginia some money to go shopping while he attended a conference. In town, Virginia met a carefree and pretty

Californian girl who was on a road trip. Always on duty, she decided to ask the girl if she wanted to make some extra money giving a rich client a massage. The girl seemed keen even when Virginia admitted the massage would have to be naked and would probably involve more than just the relaxing of muscles.

Virginia planned to meet up with her later and headed back to the apartment. Epstein was tired from the day but Virginia persuaded him to come out to a restaurant, then when they returned to the apartment, she secretly let her new friend in while Epstein was showering. When he was done, he came into Virginia's room only to see a strange and naked young girl in the bath. The girl stood up, letting the bubbles run slowly down her naked body, and Epstein smiled his approval. The two girls then massaged Epstein with the predictable results. Afterwards, the girl was paid the usual $200 and her name was entered into the little black book in which Epstein recorded the contact details of all his best encounters for future reference.

The following day after lunch, Virginia and Epstein flew to Los Angeles. On the private jet was a surprise guest – Matt Groening, the creator of *The Simpsons*. As a massive fan, Virginia fired questions at him about the inspiration for *The Simpsons* and was told it was based on Groening's own family upbringing. Less palatable than the conversation was when Epstein asked Virginia to give the cartoonist a foot massage and she saw the state of his feet. They were oddly shaped, with long, hardened yellow toenails and bits of sock fluff still stuck to his sweaty toes. Virginia couldn't bear to do the massage without first cleaning Groening's feet with a wet towel. The cartoonist didn't seem to mind, however, and even gave her two hand-drawn sketches of Homer and Bart with personal messages on them.

In LA, they met up with Sarah Kellen and another of Epstein's girls, Nadia Bjorlin, a Swedish model, singer and actress who would soon go on to star in the soap opera, *Days of Our Lives*. Nadia had brown hair and shocking blue eyes, and was one of the most beautiful women Virginia had ever seen. They all went back to the apartment that Epstein rented for Sarah on Malibu Beach, where five more young women were waiting. Sarah had provided a wide range of choices for Epstein's pleasure. However, bored and annoyed by the female conversation, Epstein took just Virginia and Nadia to the room next door, where he instructed them to use sex toys on each other while he penetrated each of them in turn. Virginia felt even more degraded than usual hearing the babble from the other room fade to silence as the girls listened in, knowing full well what was happening in the room next door.

Virginia and Epstein flew back to New York later that evening and Virginia returned late to her New York apartment, just in time to find Tony having sex with another woman. In a rage, she threw them out, aware even as she did so of the hypocrisy of the situation. She was, after all, spending most of her time with another man.

When Virginia told Epstein about her boyfriend's infidelity, he didn't commiserate or console her, but laughed it off, asking what did she expect? Men were incapable of being loyal, said Epstein, playing his favourite role, the mentor. If she just remembered that one fact, she would never be hurt again. It was hardly what a young, heartbroken girl wanted to hear, and Virginia went home feeling worse than ever.

The spat with Tony didn't last long and he soon moved back into Virginia's Palm Beach apartment. Two nights before flying back to New York to be with Epstein, Virginia threw a lavish party for all her friends at a hotel on Singer Island near Palm Beach. With her newfound wealth, she provided a cocktail of drugs for all the partygoers and they stayed up into the early hours of the next morning. The next day, on the flight to New York, Virginia felt terrible but put it down to a prolonged drug comedown. When she arrived at the 71st Street mansion, she started sweating uncontrollably and had to run to the bathroom to be sick. Later, when Epstein called for his massage, she had to refuse for the first time. She was having intense stomach cramps and put it down to something she had eaten on the plane. She managed to get some sleep, but when she woke up, she found the sheets drenched in her own blood.

Gasping with pain and vomiting, she managed to grab the phone and call the housemaid. Maxwell was soon in the room and called for Epstein. The housemaid helped her downstairs, where Jo-Jo the driver was waiting and Epstein and Maxwell accompanied her to the hospital. Inside the ward, she was given a pain-killing shot and quickly fell into unconsciousness. When she woke, a doctor informed her that she'd had a miscarriage. Epstein took the doctor aside for a private chat before taking Virginia home. He spent no energy on trying to comfort her, but he did pay the medical bills, the least he could do considering the unborn child was almost certainly his.

She was given two weeks off following the miscarriage, time she spent in her Palm Beach apartment self-medicating and sinking into a deep depression over the state of her life. But there was to be little respite. When the fortnight was up, Epstein called her with a new task – to keep a friend of his company on a trip to Little St James. The role would require occasional massages and to keep the guest happy. No more needed to be said. She packed a suitcase and jetted off to the island to meet a Harvard professor called Stephen with white hair and a mad-professor look.

Virginia showed Stephen around the island on quad bikes, then took him back to freshen up before dinner. Over food and wine, the professor began to lose his awkward mannerisms and loosen up. He even plucked up the courage to ask for one of the wonderful massages Epstein had been telling him about. Virginia downed two Xanax to ease the process, then went about her business as deftly and professionally as she had come to learn, massaging the aging man then having sex. The next day, she gave him another massage at the beach and they swam out to a water trampoline. In the evening, they had dinner and more wine but when Virginia asked if he required another massage he demurred, saying he just wanted to stay up watching movies. Surprised, but not disappointed, Virginia went to bed. Stephen had been only her second "client" other than Epstein, but already it was beginning to feel worryingly normal.

When the trip was over, Epstein invited her to New York to pick up her pay for the job with Stephen. When she arrived, she noticed another girl hanging around the mansion. She was called Rina, a teenage artist of Asian descent. Two things quickly became apparent to Virginia – Rina and Epstein had already had sex, and Epstein was using promises of selling her artwork to get her under his spell. Epstein soon asked Virginia for a massage but this time Rina was to be present, too. The three took a shower then moved to the "dungeon". Things seemed to be going normally, with Rina copying Virginia's instructions, until Epstein rose from the massage table and asked Virginia to lie down instead. Shocked, she complied, wondering what was going to happen next. She soon found out when Rina started hitting and whipping her, subjecting her to an hour of bondage for Epstein's pleasure.

Rina was a dominatrix and soon became a fixture around the Manhattan mansion, with Epstein even renting her an apartment. Rina and Virginia's double act soon became a favourite, with the artist using all kinds of toys and weapons on her lowly assistant, even cutting her and striking her around the mouth. Virginia soon learned to get her own back, however, domineering Rina during sex acts, until the sessions became like competitions, with both girls striving for mastery over the other, all of which just seemed to excite Epstein further.

Apart from her proclivities in the bedroom, Rina was a talented artist and made a painting of her and Virginia lying naked in the yin-yang position. Epstein was thrilled with the work, and as thanks got her an exhibit in New York's Metropolitan Museum of Art. But Virginia was getting tired of the physical violence and Epstein was also going off the young artist. Rina was becoming clingy and jealous, asking why she couldn't come on the longer trips with Epstein that Virginia was entitled to. It was a step too far – emotional attachment was the one thing Epstein didn't want from his girls and Rina was soon left by the wayside. Virginia couldn't say she was sorry.

One day in New York, Epstein gave Virginia $1,000 to buy new clothes and get her hair re-styled at one of New York's most exclusive beauty salons. She was also tasked with obtaining two ID photos of herself. The mystery of what this was all about was resolved when Virginia returned from her shopping trip and Epstein told her they would be flying to Europe for a special occasion – they would be attending supermodel Naomi Campbell's birthday party.

They set off in April, stopping first in London, then Paris, and finally landing in St Tropez, the Mediterranean playground of the rich and famous. They met Naomi Campbell in the famous Nikki Beach Club, where the supermodel was sipping champagne surrounded by acolytes. She spoke briefly with Epstein and Maxwell, and invited them to a party on a private yacht before the main event that evening.

Dressed in her new ball gown and refreshed after drinking in the Mediterranean sun, Virginia drank expensive champagne and was introduced to a steady stream of rich and important people. Epstein appeared to be showing her off to his rich friends and that too felt good. She continued to drink and danced with several men, even a prince, as Epstein later informed her. The whole evening was a heady mix of alcohol, dancing and socialising that left her feeling dizzy and high on life.

But the comedown was quick to follow. In the car back to the hotel, there was another passenger, a fat and balding middle-aged man. He was introduced as Rick, and was one of the Hilton hotel-owning dynasty, according to Epstein. Virginia was required to accompany him back to his room and to give him a "massage", with all that it entailed.

Back in Rick's room, she attempted to keep the encounter to a professional massage, but Rick persisted, unzipping her dress and then trying to take off her underwear while she attempted to rub his body. Disgusted and drunk, she decided to cut the encounter as short as possible, giving the drunken millionaire oral sex that was mercifully quick. Feeling as degraded as she had high earlier in the evening, she rushed back to Epstein's room, where the financier gave her a comforting hug. But the sympathy didn't last long. Epstein required his own massage before going to bed.

She celebrated her eighteenth birthday in New York and was given a pair of diamond earrings by Epstein. They flew to Little St James, where Ghislaine – who had recently acquired her helicopter pilot's licence – took them to neighbouring St John. Here they picked up Alexandra Cousteau, the granddaughter of underwater explorer Jacques Cousteau. Virginia was tasked with supplying Cousteau with massages which for once were not sexual. However, on Epstein's instigation, Virginia and Cousteau were instructed to play out lesbian scenes for the financier. Virginia was shocked to discover that someone so high profile could be so easily dragged into Epstein's sordid games, but she soon found out that he was providing funding for Cousteau's underwater projects. It wasn't just girls off the street, it seemed, who could fall under Epstein's spell.

With Cousteau around, the group did a lot of scuba diving, exploring the reefs around the neighbouring islands. On one occasion, they went out of their comfort zones, stumbling into the breeding grounds of some hammerhead sharks. Spotting the deadly shadows swimming towards them in the water, the group had to head to the surface as quickly as possible before scrambling back onto the boat. Virginia was the second from last to be pulled onto the boat as the sharks swam closer. Epstein, of course, was the first.

She spent Christmas and New Year with Epstein in New York, then accompanied him to Paris, where they stayed in a hotel overlooking the Champs-Élysées. Epstein was overseeing the construction of his new Paris apartment and seemed to revel in his power in front of the builders, bossing them around and insisting they change the smallest of details at the last minute.

From Paris, they flew to Spain and on to Tangier, where they stayed in a five-star hotel on the edge of the Moroccan city. In between massaging Epstein and visiting the sights, Virginia spent her time strolling through the local bazaars, taking in the culture and heartbeat of the city. After several days, they flew to England and spent the night in Maxwell's townhouse in London's wealthy Belgravia district.

The next morning, Virginia was woken by Maxwell entering her room, announcing breezily that they had a busy day in front of them. They would both be going shopping for new clothes and accessories, as that night they would be meeting someone very special – a royal prince no less. Virginia was slightly disappointed to find it was Andrew, the Duke of York, rather than one of the younger generation, but managed to hide it well enough. The rest of the day was spent hurrying around London's designer boutiques until Virginia had three new outfits to choose from for the evening ahead. After much deliberating, she went for the simplest – a pink mini-tee and a pair of jeans.

When the prince arrived, Virginia was feeling nervous. She listened politely as the three friends criticised Andrew's recently divorced ex-wife, Sarah Ferguson. Then the attention turned to her. Ghislaine asked Andrew how old he thought she was and the prince guessed correctly. Ghislaine laughed and said, "I guess we are going to have to trade you in soon," making light of Epstein's preference for underage girls.

The four ate at a restaurant then went on to Tramp night-club, an exclusive members-only club in Mayfair. Epstein took a seat while the others danced. Andrew soon had his hands on Virginia and was whispering compliments in her ear while she laughed embarrassedly. When she stole glances at Epstein and Maxwell, they were laughing, enjoying the spectacle of Andrew's terrible dancing and Virginia's discomfort. After an hour of this, and with Andrew drenched in sweat, they returned to Maxwell's townhouse. On the taxi ride home, Maxwell made it clear that Virginia would be expected to make Andrew happy the same way she did with Epstein. Part of Virginia was shocked at this, naively having expected better of royalty, but another part of her was already resigned.

Upstairs, Virginia requested the now-famous photo of her and Andrew, with the prince's arm around her waist and Maxwell hovering in the background. Epstein took the photo with Virginia's camera and disappeared downstairs with Maxwell, leaving Virginia and the prince alone. Virginia ran a bath and undressed. Andrew, it turned out, had a foot fetish, kissing and licking her toes and the arches of her feet. They then moved to the bedroom, where they had sex. She described it as the longest ten minutes of her life.

The next day, they flew back to New York. Elated at returning to normality, she called Tony to meet her at the airport, so they could spend the evening together. However, reality crashed in on her plans – Epstein wanted a massage back at his place when they arrived. She was forced to cancel the evening with her boyfriend and sell her body to Epstein instead. He paid her well for the Andrew encounter, but over the next few weeks she spent it all on parties, alcohol and drugs. She was gradually desensitising herself to the life she was being forced to lead.

She didn't meet Andrew again until the following spring in New York. Mooching in her palatial bedroom, waiting for the next summons from Epstein, she received a call to meet him in his study. Taking the elevator down, she was surprised to see Andrew beaming at her from the couch. Maxwell led her to the sofa and sat her on Andrew's lap. The prince had a *Spitting Image* puppet of himself which he was joking around with. He used it to grope Virginia's breast, which she obediently giggled at, then he did the same with Johanna Sjoberg – another of Epstein's "personal assistants" – while the two girls posed with him for a picture.

Virginia was asked to show Andrew to the "dungeon" for a massage. It began with a foot massage, but quickly turned into oral sex, with classical music playing in the background and the yin-yang painting of her and Rina looming heavily above Virginia's head.

The second meeting with the prince only deepened Virginia's growing depression, and she sank further into drug use, partying so much that she had permanent dark rings under her eyes and her bones were beginning to protrude. Epstein had clearly noticed the change and didn't approve.

One day, it came out of the blue – Epstein told her that she no longer looked like the girl he had first met and felt she needed a break. She was dismissed from all further duties. "I'll call you next time I'm in town," he said, and that was the last she heard from him for several months.

Back in Palm Beach, Virginia found herself a job as a waitress. The money wasn't even a fraction of what she had earned with Epstein but she was living her own life and she quickly started to feel happier and healthier, enrolling on a yoga course and kicking Tony out of the apartment after he started to become abusive on his continued spiral into drug use.

Three months went by and Virginia was feeling better than ever. She had bought a dog and was seeing her family regularly again. But it wasn't long before the bad men in her life were back on the scene. First, it was Tony banging on her apartment door, high on a cocktail of drugs and screaming down the whole building. She took him inside and soon, more out of pity than love, had agreed to take him back. It was a bad mistake. He was now stealing to fund his habit and one night he turned up at her restaurant, high, trying to pick a fight with her. She finished her shift early and went out the back to apologise to her manager, leaving Tony slumped alone at the empty bar. On the journey home, he was strangely sullen. He asked to be dropped off at his parents', which Virginia gladly agreed to, driving home alone to fume to herself about his behaviour.

The next morning, she got a call from her manager demanding angrily where the money was. The tip jar with $150 inside had gone missing the night before. Quickly putting two and two together, Virginia called Tony at his parents' house, but unsurprisingly he had gone missing and couldn't be contacted. Despite her attempts to explain and offer to pay back the $150 from her wages, the restaurant manager fired her and reported her to the police. With no money coming in and a possible prosecution looming, she was in despair. It was just at this point that she got a call from Epstein. He was back in town and wanted to meet for lunch. Seeing a quick fix for her problems, she agreed.

They met in his cabana-office outdoors by the pool at the El Brillo Way mansion. Epstein asked her if she was off drugs, and in one big rush, she explained about her new healthy and happy lifestyle, how Tony had wrecked it and the subsequent police investigation. Surprisingly, Epstein was sympathetic and not only offered to take her back, but also to help her with the police. He said he regularly made large monetary donations to the Palm Beach County Police Department and that he could smooth over the troubles she was in.

True to Epstein's word, she never again heard from the Palm Beach police. She went back to her usual role with her master, except now she felt even more indebted to him. His sexual habits hadn't diminished, either – if anything, they were more extreme than ever. His taste was ranging towards ever younger girls and to orgies involving several girls at a time. Virginia put this down to his newfound friend and business partner, Jean-Luc Brunel.

Brunel was a famous French model agent and scout with an equally infamous reputation. He ranged the world looking for the next big stars of the modelling world, usually from the poorest parts of the globe, where he could find young teenagers – fourteen to fifteen was his preferred age – who would be willing to do almost anything for the bright lights and big money of a modelling career. "Anything" usually meant sex with Brunel himself, either willingly or with the help of a drug spiked in the victim's drink. Exposed in France, Brunel had fled his home country and was now setting up a company in New York. Epstein invested $1 million in the model agency called MC2 and the two went into a fruitful partnership, with Epstein receiving young girls on tap in return for his funding.

With MC2 established in New York, a steady stream of teenage models came and went in Epstein's life. They were mostly from Eastern Europe, Russia and South America, and many of them spoke no English. They were housed at his brother Mark's East 66th Street apartments and were expected to pose nude, do pornography and sell their bodies to rich clients. Another job specification was satisfying the increasingly grotesque sexual appetites of Epstein himself, and Virginia – as his travelling sex slave – was expected to participate. She was involved in numerous lesbian orgies with handfuls of other girls, while Epstein or some other man watched, usually while masturbating. Around this time, Epstein told her of one of his most degraded exploits involving Brunel. For Epstein's birthday, the Frenchman had given him three twelve-year-old triplets who had massaged then performed oral sex on the aging financier. As Epstein described the scene, it was clear that he saw it as nothing more than another sexual exploit to brag about.

Life with Epstein proceeded as usual, with Virginia studying as much about massage therapy as she could in her spare time. She was becoming a self-taught expert and Epstein began to enjoy long two-hour sessions with her, which of course always ended in the same abusive way. Her body was still developing and she was growing from a teenager into a beautiful young woman. She felt that her role with Epstein was subtly changing at the same time, from a pure sex slave to something more like an educated escort, present as much for her charm and conversation as her body.

There were fun times, too, and sometimes Virginia, Maxwell and Epstein would roll about laughing, but fun could turn into work at any moment, and as soon as Epstein got aroused, the two women would have to flip from enjoying themselves to pleasuring him. Virginia thought of it as a confused family. They did all the things normal families did together, like eating meals and watching TV, but with the shadow of Epstein's sexual dominance hanging constantly over them. As families went, this was certainly one of the more dysfunctional examples.

It was around this time that Virginia first got to see the secret security room inside the New York mansion. She and Epstein were leaving the building one day and heading down the hall towards the massive front entrance. As they passed the rows of disembodied eyes which Epstein used to decorate the walls, he opened a secret door that Virginia had never even noticed before. Following him inside, she saw a bank of around twenty screens showing changing images of almost every view in the house, monitored by a security guard. The rows of eyes and the eerie feeling of being watched wherever she went suddenly made sense. Nowhere in this house was private, she suddenly realised; everything was captured and much of it used – for blackmail, pornography and security. Epstein had all the bases covered.

Epstein was now the happy recipient of an ever-increasing stream of young girls from Brunel. They would be sent to him at whichever home he was staying and were coached to respond to his every sexual whim. There were orgies with as many as seven girls at a time, but still Epstein wasn't satisfied, even now asking Virginia to obtain girls for him as well. To cope with the situation, she started taking Xanax again.

Her nineteenth birthday was spent on the island. There was no party, just a typical "family" evening spent watching *Sex and the City* together. Epstein gave her a pair of sapphire and diamond earrings and Maxwell a designer make-up bag. Some Russian girls arrived on the island and Epstein and Brunel arranged a model shoot in which Virginia was involved. The girls all had to pose nude and semi-nude in various positions on the beach and draped across the rocks. Then came the inevitable. They were taken to Epstein's cabana, where they engaged in a lesbian orgy for the benefit of Epstein and Brunel, who sat watching and masturbating. "The best part is they don't even speak English, so there's never a need to keep them amused," she heard Epstein say above the mass of tangled limbs.

Another time on the island, a similar photoshoot turned into an orgy, with Epstein, Prince Andrew (Virginia alleged in court documents) and eight young Russian girls. Again, Epstein joked that these were "the easiest kind of girls to get on with" because of their lack of English.

She needed someone special in her own life again and the only person she could think to turn to was Tony. She found him staying with one of Palm Beach's most notorious drug dealers. His best friend from childhood, Adam, had recently died in a drug deal gone wrong, and Tony had been hitting the narcotics harder than ever. He could hardly move or respond when she went to collect him from the dealer's house. She had to manhandle him down three flights of stairs and into her truck before driving him back to her place. Tony was in a worse state than she had expected, so she called all his friends and dealers and asked them not to supply him with drugs while he went cold turkey. Over the next few days, she nursed him through his withdrawal, forcing him out of bed once a day to eat a meal and take a shower, then giving him more of her Xanax to help him slip back into feverish sleep.

She was forced to leave Tony while his withdrawal was still in progress, as there were important visitors coming to Little St James. Al Gore and his wife Tipper were visiting. Unlike all the other men who had come to stay, Gore seemed like an honourable individual. He doted on his wife, and despite the plethora of beautiful young women coming and going, his eyes never strayed. Virginia was left with the impression of a man who, were he elected, would look after the country with the same care and respect he did his family.

The impression wasn't quite the same with the next political visitor. Bill Clinton arrived on the island and stayed for dinner, eating at the table with Virginia, Epstein, Maxwell and Emmy. The former president had two beautiful women from New York accompanying him and, after an evening of chatting and joking, he was last seen strolling into the darkness with an arm around each of them. Virginia of course retired with Epstein to give him a massage and oral sex followed by a foot massage to send him to sleep.

Back in New York, she began to notice subtle changes taking place in her and Epstein's relationship. One day after sex, a strand of hair had fallen over her eyes and Epstein brushed it aside with his fingers. The gesture was oddly tender and they gazed into each other's eyes with something that came close to intimacy. Afterwards, Epstein wanted to spend the rest of the day with her just hanging out and having fun together. The relationship continued along this unexpected arc for several weeks. They were spending lots of time alone, time that didn't just involve massages or sex. Watching a movie with the millionaire was more likely to involve snuggling up with a bowl of popcorn than having to kneel at his feet massaging them like a slave. When they went quad-biking at the ranch, Epstein preferred to have her sitting behind him than on a bike of her own. He even tried to teach her how to drive a manual car, and – most welcome of all – she was spared from procuring new girls for him. It seemed Epstein was trying to show her a softer, more caring side of his nature. But why? The answer would come soon and it was something she never could have expected.

It happened on Little St James. They had just climbed back onto the dock after a snorkel in the sea. As they were sitting warming their bodies in the Caribbean sun, Epstein shuffled closer to Virginia and put his hand on her back. She knew that something was up but could never have guessed what. Looking sincerely into her eyes, Epstein began to compliment her for her loyalty and told her that she had turned into a charming, funny and beautiful young woman. As Virginia listened, confused by the unusual outpouring of appreciation, Epstein dropped his bombshell – he wanted Virginia to bear him a child.

While Virginia was still reeling over this, Maxwell chipped in hastily with the business side of the proposal – Virginia would receive a large monthly allowance, a mansion in either Palm Beach or New York, and round-the-clock support from nannies. In return, she would have to travel with the child everywhere Epstein wanted them and would have to sign a contract stating that Epstein had sole custody of the child should the two fall out.

She was reeling and her maternal instinct kicked in straight away. There was no way she would sign over her baby to the care of this monster, no matter how many dollars or mansions he gave her. At the same time as this realisation set in, another part of her knew that it might be dangerous to refuse outright, so she stalled for time, saying she wanted to get her professional massage certificates first and become fully healthy and then, perhaps in a year, she would be ready to have Epstein's baby.

Epstein and Maxwell seemed happy enough with her response and that night they celebrated over dinner with champagne. On double her usual dose of Xanax and too much champagne, Virginia managed to get through the evening and the subsequent threesome in a state of self-induced numbness.

She stumbled back into a normal routine for the next few weeks and the proposal went unmentioned. Her twentieth birthday came around while she was staying in the New York mansion. A buzz came over the intercom while she was painting her toenails in her room. It was Epstein asking her to come down to his office. When she arrived, he asked her to sit on his lap. He wished her a happy birthday and announced a surprise present – a massage therapy course in Thailand. She would at last get her wish to become a professionally trained masseuse.

She was given a week to pack and say her goodbyes. She did the rounds of her friends and family, and spent a week getting drunk at farewell parties. Tony accompanied her to the airport and walked with her all the way to the security scanners. He cried when they had to part, not wanting to be without her for so long. Virginia cried, too. Her feelings for Tony had diminished over time but she was still fond of him and felt bad about leaving him just as his recovery from drugs was still in the balance. But this was her dream and she knew it was time to do something for herself at last. She gave Tony one last hug and turned away, not realising this would be the last time she would see him.

She first flew to New York, where Maxwell had prepared a list of everything Virginia might need in Thailand, from emergency numbers to Western Union locations and a series of dos and don'ts. It was a rare insight into a more caring side of the high-society heiress. But when Virginia went to see Epstein, she was surprised to find another woman with him. The beautiful leggy blonde was introduced as Nadia Marcinkova, Epstein's new live-in masseuse and assistant while Virginia was away. Before she left for Thailand, Virginia was to instruct Nadia on how to massage Epstein as well as on, of course, the seedier aspects of the role. Virginia couldn't help feeling a little hurt at being replaced so easily and callously, but another part of her had expected it. Women were nothing more than tools to Epstein, so why should she be surprised that he would replace an old one so readily?

Virginia spent a few sessions massaging and pleasuring Epstein with Nadia. It was amusing to watch how the Czech girl tried to compete with her, trying to massage the boss in her own ways and melodramatically faking orgasms during their sexual encounters. Virginia tried to brush it all off. She would soon be free from all this, for a short while at least.

The last few days in New York sped by and soon Virginia was touching down in Chiang Mai, the largest city in northern Thailand. She got settled down in her hotel and soon started the course. She was studying eight hours a day, five days a week and partying hard in the evenings. Having had so much experience of massage, she quickly became the star of the class and made several friends, one of whom was a girl from Wisconsin who Virginia let share her room as she was beginning to run out of money.

It was on one of her many nights out that she met Robbie, an Australian who was training and taking part in the Thai kickboxing tournaments that were big tourist attractions in Chiang Mai. She was instantly attracted to him and after their first meeting, watching a Muay Thai competition with friends, they arranged another date. They quickly fell in love and she found herself telling him everything about her life of servitude to Epstein. To her surprise, Robbie wasn't judgemental but rather was sympathetic and comforting. When she told him that they should take it easy because she would have to return soon to Epstein, he asked her to come back to Australia with him instead.

They were standing on the balcony of her room overlooking the city of Chiang Mai and the surrounding mountains. "What?" she said, shocked and confused, thinking she had somehow misheard. But she hadn't.

Robbie got down on one knee. "Please will you marry me?" Hardly hearing her own words over her thundering heartbeat, she said yes and her future was sealed.

They were married a little over a week later in a Buddhist ceremony in a mountaintop temple, but not before she had to make the call she dreaded: telling Epstein. Her news was met with silence, so nervously she went on prattling about Robbie and how they had met. Still silence. Worried, she asked Epstein what he thought of the news and he spoke the last few words she would hear from him for several years, "Have a nice life," then he hung up. She was upset at first, but with Robbie's help she put the last of her ties to Epstein behind her.

The next day at the ceremony, after the vows, birds were released from a cage. As she watched them flying freely over the mountains of Chiang Mai, she couldn't help but think of the aptness of the symbolism.

The two lovers had a six-week holiday on the island of Koh Samui before heading back to Australia, where Virginia still lives to this day. Over the years, she did her best to forget Epstein and the world she had inhabited. She came off prescription drugs, settled down to family life with Robbie and gave birth to two children.

Then one day out of the blue in 2007, she received a call from Maxwell asking if she had spoken to the FBI about Epstein. A day later, she got a similar call from Epstein himself, closely followed by one from an FBI agent informing her that they were investigating Epstein and that she had been identified as one of his victims. Wanting to forget the past, she avoided speaking to the FBI at greater length about her abuse, but six months later, when Australian Federal Police turned up on her doorstep, she decided to add her testimony to that of the other survivors.

So began a long struggle for justice that continues to this day. In 2009, she brought a civil lawsuit against Epstein for his crimes against her, and in 2011, she told her story to the press, speaking to the *Daily Mail* and releasing the damning photograph of her with Prince Andrew at Maxwell's London house. In 2014, she set up her own non-profit organisation, Victims Refuse Silence, with the aim of helping girls escape from sex trafficking and of helping survivors to recover.

On Epstein's death, Virginia, like all the other victims, was denied the chance of seeing justice done, but she remains at the front and centre of the battle to bring Maxwell, Jean-Luc Brunel, Prince Andrew and other co-conspirators to justice. With over 100,000 Twitter followers and regularly in the news, she has had a massive influence on keeping the Epstein case in the public eye. Many times on Twitter, she has teamed up with Maria Farmer to expose the super predators.

Far from the confused, depressed teenager who was seconds away from throwing herself off that Palm Beach balcony decades ago, Virginia has become an influential woman leading the fight for justice for survivors of sexual abuse. In the end, she didn't fall but took flight, and in doing so she has become a living example of how to transcend victimhood.

CHAPTER 14
RYAN DAWSON: THE MAN WHO RESEARCHED EPSTEIN FOR THIRTEEN YEARS

Ryan Dawson is an independent researcher, journalist and the author of *The Separation of Business and State*. He is a regular guest on my YouTube channel and has produced an extremely detailed Epstein map linking the key figures. This is an edited version of his interview:

Shaun: What got you interested in Epstein in 2007?

Ryan: Him being arrested. I had people on my forum in the Florida area who were talking about it. And honestly when—I don't remember if it was before or after he got arrested, I'd have to go back and look, but there were—this is not the only paedophile ring. There was the Dream Boys, and before that there was the Finders Cult, and a lot of this happens, sadly enough. I mean, even at war time, I mean Abu Ghraib and others that are tortured in prisons and DynCorp, and even Blackwater, they get involved in this human sex trafficking. And states get involved in this, Saudi Arabia and Israel in particular, which will end up very deeply involved with Epstein, too. And so, it's hard for me when I hear a claim: *Is this somebody seeking attention or is this real?* Because it was so bizarre what was going on.

And you see something on an Internet forum and I'm like, *Why are you telling me? Why don't you tell the police or something?* I was so naïve, right? *But why aren't you going to the authorities?* And the problem is they're paid off or they're the ones doing it. And so, we talked about Epstein, we were talking about his cohorts. We talked a lot about Maxwell's father and stealing Promis software, because I do a lot of digging into the Israelis, into the mafia, as you do. And so, you see these webs, and I'm not shy from conspiracy. I don't dabble with the Jones-type variety, what we call the Alex Jones variety, that's not my cup of tea, but Eric Weinstein, that's more the type of conspiracies that I dig into.

But I'm still very angry about it, and I think a lot of people are interested in this story and want to know what happened because this is a lot deeper than just some wealthy guy who was a pervert. This was an intelligence operation and we have evidence that it was an intelligence operation and we know the players. And there are still people who could be subpoenaed. We know where Dershowitz is, we know where Prince Andrew is.

Shaun: So, you talked about the transfer of nuclear technology and knowledge to Israel, and Robert Maxwell was pushing the Promis software all over the world, selling a multiple of what the other peddlers were selling. How big was his role then in that transfer of that knowledge?

Ryan: Yeah, he comes a little after the Sonneborn group, but it's an identical way of financing, the same way they originally made a group with Rudolf Sonneborn in New York in 1945 to procure weapons for the future war. Haganah was stealing weapons from all over the world, but especially in the United States because the United States had the most weapons. They didn't have any cities destroyed in World War Two, one base in Hawaii, which actually wasn't part of the United States yet, but they had the bomb and the goal was, *We're going to get the bomb.* And I just brought that up to show the scale of if you can't get a story out of the most powerful weapon in the world being stolen and the US still won't admit that, not officially, they won't admit that Israel has nuclear weapons, even though Mordechai Vanunu went and took pictures of the warheads and showed at that time they already had hundreds of nuclear weapons.

But you're right: [Robert] Maxwell was in that same clique with some of the scientists, Zalman Shapiro and so on, who were part of the tail end of the weapons theft, which I guess is most well-known for the theft they did out of Pennsylvania where Heli Trading Company, for example, is the largest Israeli arms dealer; Arnon Milchan admits it on a stage, by the way, nothing happens to him. The buyer side of that was who was taking Krytron triggers – which is something you need in the development of nuclear warheads – was none other than Benjamin Netanyahu, who's now the prime minister. And when it comes to Epstein, he's not unfamiliar with prime ministers or chief heads of the Mossad, either, like Ehud Barak.

But that's very important because Ehud Barak helped shelter other paedophiles, other incidences of international paedophilia. And also, President Katsav; Katsav was the president of the tail end of Barak's tenure as prime minister; he was convicted of rape in Israel. Israel's president was convicted of rape. I mean, in 2000 to 2007, he's president. Not many people know that the president of Israel was convicted of rape. Can you imagine if the president of Iran was convicted of a rape? That would be all over the TV. Or any other country? The president of the United States was convicted of rape and where that would be? But yes, the president of Israel – Israel has a president and a prime minister; they have a similar system to the French – was convicted of rape and that was all during this time period. And not a peep in the media about that, either.

So, when people are wondering *Why did this story die? How come there were all these questions and then it went away?* They got about as deep as Leslie Wexner and then zip. The Wexner Foundation was actually used to illegally launder money to Ehud Barak's coffers. This was the chief of the Mossad. And while he is for the Mossad, he is the chairman of the board for the Carbyne group, which used to be called Reporty, which Epstein helped to create, too – so did Peter Thiel, who is one of the principal founders of PayPal. Carbyne is kind of Israel's Blackwater; it's a security front 911 response thing. And Erik Prince gets involved in that as well. He's changed the name. I think it went from Blackwater to XZ, and then it was Academy, and they had another name and now I think it's called Frontier Secure Services Group or something, and they're making Blackwater China as we speak.

But these people have been caught in rape rings, as has Dyn-Corp. So, this isn't anything new as far as governments covering up paedophilia. But a lot of Wexner's group for the mega donors, the Bronfman family for example, have deep ties to organised crime as well as the NXIVM cult, which also was caught in raping women and branding people.

Clare and Sara Bronfman actually already admitted to trafficking young girls in the NXIVM cult, and Edgar Bronfman senior is the president of the world Jewish Congress. And Charles Bronfman, of course, is the chairman of United Jewish Communities, which would have the United Israel Appeal, the United Jewish Appeal, and the Council of Jewish Federations. And I don't want anyone to get the wrong idea, they can write the word Jewish in their name, that doesn't make them speak for an ethnic group – these people are Jewish supremacist. It's the same as *Wow, are you so shocked that white supremacists are white and black supremacists are black and a lot of Jewish supremacists are Jewish?* But that is a subset of a larger category. I don't want anybody confusing that these people have loyalty to a state, which is the state of Israel, and it can call itself the Jewish state, but that doesn't make it so. All these people are out of their minds.

And Michael Steinhardt and a lot of these Jewish billionaires – the Bronfmans, Wexner – they don't represent Jews, they don't represent anything. I don't want anybody getting the wrong picture there, but they are a supremacist clique and they do have loyalty to a foreign state. And that is their purpose, to set up a parasitic relationship really inside the US and Canada to steal technology. Because that's what Epstein was doing: he was a blackmail and spy operation. And it's been done many times before. If I had many, many hours, I could go all the way from the Forties to now, walking through it. I have taken a map starting from about the Eighties – just when Epstein got involved – onward. But they are always stealing technology and setting up honeytraps.

Right now [2020], the current president of the United States, his son-in-law is Jared Kushner, whose father was caught and convicted and thrown in prison for illegal campaign financing, which also involved sexual blackmail on his own brother-in-law, where he got in a feud with Marie Kushner, his older brother and then his sister Miriam. And he set up her husband with a hooker – who went to the Red Bull Inn – and they secretly filmed a sexual encounter and he tried to blackmail his own sister with this. His own sister and brother were feuding with him because he set up a bunch of cut-out front companies as a way of illegally feeding the campaign of the governor of New Jersey at the time, Governor McGreevey, because the governor of New Jersey is who selects the chairman of the Port Authority of New York and New Jersey.

And the Port Authority sets up lucrative real-estate contracts, which Kushner was trying to award to himself. And the president, by the way, the former chairman is the president of APAC, the largest Israeli lobby. But it's a big circle. I have a film about that called *Trump's Zionist Ball and Chain*, it goes through all these white-collar crimes. And it might be a little bit heavy in the economic jargon and whatnot in that film. But the gist of it is: they're setting up honeytraps, they're buying hookers, they're illegally financing everything. And they do it all the time. And because even when they get caught, now and then, the return is so much larger than the consequence. And so it just continues. You can use a couple of million to bribe and end up with billions. And so they just do it and do it and do it.

And it didn't hurt them at all. I mean, Jared Kushner, who has worked for his dad and whose father and mother also bribed his and his brother's way into Harvard. And it doesn't seem to escape them because it's never reported. I mean, do you think the Democrats, as much as they say, "Oh, Trump's racist" and all that, why wouldn't they bring up the fact that Charles Kushner is a convicted felon and that their son is given a high-level position in the White House, and the Kushner clan has been involved in all of these crimes linking back to Tony Salerno and all these mafia people around Atlantic City? They could, but they can't because a lot of the Clintons and the Bidens are doing the same thing, so they're not going to bring it up.

Shaun: Let's go back to Robert Maxwell and Epstein's entry into the intelligence community then. If you've seen the statements by Ari Ben-Menashe …

Ryan: Yeah, Ari Ben-Menashe, he was the agent who spent time at MCC, the same prison as Epstein was murdered in.

Shaun: He's saying that when Ghislaine and Epstein started to go out, it was Robert who brought Epstein into the fold. Do you agree with that?

Ryan: What they tried to do at first with Epstein – because Robert was more into diverting illegal arms and at the time they were working, I believe it was with Douglas Leese in a bid, because the Americans had shafted Saudi Arabia on a contract for fighter jets and the British stepped in, I think it was the Tornadoes, I don't remember which jet it was – but basically, Epstein wasn't very good at it. And you can see his earlier Ponzi scheme with the reinsurance company with Steven Hoffenberg, they knew John Lehman who was on the 9/11 commission, by the way. They had worked with Douglas Leese and tried to get Epstein in on this legal-ish—I mean, it's insider trading with his quasi-legal and illegal arms trade, but he just didn't know what he was doing. They said he was a brilliant mind and others say: "No, this guy was just a brilliant con man." I lean more toward the brilliant con man than any kind of whizz-kid hedge fund manager or arms dealer, stockbroking. The guy found his niche setting up honey-traps and getting young girls. Apparently, he had some charm and they funded him the money. I mean, Wexner gave him a house, they just gave him a house. He owned a mansion in New York, the most expensive house there was. And he figured out with Jean-Luc Brunel and MC2 modelling and other modelling agencies in the United States that rather than the traditional feeding ground of orphanages or putting up false advertisements in Eastern Europe and taking advantage of the desperate situation there after the collapse of the Soviet Union, that's how they got a lot of young girls who wouldn't be known, who were attractive that they could use in these rings.

They set up modelling agencies and the level of degeneracy worldwide had reached the point where it was perfectly okay to take twelve-year-old models and stick them in nearly naked ads and things, and they plastered them all over Leslie Wexner's businesses like Abercrombie & Fitch, and it was kind of okay, they weren't naked, but it was sketchy. But it was a way of saying, *Look, you got a grown man with a house full of twelve-to-fifteen-year-olds.* And that is something that Jean-Luc Brunel was able to do to help as almost a farm to find, to hire, purposely hire the compromised and then get them to the United States or to the Caribbean. And then of course everyone knows the story of what happened to them, unfortunately from there, with Ghislaine Maxwell and Jeffrey Epstein using them, raping them and using them as honeytraps. I would also add kidnapping some of them, and some of them lived with them and had nowhere to go. They took their passports away. Ghislaine on many occasions threatened to kill them.

But I'd like to point out, too, that Epstein's brother, Mark Epstein, has a lot of property in the New York area adjacent to the Wexner rape house where a lot of these models were housed. His properties were housing a lot of these young girls. And this is often a place that people like Prince Andrew and Ehud Barak would go and visit, spend the night. So, it wasn't just in Epstein's New York rape mansion itself, but the adjacent territories were full of young girls and they were prostituting them out, which is just disgusting. They raped a bunch of women. And a lot of people in that area knew and just had nobody to tell because to the authorities it didn't matter.

Shaun: Well, the girl at Wexner's house, Maria Farmer, she called the authorities, and they came out and they were basically in Wexner's pocket, so they wouldn't do anything for her.

Ryan: Yes. I mean, you're talking about a billionaire with multiple businesses who's friends with other billionaires that own papers and they have so much influence, versus a teenage girl with no connections. What is she supposed to do? And this had to happen over and over and over again before anything ever was done. And I guess it starts in Florida. Well, he pissed off another billionaire, Donald Trump, over the Mar-a-Largo property capture, was rubbing Trump's face in it because obviously Trump wanted to buy the property adjacent to what he already owned and he was having a lot of financial problems and Epstein and Maxwell were rubbing his nose in it. But Trump did make a lot of money in some of his hotel investments and then later through *The Apprentice*, and was able to just barely outbid Epstein and nabbed the property, which caused a rift between the two. But that's the property where Virginia Roberts was recruited from by the tennis courts. You've heard her story … She's probably been the most vocal victim out of all the victims so far, and I believe more will step up.

But with the death of Epstein, a lot of it all died even though there are plenty of players to still go after. Maxwell's also accused of rape, so is Dershowitz, Jean-Luc Brunel, Prince Andrew, there are people there, some of them who aren't hiding. And nothing seems to really go forward.

I think I mentioned earlier how Ehud Barak helps shelter other paedophiles. One of them was Arie Scher who – together with a Hebrew language teacher named George Steinberg – set up a child prostitution ring. They were homosexual and they were using little boys and little girls, and they had Israeli tourists going to the Israeli consulate in Brazil where these parties would happen with little kids. And that's how they got caught; these guys were so brash that they stupidly didn't understand that in the background of some of the photos that were going around, was the swimming pool of the Israeli consulate, which was very noticeable. So, they were doing it on government property. That doesn't mean necessarily that the Israelis set them up to do that. But as an employee of the Israeli state, Arie Scher sure was doing that and wasn't convicted and he fled back to Israel. And Katsav, the convicted rapist president of Israel, he just moved him around; they tried to send him to Australia. The Aussies looked up his past and said: "There's no way this person is coming here." And then he went to Hong Kong and they just move them around like the Catholic Church used to do the rape priests. "Oh, you got caught doing that. Well, let's just put you in this other area." Which is disgusting. I mean, they're being financed and protected by a state when they're raping children.

And I mean it was like eight, nine-year-old kids that these guys were involved with, and it just goes on and on. They're always getting Latin American kids out of Colombia. A former IDF [Israel Defense Forces] soldier set up a rape ring in Colombia, and they would get caught and maybe it's in the written news for a day and then disappears and it's never in the American media. And it doesn't matter how big it is or who it involves. And I swear the only reason they really jumped on the Epstein thing is because there was pictures of him with Donald Trump, and whatever you think about Donald Trump, there has been many sustained anti-Trump screed in the media since before he was even sworn in.

And so, when they then tried to go to Acosta, who said "I was told this is intelligence, back off," right? And with who? Which kind of intelligence? If it's the CIA, why are we busting ourselves? Why did we arrest him in New York at all, right? It's someone, it's intelligence, all right. It's not our intelligence, it's another country's intelligence. More powerful, probably, with pulling the strings than the United States is. But he was told to back off, and Barry Krischer – that gave him the sweetheart deal in Florida – was an award winner for the ADL [the Anti-Defamation League], as was Alan Dershowitz.

It's not hard to figure out who it was. The Mega Group was set up for that purpose and he's giving money to the chief of the Mossad, who's the chairman of an Israeli security network that they themselves also created. And then these people are hiding rapists. And why are you stealing tech? Why are you setting honeytraps? Why are you so interested in US technology and science? Is the US stealing that to give it to the US? That doesn't make any sense; it's a foreign state and it's Israel.

Shaun: The reason it prevails in the news here is because of Prince Andrew. Do you think Prince Andrew was just a useful idiot or was he more diabolical?

Ryan: Both. He's a useful idiot and diabolical. Prince Andrew [gave Epstein] more clout. It's like: "Look, I know a Royal," which in America, no one cares. It's like, "Prince of what? Get lost." But it's a big deal in other places. "He's a prince, he knows the Queen" and whatever, and it's a very rich, wealthy, famous person. And Epstein would brag about this to many. "Oh, I got this guy, I got that." And he liked to get actors or prominent people. His role officially was to go after US science and technology. But one way you're going to have to set up honeytraps to protect yourself politically. You mess with Hoover – what Hoover used to do with his G-Men was collect sexual blackmail on key figures that he was going after. But then, of course, Frank Costello got the goods, the sexual blackmail off Hoover and Clyde Tolson themselves. So, you blackmailed the blackmailer and now you're a blackmail over everyone else. Epstein was kind of like this. Because you have to understand when you're talking about the very, very wealthy, the very powerful, bribery doesn't really work. You can't really bribe somebody with something they already have. If you're going to bribe a billionaire or a millionaire, you're going to need an enormous amount of money because they're not going to risk everything they have for $200,000 or something.

No, if you want to go after the poor, you use bribery. If you want to go after the wealthy, you use blackmail. Blackmail conversely doesn't work so well with the poor because they have nothing to lose, but you wave money around and they're willing to do it. So, if you want to get somebody like Bill Clinton or you want to get somebody like a governor or a senator, or a Larry Summers or someone like that, then you want to go – like Bill Richardson, for example – then you're going to use blackmail. And the best kind of blackmail is sexual blackmail. And the best kind of sexual blackmail is underage sexual blackmail, because that is the one thing that will do you in, because if you look at, for whatever reason, in the UK and the US if somebody advocated murder, if somebody caused the starvation of half a million Iraqi children, if somebody was involved in intentional starvation in Yemen, if somebody reinstituted slavery in North Africa, if somebody was caught aiding Al Qaeda, that's fine. But you get caught banging a little kid, then, okay, we have a moral line somewhere that will end your career.

So, this is how deep and ugly it's got to be to get blackmail, because advocating murder and starvation and torture, that's a legitimate political platform. If you want to get up there and be pro-torture, you can sit there as an adult and actually make a case of why you should be allowed to torture human beings, even though it's been proven all it does is get them to say whatever they think you want to hear and it's not reliable and it doesn't matter. That's fine. That's okay. And you can advocate for sanctions even though we know that it's killing people collectively and you can do all that. You shouldn't be able to, but that will not tank your career. What will tank your career in the United States or the UK is sexual deviancy or racism. That's about all you could possibly do that would automatically kill your career.

Shaun: So, with Prince Andrew being in the news here, it's taken the heat off the Clintons. How tight were the Clintons with Epstein? I saw Hillary was on the flight as well.

Ryan: Yeah, it's interesting because a relative of mine was in the uniform, secret service, was a bodyguard for both Clintons. And I heard many stories about her sexual escapades, let's say. And I had Gary Byrne on my show recently and he conferred a similar story of her being walked in on with another woman. And so, she's not as well-known as Bill, because Bill actually was the president unlike Hillary, so he got a lot more attention from the accusations of rape going all the way back to when he was a governor of Arkansas and beyond during the Iran-Contra scandal, which he also assisted in. Iran-Contra, by the way, it was not an event where the Israelis helped the US by selling contraband to Iran. Israel had been getting contraband out of Nicaragua and aiding the dictatorship there since the middle of the Seventies. Somoza's grandfather helped smuggle and divert weapons out of Nicaragua to the Israeli state the generation before, so they owed them. But the Clintons ... Bill Clinton was very well known, not as a paedophile, but definitely as someone that couldn't keep his willie in his pants – he really liked the ladies. And so, it was a simple target to honeytrap Clinton. And I don't think he was just on the plane making peanut butter and jelly sandwiches, let's say that.

The best troll ever was Donald Trump bringing in Clinton's rape accusers and putting them in the front row of his debate with Hillary, so she had to look them in the face the whole time.

Shaun: Yeah, I saw that. That was a hell of a power play and Clinton deserves that. He was allegedly coked-up abusing women.

And you mentioned earlier how the president of Israel had a rape conviction. Well, I suspect that Clinton would've had one if it wasn't for his resources, connections, legal team, out-of-court settlements, non-disclosure agreements and being fully backed by the CIA protecting the cocaine operation of [George H. W.] Bush and Oliver North.

Ryan: And they tried to involve a lot of their own security personnel in North Africa, for example, where they would buy hookers for everybody and try—it was pure debauchery when the Clintons got into the White House; they brought it into that kind of sacred area and they brought all of it there with them. And the kind of people they were hiring and the kind of people they had been associated with all the way back to their mafia days in Arkansas, it never skipped a beat. So, it wasn't surprising at all. I mean, Clinton pardoned Mark Rich in his final hour in office. And Mark Rich was a commodities trader for Glencore and famous for a lot of crimes; officially he was on Interpol's most wanted list for tax evasion in the tens of millions. And his wife financed Hillary Clinton's senate campaign.

Pick a crime – they did it with the Russian mob, including narcotics, illegal smuggling of weapons, uranium and human trafficking. And so, Mark Rich, these guys in the Russian mob, they're all tied to the Clintons. So is Lewis Libby even, ironically. Libby was Mark Rich's lawyer and he was the chief of staff for Dick Cheney, and he wrote a book about paedophilia rape. He had underage Japanese girls being raped in a cage by a bear, so you can include bestiality on top of paedophilia.

Shaun: And Clinton pardoned his own brother who was buying coke, dealing coke, and who said that Bill had a nose like a vacuum cleaner. And Dan Lasater, who was laundering the money. Do you think some of Epstein's money was drug money?

Ryan: They were doing drugs, so I mean, he was involved in it. But most of his money he got because of his theft. And so he wasn't really a drugs tsar so much. But some of the people he was partying with certainly were.

Shaun: Was he moving drug money around for the CIA? Kind of like Dan Lasater, who laundered money through Arkansas.

Ryan: Oh yes, okay, as far as the money-laundering section, yes, absolutely. He wasn't the guy selling the narcotics though. Epstein was more of the one cleaning the money. And he was a frontman for the Mega Group and also for JP Morgan Chase. So, one of the things he did, and this will just be one example of the many things that he did, because we talked earlier about Steven Hoffenberg and Doug Leese and stuff, but I didn't get into the nitty gritty of that. But there's so many scandals and Ponzi schemes that he was involved with. Also, he actually was involved in another one with the Bronfmans. So, I can get to that later, too, if you put a pin in that and remind me. But one of the things he did down in the Caribbean, this is a guy buying islands. As Eric Weinstein said, he looked way richer than he was, unless they're just lying about his income.

But the Mega Group set him up well and he was sort of the cut out and had cut-out companies to hide money in to launder money for financials and hedge funds. He wasn't a hedge fund manager, like a legal hedge fund manager that's actually investing well. That's not what he did. What he did is, for example, he set up a company in Bermuda for Bear Stearns. And so, he did Bear Stearns Ltd, Ireland Ltd, to get a way round US regulations. And then they set up Liquid funding Ltd in Bermuda and put up 40% of the money for this. And there's a whole webby network of who's who, crooks involved in that. And all it was really doing was offloading toxic assets for Bear Stearns onto this subsidiary so that they looked like they had balanced books when they didn't.

And Bear Stearns, for example, the first of the following

month, would buy back the toxic assets; it just shifted them around, so it would look like they didn't have debt obligations when they did. And then, of course, Liquid Funding would look as if it was terribly in the red, and then it would just be bought back again after the rating agencies had cleared it. It's just shifting around toxic assets, there's nothing genius about it. It's actually a really low-level scheme. But to make it worse, Liquid Funding issued commercial paper into several money markets, including Dreyfus money market. They put in $139 million and then $125 million in Russell Investments, and $100 million into JP Morgan money market funds. And it was odd because, of course, he's meeting with representatives of them. James Staley of JP Morgan physically met Epstein in Florida while he's supposed to be in jail.

He had the twelve hours or six days a week he could go back to work and then stay next to the jail in an apartment. On one of his working holidays – working from home and still continuing to rape women – he met with Alan C. Greenberg and James Staley. Why can't you just call the guy on the phone? Well, we know why, you want to meet in person. You know, we all know.

Shaun: He had plain clothes police screening his guests.

Ryan: They weren't calling him the prisoner, put it that way. Cops don't have the highest salary and he's like, *Here's a wheelbarrow of cash and two girls*, right? So, JP Morgan Chase, they would end up buying out Bear Stearns in this kind of corporate takeover, but not alone – the Federal Reserve Bank in New York set up Maiden Lane LLC, and they put in the senior loan of $28.2 billion, and JP Morgan only put up $1.1 billion or maybe $1.2 billion in this takeover of Bear Stearns. So, of the $30 billion, over $28 billion of it came from Maiden Lane, which was just a Federal Reserve creation, a Federal Reserve bank of New York. Not the Fed like the DC Fed, but same difference. And they would buy out the company that Epstein was helping to hide toxic assets for and illegally putting out junk commercial paper into money markets that caused all these people to lose their fortunes.

Should he have been convicted of that? I think that story, because the paedophilia is so bad and so click-baity, I guess, that some of his other nefarious financial crimes never really get a lot of attention. But not only was he a paedophile and a spy, he was definitely a world-class white-collar criminal.

CHAPTER 15
JEAN-LUC BRUNEL: THE
FRENCH CONNECTION

Thysia Huisman arrived at the apartment on Avenue Foch near the Arc de Triomphe in Paris, just as she'd been instructed. The eighteen-year-old aspiring model carried only a small backpack of possessions and three photos of herself – not much to begin a new life, but the man she was going to live with had a reputation for making superstars. It would surely be worth it.

The apartment was as grand on the inside as its façade suggested, with antique furniture and paintings covering the walls. Its owner was equally impressive in his way. Urbane, charming, softly spoken and every inch the gentleman, Jean-Luc Brunel had met the young Dutch girl in a chocolate shop in Brussels and invited her to Paris to stay in his apartment. Thysia had initially thought the offer was strange but her agents had urged her to accept it. This was the man who had launched the careers of Monica Bellucci, Sharon Stone, Christy Turlington and Jerry Hall, after all.

But when Thysia entered the apartment, she noticed the warning signs immediately. Many of the other girls who were staying there – some of whom she recognised from magazines – looked distinctly underage. They all had a sad look about them and Thysia sensed they were being forced to sleep with the middle-aged Frenchman. Brunel began flirting with her straight away, joking that they would one day be married and that they would soon have sex. When she asked him where she would be sleeping, he told her his bed, of course.

Thysia managed to get through the first night, sleeping under a blanket on the floor of another girl's room. Part of her was screaming to get out but another part told her she just had to stay careful and ride this through – it was the opportunity of a lifetime.

Despite her reservations, Thysia was soon caught up in the lifestyle of an up-and-coming model – there were test shoots, castings and endless parties. At one point, Brunel offered to hook Thysia up with his friend, Harvey Weinstein, for a career in the movies. On another occasion, she met a man in a black turtleneck sweater that she now thinks was Jeffrey Epstein. The inevitable came one night at an after-party at the apartment. Brunel gave Thysia a drink he said he'd mixed especially for her. She drank it and immediately started to feel woozy. The rest of the night's events ran like a kind of blurry slow-motion movie with tiny moments of horrific clarity – Brunel taking her to his room, lying her on the bed and telling her to relax; the sound of her blouse being ripped open; wanting to struggle but being unable to move; and the feeling of something pushing between her legs.

Thysia woke the next morning wrapped in a kimono that wasn't hers with her clothes in a pile on the floor. Her inner thighs were marked and bruised. She got dressed, grabbed her backpack from the other room and ran out of the apartment while Brunel was on the phone. Outside, Thysia felt like the houses were moving and had a deep sense of disconnection from reality. Her world had been turned upside down, her dreams shattered. She was just another victim of the conveyor belt of abuse.

Huisman was one of dozens, maybe hundreds, perhaps even thousands of young models who fell prey to Jean-Luc Brunel. The story was always the same – first they were charmed, seduced and dazzled by the high life, plied with drink, drugs and endless parties. If none of these encouraged them to succumb to Brunel's sexual desires, then it would be a spiked drink and a half-remembered traumatic nightmare.

This was the man who became Epstein's go-to supplier of beautiful – usually underage – women, trafficking them across the Atlantic on the promise of glittering modelling careers, only to find themselves being forced to pleasure the sexual appetites of a perverted old man. The pipeline was so prolific that Epstein boasted of sleeping with over 1,000 of Brunel's models, three of whom, according to Virginia Giuffre, were twelve-year-old triplets given as a birthday present. Yet until the end of 2020, this serial child abuser and trafficker was never charged with any crimes in France, even when several media exposés revealed what he was doing.

When asked about Brunel, most people who knew him only had good things to say about him, mentioning his charming, gentlemanly and soft-spoken manner. Yes, he was a bit of a party animal and a ladies' man, but who wouldn't be, given his position and proximity to so many beautiful women? It becomes clear from the testimony of those who knew and worked with Brunel that he had two sides to his personality – the charming, pleasant side which his associates saw, and the darker, abusive aspect which only his victims witnessed. Whatever the case, he clearly lived a kind of charmed life. How did this diminutive Frenchman come to be in such a position of power over so many women, and what were his deeper links to the murky world of Epstein?

Born in 1946 in Paris, Brunel was originally named Jean-Luc-Charles-Raymond Benchamoul, according to French Epstein researcher Frederic Ponton (La French ConAction on Twitter and YouTube). His family were originally of North African Jewish descent. Like Robert Maxwell, Brunel may well have changed his name to escape anti-Semitic prejudice while trying to make a name for himself in post-war Paris. Brunel had a brother, Arnaud, and their father was a real-estate manager to the elite, so the two children were brought up around the glitz, glamour and wealth of Parisian high society.

Brunel clearly inherited his father's taste for the high life. He loved to party and socialise, to be surrounded by the most beautiful objects and of course women. He married twice, first to the Swedish model Helen Hogberg, and then to American model Roberta Chirko. Both marriages ended in divorce. Given his tastes, Brunel was perhaps destined for a career in the fashion industry. His first experience came in 1974 when he met Claude François, a famous French pop singer who hired Brunel as a model scout for his new modelling agency, Girl's. Working for François, Brunel travelled around Europe, scouring the continent for beautiful women.

In 1975, Brunel took a hiatus from his modelling career and moved to Ibiza, where he opened a bar with his first wife, Helen Hogberg. But the move did not become permanent and Brunel returned to Paris in 1977, where he joined Karin Mossberg's elite modelling agency, Karin Models. As his marriage fell apart, Brunel's career began to flourish. The following year, he became head of Karin Models, and in the next ten years he claimed to discover the likes of Milla Jovovich, Christy Turlington and Sharon Stone. However, his decade at the top of the game was to end in controversy.

In 1988, he was the subject of a *60 Minutes* investigation in which several American models described the culture of drugging and sexual exploitation that Brunel fostered. And in another investigative programme, Brunel's long-term use of cocaine was exposed. According to many models, Brunel's exploits were well known throughout the fashion industry. Models were at first seduced then coerced and, if they resisted, finally drugged and raped. And those who refused were denied work and found their careers floundering.

Although he wasn't formally charged, Brunel's reputation had taken a severe blow and in the same year he and brother Arnaud left France for America, where they set up their own modelling agency, Next Management Corporation. The following year, they partnered with Faith Kates and Joel Wilkenfeld to create a global brand, Next Management Company, with Brunel becoming the head of the Miami branch.

It was around this time that Brunel first met Jeffrey Epstein, probably in the year 1993 or 1994, according to Ponton. Although Brunel and Epstein's infamous trafficking partnership wasn't to start for another decade, the two clearly had already established a close relationship, with the name Jean-Luc Brunel or "JLB" appearing on the flight logs of the *Lolita Express* more than twenty-five times between 1999 and 2005.

Controversy continued to follow Brunel in the US and in 1996 he and Arnaud were forced to separate from Next when they were accused of siphoning models from the agency to their own newly formed company, Karin Models of America. In 1999, Brunel was the subject of a BBC *MacIntyre Undercover* report into sexual abuse in the fashion industry, and in 2002, supermodel Karen Mulder mentioned his name in association with the prevalent sexual misconduct and abuse within the Paris fashion world. In 2003, Brunel's two major funders, his brother Arnaud and business partner Etienne des Roys, pulled out and in 2004, he was forced to change the name from Karin Models of America after the Paris office filed to revoke the name.

At this time, things were looking bad for Brunel. He was living in an apartment in Trump Tower and was basically broke. This was when Epstein stepped in. According to Ponton, Epstein and Brunel first attempted to set up a partnership with Elite Models and Donald Trump. Brunel probably knew Trump through their mutual friend, Paulo Zampolli (it was Zampolli who introduced Trump to his now-wife Melania). When this attempt fell through, Epstein provided $1 million of funding for Brunel to continue with his own agency. MC2 Model Management was born, the name being a subtle reference to Epstein – the missing E coming from Einstein's famous equation $E=MC2$. MC2 opened offices in New York and Miami, and also a base in Tel Aviv, Israel. According to Ponton, the Tel Aviv office was nothing but a front, with business addresses linked to nondescript properties in residential streets. Given Epstein's close association with the Mossad, this provides an interesting link between the Israeli intelligence service and Epstein and Brunel's sex-trafficking operation, an operation that now went into overdrive.

According to Ponton, with MC2 set up, Brunel now began

travelling widely across Eastern Europe, South America and the former Soviet Bloc to find young and underage models for MC2 and Epstein. The girls were brought in on valid working visas where possible but often, according to Ponton, Brunel would smuggle them in on tourist visas – a practice that Epstein became increasingly angry about as he knew the risks it involved. Such a victim was Nadia Marcinkova, who was brought into the States at the age of fourteen and housed at Mark Epstein's 66th Street apartments before going on to become Virginia Giuffre's replacement as Epstein's masseuse and sex slave.

The fact that underage girls were coming into the States under the cover of modelling agencies is confirmed by the testimony of Miles and Cathy Alexander, who managed Little St James island from 1999 to 2007. According to the couple, numerous girls were brought to the island under the cover of modelling work, with some of the most obviously underage being smuggled onto the island by boat to circumvent immigration laws. As we have seen, Brunel provided a steady stream of these "models" for Epstein's private entertainment and he clearly knew that many if not most of these were under the legal age of consent, as is evidenced by several handwritten notes taken down by Epstein's assistants following phone calls from Brunel. One such note from 2005 reads: "He has a teacher to teach you to speak Russian. She is 2x8 years old, not blonde. Lessons are free and you can have the first one today if you call."

These girls were housed in rooms at Mark Epstein's 66th Street apartment block in New York, with up to four girls per apartment. Brunel charged the girls rent at $1,000 a month and Brunel and Epstein took a 30% cut of their earnings.

Outside the modelling agency, it was clear that Epstein and Brunel enjoyed more than just a professional relationship. In his legal testimony, former Palm Beach house manager, Janusz Banasiak, said that Brunel would often visit the house and even make lunch for himself in the kitchen. And when Epstein was sentenced to thirteen months in jail, Brunel visited him no less than sixty-seven times. Indeed, it was during Epstein's first investigation by Florida police that the two were perhaps closest. When Brunel was asked to provide testimony for the investigation in 2009, he played a game of cat and mouse through his lawyer, always ensuring that he was abroad and unavailable to talk. Six years later, Brunel himself admitted that it was Epstein who had asked him to "leave the region, and to go to Europe and Asia to delay the testimony".

This admission came in 2015, when their relationship had clearly changed for the worse. Brunel sued Epstein for damaging the reputation of his brand but the case came to nothing. Brunel claimed that he was also a victim of Epstein, as the financier had helped him re-launch his career as a model agent so he owed him a debt. According to Ponton, during the case Brunel's lawyer, Joe Titone, claimed that Brunel had lots of pictures with Epstein and his friends, and that many of them included young girls. Brunel agreed to supply these photographs but seems to have promptly changed his mind, quickly leaving the country.

Brunel was last seen in public on the night before Epstein's arrest, partying at the exclusive Paris Country Club. Although it was widely reported that Brunel had gone into hiding, possibly in Brazil, he was in fact in France preparing his defence with his lawyer, Corinne Dreyfus-Schmidt. On September 17, 2019, French police searched the offices of Karin Models in the 8th arrondissement of Paris, but it seems nothing was found. Its manager, Ruth Malka, Brunel's right-hand woman for many years before taking over the agency, says she never knew anything about Jean-Luc Brunel's attitude towards young women.

Brunel was arrested on December 16, at Paris's Charles de Gaulle Airport, carrying a one-way ticket to Dakar in Senegal. He was charged with multiple rapes against Virginia Giuffre and one charge of sexual harassment against an unknown accuser in 2016. Giuffre's testimony was crucial because two of her rape allegations occurred in 2000 and 2001, meaning they were within France's twenty-year statute of limitations for such offences.

Unfortunately, most of Brunel's misdemeanours – for which victims have been willing to step forward – seem to have occurred in the Seventies, Eighties and Nineties, thus falling outside the statute of limitations.

Amongst the other complaints filed against Brunel were those of ten alleged victims reported in 2019. The most recent was a young French woman in her twenties who described being sexually harassed by Brunel within the last four years. A former model for Karin Models, Courtney Soerensen, told the French press how Brunel sexually assaulted her after weeks of sexual harassment. She described how he lured her into his bedroom at the Avenue Foch apartment on the pretext of showing her some pictures, then: "He tried to push me on his bed. I resisted. He persisted. He then tried violently to undo my shirt. I managed to escape from the room." After the incident, Soerensen described how castings and photo shoots dried up for her and she was forced to change agency.

New Zealand model Zoe Brock also reported being sexually assaulted by Brunel and to have been professionally punished for managing to escape. And, as we have seen, Virginia Giuffre has alleged that she was forced to have sex with Brunel several times over a three-year period, as well as being forced to partake in lesbian orgies for Brunel's sexual pleasure with dozens of other girls, mostly foreign models from MC2, many of whom looked underage.

Despite the multiple allegations of sexual abuse and the links to Epstein's sex-trafficking operation, Brunel's influence, it seems, still lives on within the fashion industry. Although MC2 New York has closed and the Miami office is reportedly about to shut down, Brunel seems to have been involved in the setting up of at least three new modelling agencies – The Identity Models in New York, The Source Models in Miami and One Mother Agency in Kiev, Ukraine.

The Identity was supposedly founded in New York in 2017 by Mathias Pardo, a French-born talent scout who is listed as "vice president" of the company. The identities of the president or any other executives of the Delaware-incorporated firm aren't publicly known. Pardo, who worked for Brunel as a talent scout at MC2, claims that Brunel had nothing to do with the founding of the new agency. However, according to a report by *The Daily Beast*, one Identity model allegedly joined Pardo at New York's Mercer Kitchen for a meet-and-greet that included only one other person – Jean-Luc Brunel.

According to the model's mother, Lea Assenmacher, the young woman showed both men her portfolio during the rendezvous at the chic Soho restaurant. The model told her mother that Brunel was "very polite" and "drank a lot of champagne" as they made small-talk about the fashion world. During their conversation, Assenmacher claimed, Brunel and Pardo indicated that MC2 would cease operations and The Identity would take its place. The girl signed a contract with The Identity soon after. "She felt Jean-Luc Brunel was the final arbiter" of whether she was signed, Assenmacher told *The Daily Beast*. "Mathias was deferential to him."

Further evidence comes from the fact that initially The Identity operated out of MC2's offices on West 14th Street. "The only ones working for The Identity were Mathias and Jean-Luc Brunel," a former MC2 employee told *The Daily Beast*. The Identity also shares the same attorney as MC2 – Ian Illych Martinez of Florida – and houses its models at the same East Village apartment once used by MC2. Martinez also represents The Source Models and One Mother Agency, both of which have been linked to Brunel. And The Identity and MC2 share models together as well as one common talent agent, a former MC2 employee called Vinicius Freire.

The Source Models in Miami is run by Petra Pedraza and Jeff Fuller, who deny any links between Brunel and the company. However, the MC2 office in Miami is currently in the process of transferring its assets to The Source, according to *The Daily Beast*. Fuller was Brunel's long-time business partner at MC2 and the contact email listed on The Source's Instagram page is an mc2models.com address. Also, Fuller's wife, Hilary Altman, is the registered agent for the Ukrainian One Mother Agency in Florida which has links to Brunel.

A representative of The Source told *The Daily Beast* that Brunel's connection with One Mother was limited to an initial loan to help set up the company, which has now been paid off. However, two One Mother models told *The Daily Beast* that they thought Brunel was the owner and they saw him regularly in the Kiev office. And Ukrainian model scout Vladimir Yudashkin told *The Daily Beast* that he co-founded One Mother with Brunel and that the agency was Brunel's idea. Yudashkin claimed Brunel set up One Mother to funnel Ukrainian models to MC2 in New York by making them think it was the best fit for their careers, without telling them that the two agencies were financially linked. Yudashkin told *The Daily Beast* he quit working for Brunel in 2017 when he could no longer face lying to the models.

So, Brunel's influence clearly lives on, as probably does Epstein's. The French authorities launched their own investigation into Epstein in 2019 but it seems to have made little progress. One problem, according to Ponton, with both the Epstein investigation, and the lack of victims coming forward to testify against Brunel, is the culture of silence within the French fashion industry. Ponton refers to this as "omertà", the Italian mafia's code of silence which prevents people speaking to the authorities. However, more sinister methods may also have been in play. On October 3, 2019, three police officers and an administrative worker were stabbed to death at the Paris headquarters of the DRPP [Direction du Renseignement de la Préfecture de Police (Intelligence Directorate of the Prefecture of Police)]. Just one month after the same department had issued a call for Epstein victims to come forward.

The attack was carried out by Mikaël Harpon, a forty-five-year-old IT specialist at the DRPP. Harpon, who was deaf, was shot dead at the scene by another officer. The police and press quickly painted the massacre as an act of terrorism – Harpon had converted to Islam ten years previously and had supposedly started exhibiting radical tendencies. However, Ponton questions how a middle-aged man with physical disabilities could have overpowered three fully fit and trained police officers with just a ceramic knife. Could it instead have been the case that Harpon had come across some extremely sensitive material linking Epstein with powerful paedophile rings in France? Might Harpon have shared this material with his colleagues, necessitating that they all be taken out in an incident made to look like a classic lone-gun terrorist attack?

There are some interesting connections between Epstein and high-profile figures in France who have dubious reputations with regards to children. One of these is former Culture and Education Minister Jack Lang. Lang's name has cropped up many times in connection with paedophiles, although he has never been formally charged. In 1977, he signed a letter in French newspaper *Le Monde*, written in defence of three men imprisoned for sexually abusing twelve- and thirteen-year-old girls. The letter was written by a French writer called Gabriel Matzneff, who was famous for writing about his penchant for paedophilia. Then, in 1982, Lang's name was raised in relation to the infamous "Coral Affair" in which children at an education centre near Nimes – many of them with autism and other disabilities – were subjected to a horrific culture of abuse and paedophilia. Lang was also a long-time supporter and friend of suspected paedophile Woody Allen, and convicted paedophile Roman Polanski. And in 2011, Lang's name was mentioned by former French domestic intelligence chief, Yves Bertrand, in connection with a paedophile orgy in Morocco.

Lang first met Epstein at a dinner in celebration of Woody Allen and was a guest at Epstein's Avenue Foch apartment. In March 2019, shortly before Epstein's arrest, Lang invited him to the thirtieth anniversary of the Louvre's glass pyramid. But there were more than social ties between the two men. In 2018,

Lang co-founded an organisation called "L'Association Pour La Promotion De La Politique Culturelle Nationale Menée Dans Les Années 80 Et 90 Du Xxème Siècle", which translates as "Association for the Promotion of National Cultural Policy Conducted in the Eighties and Nineties of the Twentieth Century". This non-profit's vague-sounding goals were "to promote the major leaders and achievements of these decades' cultural policy". The organisation has no website or social media presence, and The French Observatory of Cultural Policies, a national body closely involved in cultural life across France, said it had never heard of the non-profit. Despite its vague title and goals, and its shadowy existence, Lang's organisation received a $57,897 donation from Gratitude America Ltd, an equally nebulous organisation set up by Jeffrey Epstein, with a $10 million donation by American investor Leon Black – another name that pops up frequently in regard to Epstein. The other donations Epstein's non-profit made before his arrest were to a sex clinic in Rome and a Lithuanian ballet company.

If the connection between Epstein and Lang's organisations seems shady, so too do the links to the French government. Not only is the co-founder, Lang, the former Culture Minister, but the group's treasurer, Jacques Renard, was deputy director and chief of staff under Lang's culture ministry, and its president, Christophe Degruelle, worked as Lang's chief of staff in the education ministry from 2000 to 2002. It seems valid to speculate about the real motives of Lang's non-profit and about Epstein's interest in it – did it involve the abuse of minors and the protection and funding of high-level paedophile rings in France?

France, according to Ponton, is rapidly becoming an international haven for paedophilia and child trafficking. Child porn is a big business in the country, with videos sold for up to a million Euros on the dark web. There were 51,287 reports of disappearances of minors in 2019 alone. And investigating high-level paedophilia in France is a dangerous game, according to Ponton, with the disappearance or death of many researchers who shot too close to the mark. Perhaps this is why, according to Ponton's research, Epstein was planning on retiring to France not long before he was arrested.

Perhaps it is also the reason that his paedophile partner in crime, Jean-Luc Brunel, evaded justice for so long in the country of his birth.

CHAPTER 16
EPSTEIN: THE PATRON OF SCIENCE AND TECHNOLOGY

In 2018, Epstein told *The New York Times* journalist, James B. Stewart, that he had dirt on prominent figures in Silicon Valley. Rather than the geeky images these tech leaders like to present, Epstein told Stewart, they were actually hedonists who enjoyed drugs and sex. What's more, Epstein had himself seen these people taking drugs and ordering for sex.

Given what we know about Epstein's sexual blackmail operation and his courting of prominent scientists and tech leaders, his admission to Stewart would seem to indicate that the sexual blackmail operation had shifted towards ensnaring these kinds of people after 2010. But why? And what did he hope to achieve from it?

It's certainly true that Epstein made a concerted effort to surround himself with elite scientific minds in the 2010s. Names that have been connected with him include Gregory Benford, George Church, Murray Gell-Mann, Stephen Jay Gould, David Gross, Stephen Hawking, Danny Hillis, Gerard 't Hooft, Stephen Kosslyn, Jaron Lanier, Seth Lloyd, Marvin Minsky, Martin Nowak, Oliver Sacks, Lee Smolin, Robert Trivers, Frank Wilczek, Roger Penrose, James Watson, Noam Chomsky, Lawrence Krauss and Steven Pinker.

Of this list of illustrious names, we know at least one has been directly accused of having sex with an Epstein victim. Virginia Giuffre stated in a legal deposition that she was forced to have sex with Marvin Minsky on Little St James. Another prominent scientist who Giuffre had sex with was the mysterious Harvard professor 'Stephen', who she writes about in her memoir.

Epstein courted the stellar names of the science world through science conferences, special dinners hosted at his various residences, trips to Little St James and, most of all, funding or the promise of funding. He met them through attending and hosting science conferences and via John Brockman, a literary agent whose authors included Richard Dawkins, Daniel Goleman and Jared Diamond. Brockman acted as Epstein's PR man according to journalist Evgeny Morozov, telling him: "He's been extremely generous in funding projects of many of our friends and clients."

At his dinner events, Epstein would hold court over an array of scientific talent. He would ask provocatively simple questions such as "What is gravity?" then sit back and watch the various minds at work. However, when the topic stretched beyond his interest or understanding, he would often blurt out: "What's that got to do with pussy?"

Nevertheless, many of the scientists who knew him described Epstein as having a brilliant mind and an interestingly fresh perspective. How much of this admiration was induced by the promise of funding it's hard to tell, but others saw through the masquerade. Jason Lanier, one of the founders of virtual reality, said that Epstein's ideas, while interesting, didn't amount to proper science, like when he told the scientist that atoms behaved like investors in a marketplace. But if anyone disagreed with Epstein openly or highlighted his lack of understanding, he would become peevish. Cognitive psychologist Steven Pinker wrote about a meeting at Harvard where Epstein criticised efforts to reduce poverty and ill health because it led to overpopulation. When Pinker pointed out that better standards of living actually led to reduced birth rates, Epstein looked annoyed. Pinker was later told by a colleague that he was no longer welcome to Epstein's gatherings and had been "voted off the island".

But why was Epstein spending so much time, effort and money courting these academic figures? One reason, perhaps, was his sexual blackmail operation, but it seems likely that there was more to it than that. Ego was certainly one factor. That Epstein thought of himself as a kind of maverick genius is clear, and by surrounding himself with geniuses he could keep up that particular delusion without ever really having to put it to the test. Yet ego alone can't explain all the millions of dollars Epstein spent. It seems rather that he was aiming to fund individuals and research that promoted his own, often controversial ideas.

These included, according to *The New York Times*, funding research on a particle that could trigger the feeling that someone was watching you. Then there was his ambition, cited by several guests at his dinner parties, to seed the human race with his genes by impregnating up to twenty women at a time at his New Mexico ranch, a plan that linked with his interest in eugenics, population control and transhumanism. Epstein told several scientists that he was interested in "perfecting the human genome" and improving humanity through genetics. It was to this end that his Southern Trust Company was set up to analyse the DNA of residents of St Thomas in the US Virgin Islands and sell the information to drug companies, netting $200 million in revenue and extensive tax breaks in the process. A charity set up by Epstein also donated £20,000 to the World Transhumanist Association to help research merging humanity with AI.

Given his sometimes crackpot, often worrying ideas, not to mention his 2010 conviction for sexual offences involving minors, why did so many top-level scientists continue to associate with Epstein? The answer is money. As Stuart Pivar, one of Epstein's long-term friends and a founder of the New York Academy of Art, said in an interview with *Mother Jones* magazine: "Jeffrey had lots and lots and lots of dough. Scientists are always looking for lots and lots of dough, because most scientists spend most of their time writing grant proposals to raise money. Jeffrey didn't require a grant proposal. Jeffrey would promise money and so they crowded around."

The scientists who accepted Epstein's cash included the likes of Nobel Prize-winning physicist Murray Gell-Mann, who discovered the quark; Harvard mathematical biologist Martin

Nowak; and MIT quantum physicist Seth Lloyd. Interestingly, one of the few scientists to refuse Epstein's money was a woman. Ivette Fuentes from the University of Nottingham was working on a novel method for detecting gravitational waves when she was asked by physicist Roger Penrose if she would be happy to accept funding from a convicted sex offender. Fuentes immediately said no. When she read the news that Epstein had been arrested in 2019, she called Penrose and asked if the mysterious patron was him. Penrose told her he believed it was.

Reflecting on her decision, Fuentes told *Science Magazine*: "The dream of my life is to build a gravitational-wave detector, and have it work. So, if someone were to say to me, 'I'll give you the money to make your dream come true,' it would be very tempting to say yes. But then you have your ethical standards. Even if you lose some opportunities, [saying no] is the right thing to do ... What Epstein has taught me is how important it is to do that."

However, such ethical concerns don't seem to have troubled the majority of male scientists who accepted Epstein's funding. This was never better illustrated than with the academic institution Epstein patronised the most – the Massachusetts Institute of Technology (MIT).

MIT and specifically the MIT Media Lab, headed by Joi Ito, took millions of dollars in funding either directly from Epstein or funnelled through him after his Florida conviction. Even though Epstein was marked as "disqualified" in the university's official donor database, it continued to accept funding from him, consulted him about the use of the funds, and marked his donations as anonymous, according to *The New Yorker*, which obtained dozens of pages of emails regarding Epstein's links to the university. In fact, according to *The New Yorker*, the undercover nature of Epstein's link with the Media Lab was so widely known that the Lab's head, Ito, referred to Epstein as "Voldemort" or "he who must not be named".

It turns out that Epstein had donated $1.2 million to the Media Lab in undeclared funding, as well as acting as an intermediary to secure funding from other rich donors. This included $2 million from Bill Gates and $5.5 million from Leon Black, two names which crop up around Epstein with suspicious regularity. Ito also visited Epstein several times at his residences, including two flights to Little St James, and even invited Epstein to visit the Media Lab to inspect the results of his funding and meet with faculty members. The visit was criticised by an (again) female staffer, Signe Swenson, a development associate and alumni coordinator at the lab, who told Peter Cohen, the director of development and strategy, that she felt uncomfortable with Epstein's presence on campus. Swenson told *The New Yorker*: "At that point it hit me: this pedophile is going to be in our office." The paper reported that Cohen agreed and thought that Epstein was "unsavory" but said, "We're planning to do it anyway – this was Joi's project."

Epstein's name was kept off all documentation about the visit and certain staff members were instructed to keep away from the glass-walled office where the meeting was to take place. This was probably a good idea, as Epstein had the gall to turn up with two young female "assistants" who he insisted came in with him. The appearance of the women brought home to Swenson the reality of the monster they were dealing with. She told *The New Yorker*: "They were models. Eastern European, definitely. All of us women made it a point to be super nice to them. We literally had a conversation about how, on the off chance that they were not there by choice, we could maybe help them." Swenson resigned eventually because of the Lab's relationship with Epstein. Ito likewise resigned but only after the press revelations made it almost impossible not to.

Alongside the courting of prominent scientists, there was another strand to Epstein's operation – getting in bed with the glitterati of Silicon Valley. There are few top names in the tech world that haven't been connected with Epstein at some time or another. They include Elon Musk, founder of Tesla; Mark Zuckerberg, founder of Facebook; Jeff Bezos, founder of Amazon;

Sergey Brin and Larry Page, founders of Google; Reid Hoffman, founder of LinkedIn; former YouTube CEO, Salar Kamangar; and of course Bill Gates.

Elon Musk is the pioneer of electric vehicles, reusable space rockets and interestingly – regarding his connection to Epstein – the transhumanist project of linking human brains with AI. His ties to Epstein are numerous. He reportedly introduced Epstein to Mark Zuckerberg at a dinner hosted by Reid Hoffman. Musk was also photographed with Ghislaine Maxwell at the 2014 *Vanity Fair* Oscars party. Musk claims Maxwell photobombed the shot but that seems hard to credit when Musk and Maxwell clearly have half of the photo each to themselves.

Even closer connections between Epstein and Musk appear to float beneath the surface. *The New York Times* journalist James B. Stewart described hearing rumours that Epstein was advising Musk on how to deal with the crisis caused by his tweet announcing he had secured the funding to take Tesla private. Stewart heard that Musk had authorised Epstein to search for a new chairman to replace him after he was asked to step down from the position. When Stewart visited Epstein's Manhattan mansion to chat to the tycoon, Epstein confirmed that he was working with Tesla. Epstein claimed he was trying to secure funding for the electric car company from Saudi Arabia and said that Tesla and Musk would deny all knowledge of dealing with him as his name was too toxic. True to Epstein's word, Tesla did deny all the claims; however, a later Bloomberg report confirmed that Tesla was indeed in discussion with Saudi Arabia's Public Investment Fund, so some of Epstein's claims were verified.

If there is a cover-up going on over Epstein's relationship with Musk, it doesn't compare in scope or size with the one hiding his links to Microsoft founder Bill Gates. Gates has repeatedly tried to play down his connections with Epstein; however, there is plenty of evidence to show that the two met many more times and were far more intimate than Gates wants us to believe. And that's just the official records. There is further evidence to show that the relationship went way beyond even that, as we shall see.

According to the official story, Epstein and Gates first met on the evening of January 31, 2011. Given the time period, it's hard to imagine that Gates wasn't aware of Epstein's recent conviction and prison sentence. Another warning sign was the presence of Eva and Glenn Dubin. Eva was the former Miss Sweden who had been Epstein's girlfriend in the Eighties, and her husband, Glenn, was the man Virginia Giuffre said she was forced to have sex with after massaging the pregnant Eva. According to Gates's assistant, Bridgitt Arnold, the meeting started at 8 p.m. and lasted several hours. Following the meeting, Gates praised Epstein's intelligence and emailed colleagues saying, "A very attractive Swedish woman and her daughter dropped by and I ended up staying there quite late," a sentence that sounds very suggestive. Whether what it suggests really happened or it was Gates just trying to titillate his colleagues is a moot point.

This was the first of several contacts between Epstein and Gates that year. Soon after, attendees at a TED conference in Long Beach, California spotted Gates and Epstein "engaged in private conversation" according to *The New York Times*. And on May 3, Gates visited Epstein's New York mansion, where he posed next to Epstein for a photo in the entrance hall. It was around this time that Epstein proposed working with Gates on a "vast charitable fund" for health projects around the world. Epstein envisaged a fund seeded by Gates Foundation money supplemented by donations from Epstein's wealthiest friends. Epstein thought he could gain personal profit from the fund, raking off 0.3% of any money he raised.

This didn't seem to put off Gates at first, who sent a team of delegates to Epstein's New York mansion in late 2011 to discuss the proposal. According to *The New York Times*, Epstein told the attendees: "If they searched his name on the Internet, they might conclude he was a bad person but that what he had done – soliciting prostitution from an underage girl – was no worse than 'stealing a bagel'." According to *The Times*, some of the delegates were left feeling very uncomfortable about dealing with a sex offender. However, it obviously didn't put off Gates, who sent another team to New York in early 2012. On this occasion, Epstein told the team he had access to trillions of dollars of his clients' money, "a figure so preposterous that it left his visitors doubting Mr Epstein's credibility," according to *The Times*.

Gates and Epstein continued to meet throughout 2012. Then in 2013, Gates flew on the *Lolita Express* from New York to Palm Beach. Six months later, Gates was having dinner in New York with Epstein again, discussing the Gates Foundation and philanthropic work, according to Arnold. In October 2014, Gates donated the $2 million to MIT Media Lab which, as we have already seen, was funnelled through Epstein. Soon afterwards, the relationship began to fizzle out and the charitable trust venture never got off the ground. Epstein told a colleague that Gates had stopped talking to him, according to *The Times*, and Arnold told the paper: "Over time, Gates and his team realized Epstein's capabilities and ideas were not legitimate and all contact with Epstein was discontinued."

Whatever happened to the relationship, it had clearly been far more intimate than portrayed by Gates in the three years that it had lasted. We know from Epstein's Paris butler, Gabriel, for example, that Gates – with his wife Melinda – visited Epstein's Avenue Foch apartment in the French capital. And the close relationship didn't just involve Gates, but two of his most trusted advisors as well.

Melanie Walker joined the Gates Foundation in 2006 as its Senior Program Officer after meeting Steven Sinofsky, a senior executive at Microsoft. But before this move, she had had a suspiciously close relationship with Epstein. The two had originally met after Walker graduated from the University of Texas. According to *The New York Times*, Epstein had offered to land Walker an audition at his boss Leslie Wexner's modelling company, Victoria's Secret. If this sounds worryingly familiar, wait for what happened next. Walker moved to New York and stayed in an apartment owned by Epstein, then when she graduated from medical school in 1998, Epstein employed her as his science advisor. Although Walker has never mentioned any sexual improprieties, it's hard to imagine, given the testimonies of Virginia Giuffre, Maria Farmer and so many other women who had similar stories, that something untoward didn't go on.

In any case, Walker remained friendly with Epstein and introduced him to another Gates associate. Boris Nikolic was the Gates Foundation's science advisor and a known close friend of Gates himself, having frequently travelled and socialised together, according to *The New York Times*. Nikolic and Epstein became close friends after their introduction and Nikolic was present at many of the meetings with or organised by Gates. He can be seen in the photo taken at Epstein's New York mansion, standing alongside Gates and Epstein. Epstein and Nikolic became such good friends that Epstein named Nikolic a fallback executor in his will, should either of the two main executors, Daren Indyke or Richard Kahn, be unable to serve. Nikolic declined and has of course publicly regretted his association with the paedophile; however, the strength of their relationship is there for all to see in Nikolic's nomination as an executor of Epstein's estate.

As we can see, the bonds between Gates and Epstein are numerous, but even these don't do justice to the potential extent of the two men's relationship. There is evidence to show that Epstein and Gates not only knew each other but were actively collaborating on projects at least a decade before the supposed "first meeting" in 2011.

The 2001 *Evening Standard* article that we've already looked at in relation to Epstein and Prince Andrew contains a very interesting sentence with regards Gates. It reads: "He [Epstein] has made many millions out of his business links with the likes of Bill Gates, Donald Trump and Ohio billionaire Leslie Wexner, whose trust he runs."

As this was written in 2001, we can only assume that these many millions were made with Gates in the Nineties or perhaps even earlier. We have already seen that Ghislaine Maxwell's sister, Isabel, worked closely with Gates and Microsoft co-founder, Paul Allen, in the Nineties through her Internet companies like Magellan. Ghislaine was likely also involved in this company, so it is quite possible that Epstein came into close contact with Gates via the Maxwell sisters. Backing this up, we also have the testimony of Maria Farmer, who said she heard Epstein and Maxwell talking about Gates in 1995 as if they knew him well.

If the relationship did go back that far, what did it involve and how did Epstein make the millions that were supposedly linked to Gates? Given the Maxwell sisters' connections with Israeli intelligence, as well as Epstein's own, is it too far-fetched to speculate that Gates had some involvement as well? As we shall see, links between Silicon Valley and Israeli intelligence are not far-fetched at all, but the stuff of very worrying reality.

Israel's prime minister, Benjamin Netanyahu, has driven a clear policy of funnelling ex-intelligence and military agents into tech start-ups, using their state-trained expertise to enhance private industry. These tech start-ups then export abroad, many of them to the US, where their state funding gives them a head start on rival fledgling companies. One of Israel's tech specialities is surveillance, learned from its heavy control over the Palestinian territories and the Gaza Strip. It then exports these surveillance methods to other countries, often ones with poor records on human rights. One such example is the Israeli-created Pegasus spyware which it sold to Saudi Arabia. The Saudi government used the surveillance software to track the movements of dissidents abroad and it was believed to have been instrumental in the murder of Saudi renegade journalist Jamal Khashoggi.

But Israeli technology isn't only used by authoritarian regimes; Western countries and specifically the US are being flooded with tech start-ups staffed with ex-Israeli intelligence officers. It may come as no surprise that Epstein was involved in at least one of these projects.

Carbyne 911 is a mobile app which allows 911 call centres to track and monitor emergencies. If a Carbyne user calls 911, the responder can get access to the phone's GPS and camera, and is provided with a live video feed from the phone. The system also cross-references the caller's identity with criminal databases and can access any data on the user's phone. According to the Carbyne website, the same information can be obtained from any phone as long as it calls a 911 call centre equipped with Carbyne or even another phone that is connected to the Carbyne network. Several counties in the US have already installed the software and more could be coming online in the future.

The implications of this technology for privacy alone are concerning, but when the list of people behind Carbyne 911 is revealed, the possibilities become truly alarming. Epstein invested $1.5 million in the company through his friend, Ehud Barak, former Israeli prime minister and head of its military intelligence services. Barak is a major investor in Carbyne 911 and also acts as a frontman for the company, appearing on the likes of Fox News to endorse the product. Let's not forget that he was also the man who originally recruited Robert Maxwell to Israeli intelligence and that he had a long-standing relationship with Epstein, visiting him on many occasions and turning up several times at Mark Epstein's 66th Street apartments where the young MC2 models were housed.

But the links to Israeli intelligence don't end there. Carbyne's CEO, Amir Elichai, is an ex-Israeli intelligence officer. Co-founder, Lital Leshem, is an ex-operative of Black Cube, a private Israeli intelligence service. CIO, Alex Dizengof, worked in cyber-security for Israel's prime minister's office. And company director, Pinchas Berkus, is an ex-brigadier in the elite 8200 unit which specialises in surveillance and signals intelligence. It is interesting to note that not one of the company's high-ranking staff, directors or investors has any experience in emergency response, whereas almost all of them have ties to Israeli and US intelligence.

Given all this – not to mention Israel's history of putting

trapdoors into software such as Promis – you would be forgiven for suspecting that Carbyne 911 isn't just about improving emergency response. Indeed, similar software, which was supposedly designed to report emergencies, is now being used in China to conduct mass surveillance on its population of Turkic Muslims. The phone app is used to track their movements and facilitate the arrest of possible insurgents on the mere suspicion that they might commit a future crime.

This is the technology Epstein was funding and it fits in perfectly with his role as an Israeli intelligence operative. It also casts a revealing light over Epstein's other endeavours in science and technology, and allows us to build a picture of his ultimate goals. These, I believe, were threefold: one, to ensnare prominent scientists and tech figures in sexual blackmail scandals where possible (although this side of the operation was winding down somewhat after the Florida arrest); two, to fund Israeli infiltration into the US tech market, introducing technology that could be used for surveillance purposes and incorporating software fitted with trapdoors into existing US tech; and three, through schmoozing with pioneering scientific and tech elites, to glean inside information on the latest US science and technology breakthroughs which might aid Israel.

What is perhaps more worrying is that, even after Epstein's death, the Israeli technological infiltration of the US continues and is even growing in pace. Epstein and Robert Maxwell would, I'm sure, be smiling if they could see the fruits of their labours.

CHAPTER 17
DEEP STATE PLAYERS:
EPSTEIN'S LESSER-KNOWN
ASSOCIATES

As the flight logs of his planes and the numbers in the little black book attest, Epstein's circle of influence was vast and included some of the most prominent figures in politics, science, technology, finance and popular culture.

Some of his relationships have been documented in this book and have been widely reported in the press. But so much is yet unknown, and to document all of Epstein's many links would take several volumes. This chapter aims to take a closer look at a handful of his acquaintances who have so far remained unexplored in this book and have largely escaped the kind of media scrutiny reserved for the likes of Prince Andrew, Donald Trump, Bill Clinton and others.

Indyke and Kahn

No one, it seems, is more mired in the business dealings of Jeffrey Epstein than the two co-executors of his will: Darren Indyke, his long-term attorney; and Richard Kahn, his accountant.

Indyke, now in his fifties, worked for Epstein from 1995, according to public records dug up in an investigation by Yahoo Finance. Epstein, it appears, was Indyke's biggest client during those twenty-five years; indeed, the Yahoo report could find no clients of Indyke's who *weren't* Epstein or associates of Epstein. And, as well as having his name appear on numerous charitable filings, real-estate records and trademark filings, Indyke was also listed as the treasurer and vice president of three of Epstein's charities – the C.O.U.Q. Foundation, Gratitude America Ltd, and the J. Epstein Virgin Islands Foundation.

It is interesting to note that 1995 was the beginning of Indyke and Epstein's official working relationship, because this was the same year that Epstein's financial partner, Steven Hoffenberg, pleaded guilty to fraud for the Towers Financial Ponzi scheme which Epstein was deeply involved in. Indeed, Indyke and his fellow co-executor Richard Kahn were key players in helping Epstein evade justice over the Towers Financial affair, according to Hoffenberg.

Hoffenberg told the authors of the book, *Epstein: Dead Men Tell No Tales*, that the trustee brought in to oversee Towers Financial's bankruptcy, Alan Cohen, appointed Indyke and Kahn to investigate Epstein's activities at the stricken company. Unsurprisingly, given the relationship between Epstein and Indyke and Kahn, Epstein was cleared of all wrongdoing and walked away from the second-largest Ponzi scheme in US history scot-free. Not only that, according to Hoffenberg, but Epstein even got to keep the profits he had made, using them to fund three of his fledgling companies, while Hoffenberg was sentenced to twenty years in prison.

This, it seems, was the beginning of a beautiful relationship between Indyke, Khan and Epstein. The association continued through the Noughties, and during Epstein's Florida jail sentence Indyke visited him no fewer than thirty-eight times, including his very first day of "imprisonment".

Part of Epstein's plea deal was an incredibly lenient work-release agreement which allowed him to be outside of jail at a place of work for up to twelve hours a day. It was Indyke's name that was on this agreement. According to the filings, Indyke was acting as Epstein's employer at the Florida Science Foundation, a non-profit organisation that Indyke had set up solely for this purpose – it was created the day after Epstein signed the non-prosecution agreement that included the work-release scheme. Epstein used the Florida Science Foundation to make payments totalling $128,000 to the Palm Beach Sheriff's Office between 2008 and 2009.

And these weren't the only questionable payments Indyke was in charge of. In his role as treasurer to Epstein's New York State-based C.O.U.Q. Foundation, Indyke oversaw donations to multiple educational and research organisations that included the Clinton Foundation and Friends of the Israel Defense Forces, according to the Yahoo investigation. Indyke was also the treasurer for Epstein's non-profit Gratitude America Ltd, which received a $10 million donation from billionaire investor Leon Black, a man who, over the years, donated more than $150 million to Epstein's various organisations.

Then there was Indyke's work for Epstein's inner circle. Indyke's name appears as a trustee for Ghislaine Maxwell's non-profit, the Max Foundation. And, according to the Yahoo report, Indyke helped Maxwell buy her New York townhouse at 116 East 65th Street in 2000. Indyke was also listed as secretary for the Wexner Foundation in a 1998 SEC report, and Wexner's wife, Abigail, gave Indyke power of attorney over her 15 Central Park West property.

Indyke seems to have had direct ties to the seedier side of Epstein's operations as well. Lesley Groff, one of Epstein's long-term personal assistants and procurer of underage girls, described herself as an "executive assistant" at DKI PLLC on her LinkedIn profile, according to Yahoo. DKI PLLC is listed in public records as the name of Indyke's law practice, with an office address that doesn't exist.

Indyke's real office seems to have been 301 East 66th Street for nearly a decade at least, an address which might sound familiar as it's the building owned by Epstein's brother, Mark, which was used to house dozens of Epstein's young victims and was much visited by Ehud Barak.

As for Kahn, not only did he work with Indyke on the Towers Financial investigation, and is co-executor of Epstein's will, he was also seen sneaking into Epstein's Manhattan townhouse on the day after the paedophile's death. According to the *Daily Mail*, who photographed Kahn entering and leaving the property, he was inside for around forty-five minutes and left carrying a blue shopping bag filled with items. Could this have been incriminating information on Epstein's rich and famous blackmail victims? We can only speculate, as Indyke and Kahn, as executors of Epstein's estate, have so far refused to hand them over.

So, what have Indyke and Kahn been up to since Epstein's death? As co-executors of his estate, they each stand to receive $250,000 from his will. Apart from that, they have mostly been spending their time hampering investigations into Epstein's crimes and refusing to release important information. Sigrid McCawley, an attorney representing three of Epstein's victims, told the press that Indyke and Kahn had not released a single document that she had requested, and called the pair's behaviour "obstructionist conduct".

Indyke and Kahn are estimated to be sitting on no fewer than 730,000 documents pertaining to Epstein's activity. The attorney general of the US Virgin Islands, Denise George, has brought a civil lawsuit against the Epstein estate for racketeering, which named Indyke and Kahn as co-conspirators. George called the Epstein estate an "ongoing criminal enterprise", which doesn't sound far wrong.

Mark Epstein

Mark Epstein, Jeffrey's younger brother by two years, is the sole beneficiary of his estate. He was also one of the first and loudest to cry foul play when Epstein died. Mark was insistent that Epstein had not committed suicide and even hired a second expert to observe the autopsy.

Given his close ties to his brother and his challenging of the official narrative around Epstein's death, you might think Mark was up to his eyeballs in the same nefarious games as Epstein.

However (perhaps unsurprisingly), Mark Epstein denies having any business ties to his brother. Perhaps more surprisingly, however, Mark seems to have escaped the media glare that has focused on other Epstein associates, and there has been no indication of him being investigated officially for his links to Epstein.

This is surprising because, as we shall see, there is plenty of evidence revealing extensive business connections between the two brothers, as well as links to the seedier side of Epstein's operation.

Mark grew up alongside his elder brother in Brooklyn and attended the Cooper Union School of Art in Manhattan and Stony Brook University. According to *The Daily Beast*, neighbours described the young Mark, nicknamed "Puggie", as a talented artist with a good business brain. This led him to set up an early artistic business venture silk-screening T-shirts that was described as "one of the most versatile silk-screening printing companies in New York," according to *Business Insider*.

In the Eighties, Mark headed a charter and leasing company called Atelier Enterprises before moving into real-estate investment in the Nineties. More worryingly, given his connections to his brother, he opened a modelling agency in 2005 called Saint Model and Talent. But, according to *Business Insider*, the company has no website or social media presence and has never signed a model.

Despite his chequered list of accomplishments, Mark somehow earned enough money to semi-retire at the age of thirty-nine whilst donating hundreds of thousands of dollars to charities. Perhaps that had something to do with a trait he shared with his brother – a readiness to bend the rules when it came to financial dealings. In 2002, he was named chairman of the board of trustees at his alma mater, Cooper Union, but in 2015 was forced to step down amidst claims of financial mismanagement.

Another similarity to his brother is the ease with which he moved in political circles. Mark is listed on the board of directors for the Humpty Dumpty Institute, an organisation which works with the UN to help young people from developing countries (another alarm bell, given his brother's child trafficking operation). According to *The Daily Beast*, Mark loaned the institute $100,000 in 2014 and led a delegation of Republican and Democratic representatives to an event organised by the institute in Belgium in April 2019.

But it is through his real-estate dealings that Mark's ties to Epstein become most apparent. The brothers' joint venture into property started early, according to the book *Epstein: Dead Men Tell No Tales*, in which a childhood friend of Epstein's told the authors that Jeffrey started buying property in Manhattan early on. Epstein's classmate, Gary Grossberg, told the authors: "He started buying properties in Manhattan, including 301 East 66th St. He asked his brother – did Mark want to join him? He did."

Mark's real-estate company, Ossa Properties, owned as many as 500 rented apartments around New York in the Nineties according to a *New York Times* report, and was run by a man called Anthony Barrett, a former asset manager for brother Jeffrey.

Ossa Properties also owned most of the apartments in the 301 East 66th Street building that was at the centre of Epstein's child trafficking operation. Mark told Crain's New York that he bought the units in the early Nineties from – guess who? – that's right, Leslie Wexner. Two of Epstein's companies were officially registered at the building and he used it to house his employees, including house managers and pilots. Epstein's long-term lawyer, Darren Indyke, also used the building as the primary address for his law firm, DKI PLLC. At one point, Jean-Luc Brunel had an apartment in the building, and Epstein's ex-girlfriend Eva Andersson – who later married Glenn Dubin – also lived there.

But it also saw the seedier side of Epstein's operation. Under-age models from Brunel's MC2 modelling agency were housed there, after having been trafficked from various parts of the world. Former MC2 bookkeeper, Maritza Vasquez, swore under oath that girls were staying in Epstein's rooms in the building with up to four girls per apartment. The building was also home to four of Epstein's chief procurers – Nadia Marcinkova, Sarah Kellen, Adriana Ross and Lesley Groff. Indeed, Marcinkova's aviation marketing company, Aviloop, and Kellen's design company, SLK Designs, were both registered at the 66th Street address until recently.

One of the 66th Street units, previously registered to Marcinkova, is now the business address of Joyce Anderson, a fashion photographer who specialises in children and pre-teens according to her website. Worrying? Perhaps, especially when you discover that Anderson is Mark Epstein's ex-wife and mother to his two children. According to *Business Insider*, Anderson's photography business had previously been based at 30 Vandam Street, another building owned by Mark Epstein, where the mysterious Saint Model and Talent agency was based.

As we have already seen, ex-Israeli prime minister and Epstein associate, Ehud Barak, was often seen visiting the building, usually with a security detail waiting outside which sometimes included New York police officers. One witness described seeing Barak pay a visit to the building as late as 2019. One can only guess as to the former spy head's purposes but the large number of young girls that were housed there might provide a clue.

Mark Epstein has denied knowing what went on in the 66th Street building but, given the multiple links illustrated above, it stretches credibility to breaking point that he wouldn't have some idea of what was happening at a property he largely owned. It's also baffling why he hasn't been the subject of a serious investigation given his multiple connections to his brother's operation.

Nicole Junkermann

Nicole Junkermann is not a name you will often see associated with Jeffrey Epstein. The German-born investor and entrepreneur is often touted as one of the most prominent women in tech finance.

A former model who speaks five languages, the statuesque blonde Junkermann looks like the perfect role model for women entrepreneurs around the globe. However, behind the glittery façade, there lies some very shady connections which have been largely wiped from the Internet, connections which link her to Epstein and Israeli intelligence, and which cast suspicion over her current role gathering patient data for the NHS.

What we know of the darker side of Junkermann is largely thanks to one researcher and independent investigative journalist, Johnny Vedmore. Vedmore has been researching the shadier side of Junkermann's dealings for several years and has found some intriguing connections to Epstein and the underground circles he moved in.

Junkermann's first entrepreneurial role came in 1998, immediately after graduating in Business Administration from the International University of Monaco when she co-founded Winamax, an early online gaming platform. In 2001, Winamax was sold and Junkermann invested in Infront Sports and Media AG, where she went on to become Vice Chairman of the Board of Directors. Despite being a relatively unknown company, Infront Sports and Media won the TV rights to the 2006 FIFA World Cup in Germany. This was an interesting decision by FIFA as its president, Sepp Blatter, is the uncle of Infront's chairman and CEO, Philippe Blatter.

At around this time, Junkermann also graduated from Harvard's prestigious Program for Management Development. At the same time, Epstein was heavily involved in funding the university and Vedmore speculates as to whether this might be where the two first met. It is quite possible that Epstein was using his Harvard links to scout for talent to recruit to his intelligence operation, and Junkermann would certainly have fitted the bill. Junkermann's stunning good looks would also have drawn the attention of a man who was known for his predilection for leggy blondes. However they met, the two clearly knew each other, because around this time Junkermann flew on the *Lolita Express* three times. On the first occasion, she was joined by two other guests, but on the second and third trips, intriguingly, she and Epstein flew alone.

These flights were part of a three-day trip to England, which

Vedmore has researched in-depth and dug up some fascinating information on. On Saturday, August 31, 2002, Epstein and Junkermann flew from Paris to Birmingham. From there, as Vedmore discovered from an inside source, a private helicopter picked them up and flew them twenty-five miles south to the stunning eighteenth-century manor, Foxcote House in Warwickshire. Foxcote House is of particular interest because it belonged to none other than Leslie Wexner, who bought the property in 1997 for around £3 million.

According to Vedmore's insider, the Wexners weren't in residence on the weekend Epstein and Junkermann visited, but a couple of notable guests were – two serving members of the United States Senate no less. Vedmore's insider didn't provide the names of the two senators but did mention they had trouble with the estate's Internet connection, which necessitated calling in an engineer to fix the problem. The source also said that security for the meeting was mostly provided by off-duty British police. On Sunday, the small group went hunting and that evening Epstein turned up to dinner with two stunning women – a brunette on one arm and a blonde on the other.

The blonde was Junkermann but the brunette's identity is unknown. It could have been Epstein's assistant, Sarah Kellen, who was listed on the return flight from Paris to New York. Or it could have been a young girl called Cindy Lopez, who was logged multiple times on the *Lolita Express* and was also listed on the return flight to New York. Cindy Lopez was a model for Jean-Luc Brunel's Karin Modelling Agency and was photographed arm in arm with Bill Clinton on the *Lolita Express* on a separate occasion.

It is unclear what was discussed over the weekend at Foxcote House but the timing, the location and the presence of two sitting senators provide some important clues. September 2002 was one year after 9/11 and just one month before the Joint Resolution was passed, which paved the way for the invasion of Iraq. As we have already seen, Wexner was pushing for such an invasion in the interests of Israel and had even published a document on how to win the propaganda battle in supporting the war. Given Wexner's involvement in promoting the invasion of Iraq and the fact that the meeting was arranged at a Wexner property, Vedmore makes the reasonable speculation that Epstein was there to lobby the senators on behalf of his master, Wexner.

As to the identity of the senators, Vedmore believes he has narrowed it down to five, based on personal donations given by the Wexners between 2000 and 2004. Of these five, the two closest donations to the Foxcote House meeting were paid to Montana Democrat Max Baucus, and Ohio Republican George Voinovich. Vedmore also notes that Abigail Wexner donated $5,000 to the Ohio Democratic Party on August 31, 2002, the first night of the Foxcote House meeting. Could this have been an expenses payment for the trip?

Vedmore's other guess is that one of the senators was John Kerry. At the time, Senator Kerry was a prime contender to challenge George Bush in the 2004 election. Kerry was a keen huntsman and Epstein had been courting the contender for some time, with several donations between 1991 and 2002. Kerry's name also appears in the little black book and it is reasonable to suggest that Epstein was grooming Kerry to be his next Clinton – an American Democratic president who owed him "favours".

Whatever was decided at the meeting, the group disbanded on Monday, September 2. Epstein and Junkermann flew back to Paris, where they went their separate ways, and Epstein took the *Lolita Express* back to New York, accompanied by Jean-Luc Brunel, Sarah Kellen and Cindy Lopez.

It was the last recorded time that Junkermann flew on Epstein's plane but their links didn't end there. Junkermann went on to found and invest in many other tech start-ups, one of which was Carbyne 911. As we have already seen, Epstein was a major funder of the company, and Carbyne 911's list of directors and investors reads like a who's who of Israeli intelligence operatives. Junkermann became a director of the firm alongside former

Israeli prime minister and head of intelligence, Ehud Barak, who is a long-time Epstein associate and probable fellow paedophile. According to Vedmore, negative content about Junkermann has readily disappeared from the Internet. As part of this purge, her picture has been removed from Carbyne's board of directors, perhaps a wise move, as her links to Israeli intelligence don't particularly square well with her current role gathering data on NHS patients.

In 2018, UK Health Secretary Matt Hancock appointed Junkermann to the NHS's HealthTech Advisory Board, which is tasked with providing technological solutions to improve "patient outcomes and reducing the workload on NHS staff". Apart from her prominent position on the HealthTech Advisory Board, Junkermann is an investor in OWKIN, an AI start-up that uses machine learning to augment medical and biology research. In 2019, OWKIN announced that London hospitals had promised the company patient data in order to "develop better drugs".

Should the NHS be handing over UK citizens' private medical data to a firm with such clear links to a foreign intelligence agency? Probably not, but that's what it seems is about to happen. Epstein must be laughing in his grave.

Mohammed bin Salman

Epstein's relations with foreign heads of state weren't limited to the Israelis, it seems. He was also, according to his own testimony, good friends with Mohammed bin Salman, the crown prince of Saudi Arabia.

As we have seen, when *The New York Times* journalist Edward Jay Epstein interviewed Jeffrey Epstein in his 71st Street mansion, he noticed a photo of Mohammed bin Salman. When questioned about the relationship, Epstein told him he was close friends with the heir to the Saudi throne and often played host to him. Epstein also mentioned that he wanted to buy a house in Riyadh as he thought it would soon become one of the financial centres of the world.

Epstein was fond of playing up his relationships with famous people and he wasn't averse to downright lying, but other evidence points to the relationship being real. As well as the photo, bin Salman, or MBS as he is often known, appeared in the little black book. And when the police raided Epstein's Manhattan home, they found a fake Austrian passport that contained several stamps for Saudi Arabia. The passport also listed Saudi as Epstein's official place of residence.

Even more intriguing, flight data reveals that Epstein's plane flew into Riyadh on November 7, 2016, the eve of the US election which would see Trump come to power. It is not known what Epstein was doing in Riyadh for the forty-eight hours he stayed there, but Mohammed bin Salman was also there at the time. According to *Insider*, the Saudi Press Agency reported that MBS was in Riyadh on November 8 to present a distinguished service award to General Joseph F. Dunford Jr, Chairman of the US Joint Chiefs of Staff. Another important figure who happened to be in Riyadh at that time was Jeff Bezos, the CEO of Amazon. Bezos had a meeting with MBS on November 9 to discuss, according to the Saudi Press Agency, "Fields of cooperation and investment opportunities available according to the Kingdom's Vision 2030."

Could it be that Epstein met with both MBS and Bezos at some point during his forty-eight-hour stay? We already know of his connections to the crown prince and Epstein also knew Bezos, at least in passing. They had met twice before at meetings hosted by the Edge Foundation in 2004 and 2011. There is no official record of the three men meeting in Riyadh, but given the timing and the fact that they all knew each other, it seems likely that some kind of get-together was arranged.

Interestingly, perhaps taking a leaf out of Epstein's book, MBS tried to blackmail Bezos at a later date. The incident concerned the murder of Saudi dissident journalist Jamal Khashoggi, who had written several articles critical of Saudi Arabia and bin Salman for *The Washington Post*, a paper owned by Bezos. On October 2, 2018, Khashoggi was murdered horrifically at the

Saudi Embassy in Istanbul. Despite official denials, it is widely believed that the Saudi regime, and specifically bin Salman, were behind the murder. Following Khashoggi's death, *The Washington Post* ramped up its criticism of the Saudi regime and bin Salman, linking them to the murder.

In April 2018, bin Salman attended a small dinner with Bezos and the two exchanged WhatsApp numbers. On May 1, MBS sent Bezos a video file which, according to a later UN investigation, infected Bezos's phone with malicious code. Then, in January 2019, the *National Enquirer* ran a scoop about Bezos having an extramarital affair. The *National Enquirer's* parent company, American Media Inc., had been investigated before for links to the Saudi regime, and bin Salman and American Media CEO David Pecker also had a close relationship. It seems reasonable, therefore, to assume that the *National Enquirer's* source for the story had been Bezos's hacked phone.

Back in 2016, when the meeting between Epstein, MBS and Bezos might have taken place, Khashoggi was already under suspicion by the Saudi government and indeed later that year he was banned from appearing in Saudi publications and on Saudi TV. This ban was officially for criticising US president-elect Donald Trump, although it was probably more likely connected to Khashoggi's increasing disaffection with the Saudi government. Could the meeting between MBS, Epstein and Bezos have been about Khashoggi, or at least touched on him at some point? It's interesting to note that Jamal Khashoggi was the nephew of Saudi arms dealer Adnan Khashoggi, who, as we have seen, worked closely with Epstein throughout the Eighties.

Could Bezos and Epstein have persuaded bin Salman to let Khashoggi out of the country, thus securing his relocation to the US in June the following year? As with much of Epstein's clandestine dealings, we may never know. One thing seems sure, though – Epstein had ties to the highest levels of the Saudi regime and, given similar connections to Israel and the US, and his involvement with international arms trading and child trafficking, any number of worrying transactions could have taken place between him and bin Salman.

John Brockman

John Brockman is a writer and literary agent for many of the world's top science writers. He created the Edge Foundation to bring together top thinkers in their scientific fields to share knowledge and catalyse new ideas. He is, above everything else, a networker, a super-connector of the world's most interesting minds. We met him briefly in an earlier chapter where he seemed to have played a role in Epstein's post-2010 rehabilitation as a patron of science and technology.

One of Brockman's clients, technology writer Evgeny Morozov, described Brockman at that time as a kind of PR agent for Epstein, connecting him with various scientists to add to Epstein's own, more sordid network. But why was Brockman doing this and how deep did the relationship go?

As far as motives go, we don't have to look much further than the money. Morozov found that Epstein had funded Brockman's Edge Foundation to the tune of $638,000 between 2001 and 2015. Epstein donated at least $50,000 a year in 2009, 2010 and 2011, according to *BuzzFeed News*, at just the time when his reputation most needed laundering. In many years, Epstein was the Edge Foundation's sole donor and it seems that it was his money that paid for the organisation's "Billionaires' Dinners", star-studded events linked to TED Talks where science and tech gurus would schmooze and exchange ideas. Indeed, after Epstein's last donation of $30,000 in 2015, the Billionaires' Dinners promptly stopped.

Epstein himself attended many of the Edge Foundation events, like the 2011 Billionaires' Dinner at Long Beach, California alongside Jeff Bezos, Sergey Brin and Elon Musk. So, too, did one of Epstein's procurers, Sarah Kellen. Kellen was photographed at the 2002 Billionaires' Dinner with Brockman, and at the 2003 event with Brockman's son, Max. Brockman and his wife flew to the 2002 event on the *Lolita Express* with Epstein and his entourage, in addition to several famous scientists, including Richard Dawkins and Steven Pinker.

But Brockman's science connections weren't only established through the Edge Foundation. His literary agency, Brockman Inc., has signed some of the best scientific minds in the world, clients who all too often had links to Epstein as well. Marvin Minsky, who Virginia Giuffre claims she was forced to have sex with, was a client of Brockman. Joi Ito, who as we have seen was accepting large donations from Epstein for the MIT Media Lab, was also a Brockman client. And Steven Pinker and Daniel Dennett, who both have associations with Epstein, are Brockman clients, too.

Brockman and Epstein's association appears to go back to at least 1991. In that year, Brockman wrote a massively influential essay entitled "The Third Culture" for the science magazine *Seed*. Epstein was, according to court documents, a board member of *Seed*'s parent company, Seed Media Group, at the time. But it was after Epstein's release from his Florida sentence that the relationship went into overdrive. Brockman appeared to go out of his way to connect Epstein with scientists and technologists from his circle.

One example comes from Morozov, who was one of Brockman Inc's clients at the time. Morozov related in an article in *The New Republic* in 2019 how Brockman had emailed him in 2013, saying of Epstein: "He'll be in Cambridge in a couple of weeks, asked me who he should meet. You are one of the people I suggested and I told him I would send some links." In the email, Brockman made it clear that he knew about Epstein's crimes, saying: "He also got into trouble and spent a year in jail in Florida." Brockman also mentioned Epstein's predilection for travelling with beautiful young "assistants", saying: "Jeffrey Epstein, the billionaire science philanthropist, showed up at this weekend's event by helicopter (with his beautiful young assistant from Belarus)."

Brockman went on to recount an anecdote about a meeting

with Epstein in his New York mansion. The story is extremely revealing, not only about Brockman and Epstein's relationship, but also about Prince Andrew's final visit to Epstein in New York. Brockman wrote:

"Last time I visited his house (the largest private residence in NYC), I walked in to find him in a sweatsuit and a British guy in a suit with suspenders, getting foot massages from two young well-dressed Russian women. After grilling me for a while about cyber-security, the Brit, named Andy, was commenting on the Swedish authorities and the charges against Julian Assange.

"'We think they're liberal in Sweden, but it's more like Northern England as opposed to Southern Europe,' he said. 'In Monaco, Albert works twelve hours a day but at 9 p.m., when he goes out, he does whatever he wants, and nobody cares. But, if I do it, I'm in big trouble.' At that point, I realized that the recipient of Irina's foot massage was his Royal Highness, Prince Andrew, the Duke of York.

"Indeed, a week later, on a slow news day, the cover of the *NY Post* had a full-page photo of Jeffrey and Andrew walking in Central Park under the headline: 'The Prince and the Perv.' (That was the end of Andrew's role as the UK trade ambassador.)"

Apart from illustrating Brockman and Epstein's close relationship, this casts intriguing light on what Andrew was doing at Epstein's 71st Street mansion. If we remember from earlier, in Andrew's car crash BBC *Newsnight* interview, the prince told interviewer Emily Maitlis that although he did stay at Epstein's New York mansion in 2010, he had hardly seen Epstein except at a brief dinner party and in passing in the corridor. Brockman's email not only contradicts that claim – having a foot massage alongside Epstein is hardly passing in the corridor – but also throws into question Andrew's activities during a trip which was supposed to act as an end to their friendship. If Andrew was receiving foot massages from young Russian girls when guests like Brockman were present, what was he doing with them when they were alone?

Given Brockman's close links to Epstein and his fervent attempts to network on the paedophile's behalf, as well as the photographs showing him alongside Epstein assistants, it is tempting to ask whether Epstein had something over Brockman other than just the funding. Was Brockman one of the many victims of Epstein's sexual blackmail operation?

Brockman has so far refused to comment on his ties to Epstein. No evidence of any sexual misconduct on Brockman's part has yet come to light, but there is still a lot of information to come out, and some that may stay forever hidden. As with many of Epstein's associates, we may never know the truth, but it would certainly explain the fervour with which Brockman was promoting Epstein, a convicted paedophile, within his circle of high-profile scientists.

CHAPTER 18
WHO KILLED EPSTEIN?

Immediately after his arrest on July 6, 2019 at New York's Teterboro Airport, Epstein was taken to the Metropolitan Correctional Center (MCC), where he was incarcerated in a section known as 9-South or "The Hole", an extra-high-security zone for violent criminals or those requiring protection, such as paedophiles and sex offenders. His cellmate was Nicholas Tartaglione, a retired police officer who had killed four men over unpaid drug money. Tartaglione looked like the Hulk and probably could have killed four men with his bare hands. Prosecutors were seeking the death sentence for his crimes at the time Epstein moved in with him, so it's hard to think of anyone more intimidating as a cellmate, which was perhaps an intentional move on the part of the guards.

Initially, other inmates and Tartaglione's lawyers claimed that he and Epstein were "friends". Perhaps Epstein was buying off Tartaglione, like he had so many before with promises of money and legal help. We know Epstein was playing the same trick with other inmates, buying commissary items such as snacks, drinks and special meals at inflated prices, which the other prisoners could use to buy their own items.

One of the inmates who Epstein first got to know was William "Dollar Bill" Mersey, a man who had run an escort website and been imprisoned for tax fraud. According to the book, *The Spider: Inside the Criminal Web of Jeffrey Epstein and Ghislaine Maxwell* by Barry Levine, Epstein and Mersey were put together by another inmate, Michael "Miles" Tisdale, as part of a scheme Tisdale ran to partner new, at-risk inmates with experienced companions to help them learn the ropes. According to Levine, Mersey said Epstein was worried about being attacked, specifically by black inmates, saying he had been bullied by black kids at school. Mersey advised Epstein to "look fellow prisoners in the eye and stand his ground". However, Epstein's worries grew and, according to Levine, he even considered hiring another inmate to work as his bodyguard.

Another problem for Epstein was the guards, who seemed to take a dislike to him, supposedly because of the way he was throwing his money around to buy off other prisoners, and because he was using meetings with his lawyers as an excuse to get out of his cell for prolonged periods of time. According to the book, *Epstein: Dead Men Tell No Tales*, an inmate said that the guards treated Epstein worse than any other prisoner, denying him toilet rolls and essential cleaning items when he requested them. For the fastidious Epstein, it must have been a nightmare.

In the meantime, he had been formally charged with sex trafficking and conspiracy to traffic minors, to which he pled not guilty. He was also waiting to find out if he would be granted bail. His lawyers' case was built around the fact that Epstein had not been charged with any further crimes since his Florida sentence, thus "proving" that Epstein had controlled his unnatural urges. However, on July 17, something happened which blew that argument to smithereens. A case was filed by a woman identified as Kaitlyn Doe, who testified that Epstein had sexually abused her while on work release during his Florida prison sentence. The woman claimed that Epstein had forced her to perform sex acts on him at the office of his specially created non-profit, the Florida Science Foundation, while a deputy stood outside the door, allowing the attack to happen.

Following these revelations, Epstein's case crumbled, and on July 18, his request for bail was denied. Five days later, Epstein supposedly made his first "suicide" attempt.

On July 23 at 1.28 a.m., the guards heard someone calling for help and rushed to the cell Epstein shared with Tartaglione. They found Epstein lying on the floor, his face, feet and hands a light blue colour. According to *Epstein: Dead Men Tell No Tales*, an inmate who witnessed the incident said the guards threw the lifeless form of Epstein face-down onto the floor, then again onto the stretcher as if they thought – or expected – him to be dead. However, he was revived using CPR and taken to the infirmary, where he stayed for the rest of the night.

Like so much of Epstein's life, what truly happened on that night may forever be a mystery. Had he really attempted suicide? He'd certainly had a hard introduction to prison life. He was constantly in fear of being attacked or hit up to buy overpriced commissary items because of his known wealth. He was used to a life of the most rigorous cleanliness and health, not to mention good food and pampering, whilst here he was neglected, openly disliked and forced to live in squalid and unsanitary conditions. By his own admission, he needed three orgasms a day, preferably at the hands of a young girl, and in New York there was no fake work-release scheme where he could continue to get his kicks. Add to all that the recent news that he wasn't getting bail and it might just have broken him.

On the other hand, the marks on his neck were slight and had practically faded by the time he reappeared in court a few days later. The injuries didn't reflect a serious suicide attempt in the guards' opinions, so perhaps he had staged the attempt to get sympathy and a cushier deal? It's certainly the kind of mind game you could imagine him playing, but he did have to be revived, so if it was a stunt, it went dangerously close to the edge.

Another possibility is that Tartaglione had tried to murder him. As we've already seen, there is a code in prison to kill pae-dophiles on sight; however, if that was the motivation, why hadn't Tartaglione tried to kill him before? Facing the death penalty, Tartaglione might have been hired to perform the hit in exchange for a reduced sentence. Five years after the killings, Tartaglione still has no trial date.

Epstein later claimed that Tartaglione had tried to strangle him. Nearer the time of the incident, he told Tisdale that he'd been strangled but didn't name the culprit. According to Barry Levine's book, Tisdale told Levine: "All he did is make a strangling motion to himself with his hands around his neck and I said, 'Someone else tried to strangle you?' and he gave me a little nod."

However, Epstein told another inmate, Mersey: "I woke in the middle of the night to get a glass of water and that's the last thing I remember." This leaves open a fourth option – that someone outside of Epstein's cell, perhaps the prison staff itself, had tried to kill him. As we have already seen, it is not hard to organise a hit within a jail. However, if that was the case, why did the person not finish the job? Had they been disturbed by Tartaglione? But how would they have gotten away? Alternatively, had the guards arranged with Tartaglione himself that he would murder Epstein and they would cover it up, in return for favours? This would explain their rough handling of Epstein's body, as if they expected him to remain dead. Perhaps they hadn't bargained on the staff at the infirmary actually being able to resuscitate him?

Whatever the case, the implications for Epstein weren't good. He was promptly relocated to the ultra-secure suicide prevention wing, where life rapidly became even more restricted. He was kept in solitary confinement with little or no luxuries, dressed in a gown made of paper and forced to sleep in paper bed sheets so he couldn't hang himself. He was allowed no books and at night the lights remained switched on so he could be observed at all times.

It was now that Epstein claimed Tartaglione had tried to kill him. Either using this line or some other approach, he appears to have convinced the visiting psychologist that he was no longer a suicide threat and, incredibly, within just six days of his suicide attempt – if that's what it was – Epstein was returned to his old wing. Again, there is more than one possibility here; was it Epstein's persuasiveness alone that released him from suicide watch or did the prison staff have a hand in it – staff who hated Epstein and would be more than happy for him to take his own life?

Whatever the case, when Epstein turned up for a hearing two days later on July 31, he appeared "out of it," according to victims' attorney Gloria Allred. The smug perma-smirk had vanished and he remained silent and unresponsive throughout the brief hearing in which a trial date was set for June 2020.

Had Epstein given up? Apparently not. On August 1, he arranged a meeting with Atlanta-based lawyer David Schoen to discuss him taking over the case. Schoen said that Epstein was in good spirits and they had agreed to meet again the following week. On August 8, Epstein had another meeting with his attorneys, this time to update his will. The outcome saw his fortune placed in a sealed trust that would make it much more difficult for his victims to get their hands on it.

The newly formed "1953 Trust", named after the year of his birth, would protect the identities of his beneficiaries and would erect several more barriers between the survivors and his estate. As well as having to win their case in court to receive a portion of the estate as compensation, the survivors would first have to persuade a judge to release the details of the beneficiaries. The beneficiaries would also get a chance in court to argue their right to any funds that might be taken from them to pay the survivors. With all the loopholes and red tape, one expert estimated it could take as long as a decade to sort out the various conflicting claims.

In retrospect, it looks like a cynical ploy from a man who knew his life was about to end, either by his own hand or because he knew he was going to be murdered. But there is another intriguing possibility behind the last-minute change to his will which we will explore later in this chapter.

Whatever the motive, the move was prescient. In just forty-eight hours, Epstein would be dead. Developments came thick and fast on the next day, August 9. Firstly, it was announced that a court had decided to unseal the documents relating to Virginia Giuffre's 2017 defamation case against Ghislaine Maxwell, revealing to the world the full scope of Epstein's operation and dragging in names like Glenn Dubin, Bill Richardson, Murray Gell-Mann and Alan Dershowitz. Secondly, his cellmate was removed from his cell, leaving the paedophile on his own. Was this the set-up for the murder? Or perhaps a staff-assisted suicide? Or even a faked death and subsequent jail break? All three options remain on the table.

The night of August 9/10 was the night that Epstein finally met his fate. The events surrounding it push credibility to the limits if one believes the official story that they were all just unfortunate coincidences. The guards on duty were due to perform half-hour checks on the recently suicidal prisoner. Not one of these checks actually occurred and it was later claimed that both guards fell asleep or were too engrossed online to perform any checks between 3.30 a.m. to 6.20 a.m. Additionally, the two cameras that constantly monitored Epstein's cell both malfunctioned on the night of his death. When combined with his early release from suicide watch and the removal of his cellmate, leaving him alone on the very evening of his death, the circumstantial evidence multiplies to make it extremely improbable that all of these incidents were mere coincidences. Then there was the autopsy, which found that he had strangled himself by tying a sheet to his bed and leaning forward in a kneeling position, even though he had broken several bones in his neck, injuries which were much more consistent with suicides involving jumping – impossible for Epstein as his bed wasn't high enough – or murder by strangulation. More on this later.

There are three main explanations for Epstein's death. The first is the official story, which is that he committed suicide by self-strangulation. Evidence to back this up is the last-minute change to his will and the fact that his mental health was visibly deteriorating prior to his death. However, it doesn't explain the massive anomalies around the "coincidences" that surrounded his death that night – his cellmate being suddenly moved out of his cell, the cameras failing and both prison guards failing to check on him, as well as the broken bones in his neck.

The suicide story becomes more plausible if we assume the guards were complicit. This would explain the security anomalies on the night of his death, but it still wouldn't account for the broken bones. Also, is it really plausible that the guards would have arranged with Epstein to allow him to commit suicide? We know they disliked him but I'm sure they disliked a lot of prisoners. Was that motive enough to risk their jobs and even criminal charges by so obviously tampering with the security measures that evening?

The second explanation is that he was murdered. Implicit in this description of events is the assumption that whoever organised the hit was powerful enough to arrange the security anomalies that occurred that evening. This would explain the guards, the cameras and the absence of a cellmate, and also, of course, the broken bones which were evidence of violent strangulation. If we also assume that he knew, or was at least suspicious, that a hit was out on him, it would explain the change of will and the mental deterioration of a man who knew he was going to die.

The release of pictures of his cell and autopsy photos showing the marks on his neck triggered memories of when I had interviewed, in Tucson prison, Two Tonys, a multiple-homicide murderer who was an associate of the Bonanno crime family. Serving 141 years, he had left the corpses of rival gangsters from Arizona to Alaska.

He said that he had so many enemies, he was always ready to kill someone quickly if an assassin entered his cell. Writing his life story, I was getting the details of the things he had done. So, I just said to him one day: "How would you kill me right now?" In a split second, he jumped up, grabbed an electrical cord attached to a heating filament, wrapped it around my neck and applied pressure (detailed in my book, *Prison Time*).

Having expected him to describe how he would kill me, I hadn't anticipated getting strangled. Although taken by surprise, I trusted him, so I didn't struggle. With my breath getting cut off, I allowed him to proceed. Eventually, I was gasping and on the verge of panicking. He kept the cord tight just long enough for me to regret having asked the question. After releasing it as expertly as he had applied it, he grinned. Speechless, I was panting and massaging my throat, but eventually I managed to smile because I had such a close relationship with him.

At the request of Epstein's attorneys, New York Chief Medical Examiner Dr Barbara Sampson's autopsy was observed by the private pathologist, Dr Michael Baden. Paid for by Epstein's brother, Baden said that the three fractures on Epstein's neck had required much more pressure than from the supposed suicide method. These fractures were "more indicative of homicide," according to Baden. He added that the ligature mark on Epstein's neck didn't match the bed sheet noose seen on the photos from Epstein's cell. "It was too wide and too smooth," he said, during a Fox News interview. "This is a rougher injury." He also said there was no blood on the noose, and that the three neck fractures would not have been caused by hanging.

Baden continued: "I think there's a lot of information that hasn't been revealed yet that is essential in order to arrive at a conclusion whether this is a suicide or a homicide. I think the important thing is to find out what was seen when the guards first went into the cell. Was he hanging? Was he on the ground, as some people reported when he was found?" He added that the first responders destroyed a lot of the forensic evidence by removing Epstein's body too quickly. Surprise, surprise! Why would they want to provide any forensic evidence of him being killed by the deep state with a role played by the Clintons?

"EMS is not supposed to remove dead bodies from jails," Baden said. "They're supposed to have a whole forensic work-up – what kind of forensic evidence is in the clothing, how long the person was dead? We can tell from the ligature mark that he had been—there was a tight ligature around his neck for many hours, and the front of the neck, before he was found, so he was dead for a long time. But we could be more specific about that if somebody tested the stiffness of the body, etc. at the scene."

A photo of Epstein's cell shows a combination sink-toilet and double bunks with a little ladder up to the top cell, orange bedding and breezeblock walls. A close-up of his bunk shows a skinny mattress with orange bedding. The photo reveals that fragments of material were hanging from a window while a large strip of bedding was also looped through a hole on the top bunk. Another photo shows Epstein on the bunk – grey, ashen and freshly wrapped. Another shows the broken bones in his neck, including the hyoid near his Adam's apple.

On CBS, Baden repeated his allegations that it had not been a suicide. "There were multiple fractures of the Adam's apple, the thyroid … and the hyoid bone that are more indicative of a homicidal strangulation than a suicidal strangulation. With hanging suicide, 90% of the time there are no fractures. Maybe 10% or 15% they have hyoid or thyroid fracture. You don't have three fractures with the weight of the body in the ligature. You have to have a lot more pressure by ligature or by hands to get those fractures."

When Two Tonys had wrapped that cord around my neck, he had done it in a friendly way. There had been enough pressure to render me unconscious and if he had applied more, my oxygen would have been cut off and I could have died. My life could have been rapidly and efficiently ended; that brief time is all it would have taken for someone to have accessed Epstein while the two guards were conveniently asleep. An assassin could have entered his cell, done the damage and strung him up to make it look like suicide. Lots of evidence suggests that's what happened.

On *60 Minutes*, Baden said: "The investigators have not said whether there was DNA on the noose. The FBI or the medical examiner would have done swabs for DNA on the ligature. Whose DNA is on it? Was it Epstein alone or Epstein and somebody else?" He added that Epstein's family believed that his death was more likely a homicide, based on the autopsy results, and that they were desperate for the truth. "There is no advantage to the family whether it is homicide or suicide. There is no money involved. They just want the truth. The brother Mark or the estate would just as soon have this to be a suicide because there is no advantage to them for it to be a homicide. Mark Epstein is now concerned about a homicide. If his brother was killed because he knew too much, is he also in jeopardy? Are other people in jeopardy?" Baden rejected the claim that he made the homicide call because he was paid by Epstein's family. He said that during his time as a medical examiner in New York in the late 1970s, his professional opinion was never swayed by who had hired him.

The CBS reporter asked Baden about the position of Epstein's body, the damage to the neck, and the blood revealed for the first time in the graphic photos in the *60 Minutes* show. Multiple nooses fashioned from orange bedding were found. Photos showed prescription pill bottles, several electrical cords, and enough bed sheets for several inmates dumped on the floor. Note: several electrical cords!

If Two Tonys had been assigned to suicide Epstein, he would have gone straight for the cords. Anyone trained in the art of killing efficiently would have gone for the cords. So, in all likelihood, the murder weapon was present in the cell.

One possibility is that a guard performed the hit. Interviewing Ori Spado, a former mob boss, I learned more about how the mafia and the elites work together. He said that there is an overworld and an underworld. He was in the underworld, and the elites are in the overworld. He believed that the guards could have easily carried this out.

Also found in Epstein's cell was a handwritten note in ballpoint pen. Epstein had been documenting the prison conditions. A guard had kept him in a locked shower stall for an hour. The note included: "Sent me for burnt food. Giant bugs crawling over my hands. No fun." High-security-level jails do not allow ballpoint pens. Maybe his lawyer had slipped him one.

One photo from inside the cell showed multiple prescription pill bottles with Epstein's name on them and food on the top bunk. The final photo released to *60 Minutes* was of the noose from bed sheets found elsewhere in his cell, which we are supposed to believe was the suicide instrument.

60 Minutes also showed a photo of the cell door with police tape on it: NOW CRIME SCENE DO NOT CROSS. There was also a photo of a barred door, which separated the guards from Epstein's cell – a mere 15 feet away from them! Another photo showed the hall.

Charged with falsifying records and conspiracy, the two sleepy guards pled not guilty. They were allegedly shopping online for furniture and sleeping instead of checking on Epstein. And then when they did finally check on him, they said they told their supervisor that they had messed up and hadn't done any checks in the hours before. Then they went and altered the records.

Depending on your security level, there are headcounts every so many hours, and there are security walks every twenty to thirty minutes. In the MCC, they were required to walk every thirty minutes to make sure that Epstein was still alive and accounted for. A surveillance video that was made available showed the absence of security walks. However, the video showing what was happening around the time of his death – probably who went in and suicided him – had mysteriously disappeared.

Epstein had been on suicide watch, taken off it, his cellmate conveniently removed, guards had fallen asleep, the cameras had malfunctioned and with all the stars aligned, he was most likely taken out in a deep-state operation.

If we take this murder scenario seriously – which this book does – the next obvious question is: who pulled the strings?

Let's look at the major contenders who have been outlined in this book and summarise the evidence and possible motives for them ordering the hit.

My main suspect is Bill Clinton, or perhaps we should say the Clinton crime family. When news of Epstein's death was first announced, fingers were immediately pointed at Hillary Clinton with the hashtag #Clintonbodycount trending on Twitter and tweeted by President Trump. As we've seen in this series of books, the Clintons are certainly not averse to bumping off those who threaten to expose their sordid secret lives.

A YouTube viewer kindly sent a list of the #Clintonbodycount.

Researching the Clintons over the years, reading books like *Partners in Power*, *The Clintons' War on Women*, and Terry Reed's *Compromised*, I was familiar with many of the names of the deceased.

1: James McDougal, Bill Clinton's convicted Whitewater partner. He was a key witness in Ken Starr's investigation. Supposedly, he had a heart attack while in solitary confinement.

2: Mary Mahoney, former White House intern, was murdered in July 1997 at a Starbucks coffee shop in Georgetown, Washington, D.C. The murder happened after she had decided to go public with her story of sexual harassment in the White House.

3: Vince Foster. I urge you to go online and research about Vince Foster. His story will absolutely blow your mind. As a former White House counsellor and colleague of Hillary Clinton's Little Rock Rose Law Firm, he died of a gunshot wound to the head. Although it was ruled a suicide, the body was obviously moved and the evidence doctored. He knew a lot about the dirty deeds done at Hillary's law firm.

4: Ron Brown, former secretary of Commerce and DNC chairman. Reportedly, he died from the impact in a plane crash. A pathologist close to the investigation stated there was a hole in the top of Brown's skull resembling a gunshot wound. At the time of his death, Brown was being investigated and had spoken publicly of his willingness to cut a deal with the prosecutors. The rest of the people on the plane also died. A few days later, the air traffic controller committed suicide, and on and on it went.

5: C. Victor Raiser II, a major player in the Clinton fundraising machine, who died in a private plane crash in July 1992.

6: Paul Tully, Democratic National Committee political director, found dead in a hotel room in Little Rock, September 1992. Described by Clinton as a dear friend and trusted advisor.

7: Ed Willey, Clinton fundraiser, found dead in 1993 of a gun-shot wound to the head, deep in the woods in Virginia. Ruled a suicide. Ed Willey died on the same day his wife, Kathleen Willey, claimed Bill Clinton had groped her in the Oval Office of the White House. Willey was involved in several Clinton fundraising events.

8: Jerry Parks, the former head of Bill Clinton's gubernatorial security team in Little Rock, gunned down in his car at a deserted intersection outside of Little Rock's park. His son said that his father was building a dossier on Clinton and that he had allegedly threatened to reveal this information. After he died, the files were mysteriously removed from his house.

9: James Bunch, who supposedly died from a gunshot suicide. It was reported that he had a black book of people which included elites who visited prostitutes in Texas and Arkansas. Again, the Epstein theme of blackmail and suicide.

10: James Wilson, who was found dead in May 1993 from apparent hanging suicide. He had ties to Whitewater.

11: Kathy Ferguson, the ex-wife of Arkansas trooper Danny Ferguson, was found dead in May 1994 in a living room with a gunshot to the head. Ruled a suicide even though there were several packed suitcases as if she were planning to flee. Danny Ferguson was a co-defendant with Bill Clinton in the Paula Jones lawsuit. Kathy Ferguson was a possible corroborating witness with Paula Jones.

12: Bill Shelton, the Arkansas state trooper and fiancé of Kathy Ferguson. Critical of the suicide ruling of his fiancée, he was found dead in June 1994, with a gunshot wound, also ruled a suicide.

13: Gandy Baugh, attorney for Bill Clinton's friend, Dan Lasater. Gandy Baugh died by jumping out of a window of a tall building in January 1994. One of the biggest contributors to the Clinton campaigns, Lasater was laundering money for the CIA-backed Arkansas cocaine operation. Barry Seal, the pilot who was killed, was dropping off money directly to Lasater. As a money manager, he sold bonds, which were an integral part of the money-laundering operation. Lasater had easy access to Clinton through the back door of the State Capitol building.

14: Florence Martin, a former accountant and subcontractor for CIA activity related to Barry Seal's Arkansas drug-smuggling case. He died of three gunshot wounds.

15: Susan Coleman, who reportedly had an affair with Clinton when he was the Arkansas attorney general. Pregnant at the time of her death, she died of a gunshot wound to the back of the head, which was ruled a suicide.

16: Paula Grover, Clinton's speech interpreter for the deaf from 1978 until her death in December 1992. Died in a one-car accident.

17: Danny Casolaro, investigative reporter investigating Mena Airport and the Arkansas Development Finance Authority, who supposedly slit his wrists in the middle of the investigation. He was found dead in a bathtub in room 517 of the Sheraton Hotel in Martinsburg, West Virginia. His wrists had been slashed ten to twelve times. The Arkansas Development Finance Authority was supposedly set up to bring jobs to Arkansas and boost the economy, but it was a money-laundering scheme for cocaine proceeds. The amount of cash in the banks in Arkansas surged due to all the money laundering.

18: Paul Wiltshire, an attorney investigating corruption at Mena Airport with Casolaro in the 1980 October Surprise, was found dead on the toilet on June 22, 1993, in a Washington,

D.C. apartment. He had delivered a report to Janet Reno three weeks before his death.

19: Jon Parnell Walker, a Whitewater investigator for Resolution Trust, who jumped to his death from an apartment balcony in Darlington, Virginia, August 15, 1993. He was also investigating the Madison Guaranty scandal. Madison Guaranty Savings and Loan Association was a savings and loan company in Little Rock, Arkansas. In 1989, after ten years of operation, it was closed by federal regulators due to bank failure, leading to a $60 million loss for the Federal Deposit Insurance Corporation. The bank had been owned and managed by Jim McDougal, a friend of Bill and Hillary.

20: Barbara Wise, a Department of Commerce staffer who had worked closely with John Huang (a senior DNC fundraiser who had solicited Indonesian gardeners and Buddhist nuns living under a vow of poverty). On November 29, 1996, her bruised and naked body was found locked in her office at the Department of Commerce. The cause of death is unknown.

21: Charles Meissner, the assistant secretary of Commerce who had given John Huang special security clearance, died shortly thereafter in a small plane crash.

22: Dr Stanley Heard, the chairman of the National Chiropractic Healthcare Advisory Committee, died with his attorney, Steve Dickson, in a small plane crash. Dr Heard, in addition to serving on Bill Clinton's advisory council, had personally treated Clinton's mother, stepfather and brother.

23: Barry Seal, the drug-running CIA pilot. A federal judge had ordered Barry Seal to live in a halfway house with no bodyguards and no weapons, with the address publicly available. The Bush and Clinton crime families knew that the Colombians had a hit out on Seal, so by forcing him to stay at a public address and removing his armed bodyguards, they enabled his assassination.

24: Johnny Lawhorn Jr, a mechanic who found a cheque made out to Bill Clinton in the trunk of a car left at his repair shop. Found dead after his car hit a utility pole.

25: Stanley Huggins, who investigated Madison Guaranty. His death was a purported suicide and his report was never released.

26: Herschel Friday, an Arkansas bond lawyer and major donor to Clinton fundraisers, who died March 1, 1994 when his plane exploded.

27: Seth Rich, a D.C. staffer, murdered and robbed. WikiLeaks claimed that he had info on the DNC emails scandal.

28: Kevin Ives and Don Henry, known as "the boys on the tracks". Murdered after discovering CIA drug drops protected by Bill Clinton's Arkansas state police. A controversial case because the coroner, Malak, who was in Clinton's pocket, said that the boys had smoked cannabis and fallen asleep on the train tracks next to each other and been run over. One of the dads of the boys worked on the tracks and he knew that was impossible. A later report claimed they were slain before being put on the tracks. Many linked to the case died before being able to give testimony. All detailed in my book, *Clinton Bush and CIA Conspiracies: From the Boys on the Tracks to Jeffrey Epstein.*

Here are some of the people who died who had information on the boys on the tracks case:

29: Keith Coney, whose motorcycle slammed into the back of a truck.

30: Keith McCaskill, who was stabbed 113 times.

31: Gregory Collins, who died from a gunshot wound.

32: Jeff Rhodes, who was shot, and his mutilated body burned in a trash dump.

33: James Milan, who was decapitated, but the coroner ruled his death as natural causes.

34: Richard Winters, a suspect in the Ives-Henry deaths, was killed in a set-up robbery in July 1989.

A lot of the #Clintonbodycount information came from former Clinton bodyguards, including Arkansas state police troopers. Some are now dead:

35: Major William Barkley.

36: Captain Scott Reynolds.

37: Sergeant Brian Hanley.

38: Sergeant Tim Sable.

39: Major General William Robertson. On February 23, 1993, a Blackhawk helicopter crashed in Weisbaden, Germany, killing five of Bill Clinton's bodyguards and associates (40-43 below).

40: Colonel William Densberger.

41: Colonel Robert Kelly.

42: Gary Rhodes.

43: Jarrett J. Robertson

44: Steven Willis.

45: Robert Williams.

46: Conway LeBleu.

47: Todd McKeehan.

I believe that one of the most recent in the #Clintonbodycount is Jeffrey Epstein and that the Clintons were big players in the murder conspiracy, but that does not preclude other heavyweights – including Prince Andrew – having input.

Epstein clearly had something over Bill Clinton. In his own words, Epstein said that Clinton owed him "favours". Given the nature of Epstein's operation and Clinton's intemperate sex drive, it's reasonable to assume that whatever it was involved sexual blackmail. With Epstein's arrest, all the dirt on Clinton was threatening to spill out in court, so the motive was clearly there, and again, with their connections, murdering someone in prison is something Bill and Hillary would have had the power and influence to pull off.

The Clinton connection could also throw light on Epstein's mysterious forty-eight-hour trip to Saudi Arabia on the eve of the presidential election in 2016. Had Epstein fled the country on the expectation that Hillary would win? Did he have reason to believe that, with Hillary in power, he would have to be eliminated because of the dirt he had on her husband? Was his intention to stay permanently outside of the US? And did he return forty-eight hours later when he knew Trump was in office and thus it was safe – or safer – to return?

Then there is Prince Andrew and the UK's Royal Family. That Epstein had dirt on Andrew is unequivocal. There is enough evidence exposing Andrew in compromising situations involving Epstein and girls. Given that these alleged crimes – Andrew denies everything – occurred on so many occasions within multiple Epstein properties, it is almost ludicrous to think that Epstein didn't have video and photographic evidence. And what other nefarious secrets could Epstein have spilled on Andrew?

It's almost certain that Andrew's documented alleged crimes are just the tip of the iceberg. And what about other royals? We know that Epstein and Maxwell were also close to Andrew's ex-wife, Sarah Ferguson, and that Epstein had loaned Fergie £15,000 – according to mainstream media, but more likely a multiple of £15,000 as that amount would have been meaningless to Fergie – probably to pay off debts. We know from Maria Farmer's testimony that Epstein, and especially Maxwell, had intimate chats with Andrew and Fergie in which many secrets might have been divulged, like their shared hatred and mockery of Diana. Could one of these secrets have been information on Diana's death, information that could not be allowed to become public?

Unless we forget the huge power and influence of the Royal Family, we just need to remember how ABC news anchor Amy Robach was secretly filmed admitting that her network had been forced to pull her 2015 interview with Virginia Giuffre exposing Andrew, due to threats from Buckingham Palace. If the royals could keep such a massive story quiet for several years, could they have the power to assassinate Epstein inside a New York prison cell, perhaps via MI6 and with the collusion of US intelligence agencies? I think it's not at all unreasonable to suggest that this is a possibility.

Talking of intelligence agencies, let's not forget the Mossad. Throughout this book, we have looked at Epstein's links to Israeli intelligence, which go back as far as the 1980s – when Robert Maxwell probably introduced him into the fold. Via his links to Wexner and the Mega Group, Epstein was clearly an agent of an international Israeli intelligence and crime syndicate involved in drug and weapons smuggling, child trafficking and money-laundering enterprises. His main role throughout the 1990s and 2000s, it appears, was sexual blackmail of prominent political figures to further the aims of this spiderweb of intrigue.

With his dirty laundry about to be aired in court, the threat of these secrets, especially the use of paedophilia for political blackmail purposes, would have been utterly disastrous for Israel's reputation. There would have been only one option left in such a situation – get rid of Epstein. Did the Mossad have the power and capability to pull off hits like this in secure locations on foreign soil? The question is almost laughable; there are so many historical examples of them doing exactly this.

We also have the almost exact historical template for the Epstein hit in the case of Robert Maxwell – a man who was at the forefront of an international Mossad-linked crime operation, who then started to become a liability. He was about to face a court trial and thus might spill the beans. Regardless of his renown, wealth and position, I believe that the man was quickly and quietly taken out by a Mossad hit team and the murder presented – credibly – as a suicide.

The Clintons, the royals and Israeli intelligence all had the motives and the power to have Epstein suicided. However, despite all of the above, there remains one intriguing possibility that we have not yet covered – the chance that Epstein didn't die at all in that prison cell, that his death was faked, that he was smuggled away, and that he is still at large today.

It sounds incredible, but it might not be as far-fetched as it seems. Firstly, presuming Epstein knew about his imminent escape, it would explain the last-minute change to his will, as he would have known he was about to officially "die". It would have accounted for his apparent mental deterioration, as Epstein would have been play-acting at being suicidal in preparation for the fake death. It would also explain the apparent security anomalies as, clearly, whoever bust him from jail would have to have fixed the "suicide" with the collusion of the prison authorities.

It would also explain that mysterious visit to Epstein's Manhattan mansion the day after his death. As we have already seen, Epstein's long-term accountant, Richard Kahn, was seen sneaking into the 71st Street townhouse on the day after Epstein's death and was photographed emerging with a shopping bag full of items about forty-five minutes later. If this was sensitive material that the FBI wanted to get their hands on, why hadn't someone removed it earlier? The house had already been swept with a fine-tooth comb for incriminating evidence.

It would make more sense that the bag contained vital items required for Epstein's safe passage away from New York and on to a new life, items like a passport and other important documents as well as cash, or diamonds (we know there were lots of these floating around the mansion). We know the 71st Street house was riddled with secret doors and hidden rooms and passages. No doubt these critical possessions had been stashed away somewhere even the FBI had been unable to find, waiting for the moment when Kahn or another of Epstein's cronies would come to smuggle them out.

Epstein researcher Frederic Ponton believes that towards the end, Epstein was becoming increasingly paranoid for his safety and was planning on retiring somewhere outside the US to enjoy a life of relative peace. Ponton believes Epstein had decided upon Paris — a place that he loved — to retire, so perhaps Epstein had been preparing for such a sudden and secretive move for some time even before his arrest. In such a case, everything would have been lined up in advance for just such a hasty and secretive departure as his fake death would necessitate.

Another anomaly that this theory would clear up is the fact that Epstein's estate continued transferring money to other Epstein accounts even after his death. A *New York Times* article from February 2021 revealed that Epstein's estate had transferred no less than $15.5 million to an organisation called Southern Country International in December 2019, four months after his death. Southern Country was a bank operating out of the US Virgin Islands that Epstein had set up in 2014. However, despite some generous tax breaks from the US Virgin Islands authorities, the bank had done no business from that time until Epstein's death. At the time of his death, according to *The Times* article, the bank had assets of $693,157. Then in December 2019, two cheques totalling $15.5 million were paid in by Epstein's estate. Southern Country sent back $2.6 million, leaving the total it received at $12.9 million. But by the end of the year, Southern Country's funds amounted to just $499,759, indicating that the bulk of the money had been transferred elsewhere. None of the transfer documents indicated the reason for these movements and, when pressed for information on the payments by the US Virgin

Islands authorities, a lawyer for Epstein's estate said merely that some of the transfers were made in error.

What could explain these mysterious payments to Epstein's own private bank better than that the proceeds were going to Epstein himself, wherever he had set up his new secretive life?

Then there were the anomalies with the autopsy. At the request of Epstein's attorneys, the autopsy was observed by the private pathologist Dr Michael Baden. Why did the controversial pathologist, who had been an expert witness in the O. J. Simpson trial and the head of the pathology panel on the investigation into the JFK assassination, need to be involved in the study of Epstein's body? Why was the evidence of several broken bones, including the hyoid bone, discounted in ascribing the death as suicide? And why did the medical examiner's office stall on releasing the autopsy report, which should by law have been sent to Epstein's family as soon as the death certificate was released, but which was actually delayed for two weeks after the cause of death was first announced?

All of these questions could point to some kind of tampering with the corpse, or even the use of a body double. Body doubles might sound like the stuff of Hollywood movies, but they are not as far-fetched as they appear. Prominent politicians and high-profile figures around the world have been using body doubles for centuries, and the CIA has a long history of utilising body doubles in its espionage work. There is a credible theory that the CIA switched a body double for JFK's corpse after the president's assassination to make the wounds fit more accurately with the official narrative. Is it a coincidence then that the head of the investigation into JFK's murder was also present at Epstein's autopsy?

A similar mystery surrounds the initial finding of Epstein's body. Why did guards remove the corpse from Epstein's cell, thus violating Bureau of Prisons protocols which state that suicide scenes should be treated with the "same level of protection as any crime scene in which a death has occurred"? Why did the guards not take any photographs of Epstein's body as it was found? And why did they put out an emergency call for Epstein to be taken to hospital rather than a death report, thus ensuring that few or no press would be waiting outside to photograph the corpse?

The theory that Epstein didn't die was resurrected in 2021 by pro-Trump attorney Lin Wood, who claimed he knew of three high-level, credible sources who had all told him Epstein was alive and well. Although he wouldn't name his sources or give any evidence for the claim, Wood did make a very sound argument for the case that Epstein is still alive. Wood said that someone like Epstein, who was up to his neck in espionage and organised-crime and sexual-blackmail operations, would have been acutely aware of the possibility of being "suicided". Bearing this in mind, it is almost certain that he would have set up a so-called "dead man's switch" which would effectively make public all the dirt he had on everyone – or selected targets – in the event of his death. As we have seen from Ponton, Epstein was growing increasingly worried about being murdered in the last years of his life and was making plans to extricate himself from the web he had built. It hardly seems plausible, given this paranoia and planning, that Epstein wouldn't have set up a dead man's switch to mitigate the possibility of being taken out.

It's also implausible that, given Epstein's sexual blackmail operation, organisations like the CIA and the Mossad wouldn't have expected Epstein to have such an insurance policy. The risk to either agency's reputation of this switch being activated would have been too great. Far safer to arrange a fake death and let Epstein live out the rest of his life in secrecy and peace.

The idea that Epstein might still be alive is both intriguing and extremely unsettling. Where is he living? What is he doing? Is his perverse sexual appetite undiminished and is he still being served up a string of underage girls each day? Which of his close associates knows the answers to all these questions?

Perhaps we will never know whether Epstein died – or how he died – in that New York prison cell on August 10, 2019, but one thing is certain – the secrets haven't stopped emerging and they will continue to do so for months, perhaps years, into the future.

The Epstein story is far from over. Watch out for *Who Killed Epstein? Part 2* – which will incorporate the developments since the publication of this book, including a greater focus on Ghislaine Maxwell.

GET A FREE BOOK

Sign Up For My Newsletter:

http://shaunattwood.com/newsletter-subscribe/

REFERENCES

Ben-Menashe, Ari. *Profits of War: Inside the Secret US-Israeli Arms Network*. Trine Day, 2015.

Bowden, Mark. *Killing Pablo*. Atlantic Books, 2001.

Bowen, Russell. *The Immaculate Deception*. America West Publishers, 1991.

Castaño, Carlos. *My Confession*. Oveja Negra, 2001.

Caycedo, Germán Castro. *In Secret*. Planeta, 1996.

Chepesiuk, Ron. *Crazy Charlie*. Strategic Media Books, 2016.

Chepesiuk, Ron. *Drug Lords: The Rise and Fall of the Cali Cartel*. Milo Books, 2003.

Chepesiuk, Ron. *Escobar vs Cali: The War of the Cartels*. Strategic Media, 2013.

Cockburn, Leslie. *Out of Control*. Bloomsbury, 1988.

Cockburn and Clair. *Whiteout*. Verso, 1998.

Dawson, Ryan. *The Separation of Business and State*. CreateSpace, 2018.

Don Berna. *Killing the Boss*. ICONO, 2013.

Escobar, Juan Pablo. *Pablo Escobar: My Father*. Ebury Press, 2014.

Escobar, Roberto. *Escobar*. Hodder & Stoughton, 2009.

Grillo, Joan. *El Narco*. Bloomsbury, 2012.

Gugliotta and Leen. *Kings of Cocaine*. Harper and Row, 1989.

Hari, Johann. *Chasing the Scream*. Bloomsbury, 2015.

Hersh, Seymour. *The Samson Option: Israel's Nuclear Arsenal and American Foreign Policy*. Random House, 1991.

Hopsicker, Daniel. *Barry and the Boys*. MadCow Press, 2001.

Howard, Dylan and Cronin, Melissa and Robertson, James. *Epstein: Dead Men Tell No Tales*. Skyhorse, 2020.

Leveritt, Mara. *The Boys on the Tracks*. Bird Call Press, 2007.

Levine, Barry. *The Spider: Inside the Criminal Web of Jeffrey Epstein and Ghislaine Maxwell*. Crown, 2020.

Levine, Michael. *The Big White Lie*. Thunder's Mouth Press, 1993.

MacQuarrie, Kim. *Life and Death in the Andes*. Simon & Schuster, 2016.

Maisey, Michael. *Young Offender: My Life from Armed Robber to Local Hero*. Macmillan, 2019.

Márquez, Gabriel García. *News of a Kidnapping*. Penguin, 1996.

Martínez, Astrid María Legarda. *The True Life of Pablo Escobar*. Ediciones y Distribuciones Dipon Ltda, 2017.

Massing, Michael. *The Fix*. Simon & Schuster, 1998.

McAleese, Peter. *No Mean Soldier*. Cassell Military Paperbacks, 2000.

McCoy, Alfred. *The Politics of Heroin in Southeast Asia*. Harper and Row, 1972.

Mollison, James. *The Memory of Pablo Escobar*. Chris Boot, 2009.

Morris, Roger. *Partners in Power*. Henry Holt, 1996.

Noriega, Manuel. *The Memoirs of Manuel Noriega*. Random House, 1997.

North, Oliver. *Under Fire*. Harper Collins, 1991.

Paley, Dawn. *Drug War Capitalism*. AK Press, 2014.

Porter, Bruce. *Blow*. St Martin's Press, 1993.

Reed, Terry. *Compromised*. Clandestine Publishing, 1995.

Rempel, William. *At the Devil's Table: Inside the Fall of the Cali Cartel, the World's Biggest Crime Syndicate*. Random House, 2011.

Robinson, Charlie and Berwick, Jeff. *The Controlled Demolition of the American Empire*. Indie, 2020.

Robinson, Charlie. *The Octopus of Global Control*. Indie, 2017

Ross, Rick. *Freeway Rick Ross*. Freeway Studios, 2014.

Ruppert, Michael. *Crossing the Rubicon*. New Society Publishers, 2004.

Salazar, Alonso. *The Words of Pablo*. Planeta, 2001.

Salazar, Alonso. *Born to Die in Medellín*. Latin America Bureau, 1992.

Samworth, Neil. *Strangeways: A Prison Officer's Story*. Sidgwick & Jackson, 2018.

Saviano, Roberto. *Zero Zero Zero*. Penguin Random House UK, 2013.

Schou, Nick. *Kill the Messenger*. Nation Books, 2006.

Shannon, Elaine. *Desperados*. Penguin, 1988.

Stich, Rodney. *Defrauding America* 3rd Ed. Diablo Western Press, 1998.

Stich, Rodney. *Drugging America* 2nd Ed. Silverpeak, 2006.

Stokes, Doug. *America's Other War: Terrorizing Colombia*. Zed Books, 2005.

Stone, Roger. *The Clintons' War on Women*. Skyhorse, 2015.

Stone, Roger. *Jeb and the Bush Crime Family*. Skyhorse, 2016.

Streatfield, Dominic. *Cocaine*. Virgin Publishing, 2001.

Tarpley and Chaitkin. *George Bush*. Progressive Press, 2004.

Thomas, Gordon and Dillon, Martin. *The Assassination of Robert Maxwell.* Robson Books Ltd, 2002.

Tomkins, David. *Dirty Combat.* Mainstream Publishing, 2008.

Valentine, Douglas. *The Strength of the Pack.* Trine Day LLC, 2009.

Vallejo, Virginia. *Loving Pablo, Hating Escobar.* Vintage, 2018.

Velásquez Vásquez, Jhon Jairo. *Surviving Pablo Escobar.* Ediciones y Distribuciones Dipon Ltda, 2017.

Webb, Gary. Dark Alliance: *The CIA, the Contras, and the Crack Cocaine Explosion.* Seven Stories, 2014.

Webb, Whitney. *One Nation Under Blackmail: The Sordid Union Between Intelligence and Crime that Gave Rise to Jeffrey Epstein.* Trine Day, 2021.

Woods, Neil. *Good Cop Bad War.* Ebury Press, 2016.

Woods, Neil. *Drug Wars: The Terrifying Inside Story of Britain's Drug Trade.* Ebury Press, 2019.

SHAUN'S BOOKS

English Shaun Trilogy
Party Time
Hard Time
Prison Time

War on Drugs Series
Pablo Escobar: Beyond Narcos
American Made: Who Killed Barry Seal? Pablo Escobar or
George HW Bush
The Cali Cartel: Beyond Narcos
Clinton Bush and CIA Conspiracies:
From the Boys on the Tracks to Jeffrey Epstein

Un-Making a Murderer: The Framing of Steven Avery and
Brendan Dassey
The Mafia Philosopher: Two Tonys
Life Lessons

Pablo Escobar's Story (4-book series 2019-21)
T-Bone (Expected 2022)

SOCIAL-MEDIA LINKS

Email: attwood.shaun@hotmail.co.uk
YouTube: Shaun Attwood
Blog: Jon's Jail Journal
Website: shaunattwood.com
Instagram: @shaunattwood
Twitter: @shaunattwood
LinkedIn: Shaun Attwood
Goodreads: Shaun Attwood
Facebook: Shaun Attwood, Jon's Jail Journal,
T-Bone Appreciation Society

Shaun welcomes feedback on any of his books
and YouTube videos. Thank you for the Amazon and
Goodreads reviews and to all of the people who
have subscribed to Shaun's YouTube channel!

SHAUN'S JAIL JOURNEY STARTS IN HARD TIME NEW EDITION

CHAPTER 1

Sleep deprived and scanning for danger, I enter a dark cell on the second floor of the maximum-security Madison Street jail in Phoenix, Arizona, where guards and gang members are murdering prisoners. Behind me, the metal door slams heavily. Light slants into the cell through oblong gaps in the door, illuminating a prisoner cocooned in a white sheet, snoring lightly on the top bunk about two thirds of the way up the back wall. Relieved there is no immediate threat, I place my mattress on the grimy floor. Desperate to rest, I notice movement on the cement-block walls. *Am I hallucinating?* I blink several times. The walls appear to ripple. Stepping closer, I see the walls are alive with insects. I flinch. So many are swarming, I wonder if they're a colony of ants on the move. To get a better look, I put my eyes right up to them. They are mostly the size of almonds and have antennae. American cockroaches. I've seen them in the holding cells downstairs in smaller numbers, but nothing like this. A chill spread over my body. I back away.

Something alive falls from the ceiling and bounces off the base of my neck. I jump. With my night vision improving, I spot cockroaches weaving in and out of the base of the fluorescent strip light. Every so often one drops onto the concrete and resumes crawling. Examining the bottom bunk, I realise why my cellmate is sleeping at a higher elevation: cockroaches are pouring from gaps in the decrepit wall at the level of my bunk. The area is thick with them. Placing my mattress on the bottom bunk scatters them. I walk towards the toilet, crunching a few under my shower sandals. I urinate and grab the toilet roll. A cockroach darts from the centre of the roll onto my hand, tickling my fingers. My arm jerks as if it has a mind of its own, losing the cockroach and the toilet roll. Using a towel, I wipe the bulk of them off the bottom bunk, stopping only to shake the odd one off my hand. I unroll my mattress. They begin to regroup and inhabit my mattress. My adrenaline is pumping so much, I lose my fatigue.

Nauseated, I sit on a tiny metal stool bolted to the wall. *How will I sleep? How's my cellmate sleeping through the infestation and my arrival?* Copying his technique, I cocoon myself in a sheet and lie down, crushing more cockroaches. The only way they can access me now is through the breathing hole I've left in the sheet by the lower half of my face. Inhaling their strange musty odour, I close my eyes. I can't sleep. I feel them crawling on the sheet around my feet. *Am I imagining things?* Frightened of them infiltrating my breathing hole, I keep opening my eyes. Cramps cause me to rotate onto my other side. Facing the wall, I'm repulsed by so many of them just inches away. I return to my original side.

The sheet traps the heat of the Sonoran Desert to my body, soaking me in sweat. Sweat tickles my body, tricking my mind into thinking the cockroaches are infiltrating and crawling on me. The trapped heat aggravates my bleeding skin infections and bedsores. I want to scratch myself, but I know better. The outer layers of my skin have turned soggy from sweating constantly in this concrete oven. Squirming on the bunk fails to stop the relentless itchiness of my skin. Eventually, I scratch myself. Clumps of moist skin detach under my nails. Every now and then I become so uncomfortable, I must open my cocoon to waft the heat out, which allows the cockroaches in. It takes hours to drift to sleep. I only manage a few hours. I awake stuck to the soaked sheet, disgusted by the cockroach carcasses compressed against the mattress.

The cockroaches plague my new home until dawn appears at the dots in the metal grid over a begrimed strip of four-inch-thick bullet-proof glass at the top of the back wall – the cell's only source of outdoor light. They disappear into the cracks in the walls, like vampire mist retreating from sunlight. But not all of them. There were so many on the night shift that even their vastly reduced number is too many to dispose of. And they act like they know it. They roam around my feet with attitude, as if to make it clear that I'm trespassing on their turf.

My next set of challenges will arise not from the insect world, but from my neighbours. I'm the new arrival, subject to scrutiny about my charges just like when I'd run into the Aryan Brother-hood prison gang on my first day at the medium-security Towers jail a year ago. I wish my cellmate would wake up, brief me on the mood of the locals and introduce me to the head of the white gang. No such luck. Chow is announced over a speaker system in a crackly robotic voice, but he doesn't stir.

I emerge into the day room for breakfast. Prisoners in black-and-white bee-striped uniforms gather under the metal-grid stairs and tip dead cockroaches into a trash bin from plastic peanut-butter containers they'd set as traps during the night. All eyes are on me in the chow line. Watching who sits where, I hold my head up, put on a solid stare and pretend to be as at home in this environment as the cockroaches. It's all an act. I'm lonely and afraid. I loathe having to explain myself to the head of the white race, who I assume is the toughest murderer. I've been in jail long enough to know that taking my breakfast to my cell will imply that I have something to hide.

The gang punishes criminals with certain charges. The most serious are sex offenders, who are KOS: Kill On Sight. Other charges are punishable by SOS – Smash On Sight – such as drive-by shootings because women and kids sometimes get killed. It's called convict justice. Gang members are constantly looking for people to beat up because that's how they earn their reputations and tattoos. The most serious acts of violence earn the highest-ranking tattoos. To be a full gang member requires murder. I've observed the body language and techniques inmates trying to integrate employ. An inmate with a spring in his step and an air of confidence is likely to be accepted. A person who avoids eye contact and fails to introduce himself to the gang is likely to be preyed on. Some of the failed attempts I saw ended up with heads getting cracked against toilets, a sound I've grown familiar with. I've seen prisoners being extracted on stretchers who looked dead – one had yellow fluid leaking from his head. The constant violence gives me nightmares, but the reality is that I put myself in here, so I force myself to accept it as a part of my punishment.

It's time to apply my knowledge. With a self-assured stride, I take my breakfast bag to the table of white inmates covered in neo-Nazi tattoos, allowing them to question me.

"Mind if I sit with you guys?" I ask, glad exhaustion has deepened my voice.

"These seats are taken. But you can stand at the corner of the table."

The man who answered is probably the head of the gang. I size him up. Cropped brown hair. A dangerous glint in Nordic-blue eyes. Tiny pupils that suggest he's on heroin. Weightlifter-type veins bulging from a sturdy neck. Political ink on arms crisscrossed with scars. About the same age as me, thirty-three.

"Thanks. I'm Shaun from England." I volunteer my origin to show I'm different from them but not in a way that might get me smashed.

"I'm Bullet, the head of the whites." He offers me his fist to bump. "Where you roll in from, wood?"

Addressing me as wood is a good sign. It's what white gang members on a friendly basis call each other.

"Towers jail. They increased my bond and re-classified me to maximum security."

"What's your bond at?"

"I've got two $750,000 bonds," I say in a monotone. This is no place to brag about bonds.

"How many people you kill, brother?" His eyes drill into mine, checking whether my body language supports my story. My body language so far is spot on.

"None. I threw rave parties. They got us talking about drugs on wiretaps." Discussing drugs on the phone does not warrant a $1.5 million bond. I know and beat him to his next question. "Here's my charges." I show him my charge sheet, which includes conspiracy and leading a crime syndicate – both from running an Ecstasy ring.

Bullet snatches the paper and scrutinises it. Attempting to pre-empt his verdict, the other whites study his face. On edge, I wait for him to respond. Whatever he says next will determine whether I'll be accepted or victimised.

"Are you some kind of jailhouse attorney?" Bullet asks. "I want someone to read through my case paperwork." During our few minutes of conversation, Bullet has seen through my act and concluded that I'm educated – a possible resource to him.

I appreciate that he'll accept me if I take the time to read his case. "I'm no jailhouse attorney, but I'll look through it and help you however I can."

"Good. I'll stop by your cell later on, wood."

After breakfast, I seal as many of the cracks in the walls as I can with toothpaste. The cell smells minty, but the cockroaches still find their way in. Their day shift appears to be collecting information on the brown paper bags under my bunk, containing a few items of food that I purchased from the commissary; bags that I tied off with rubber bands in the hope of keeping the cockroaches out. Relentlessly, the cockroaches explore the bags for entry points, pausing over and probing the most worn and vulnerable regions. *Will the nightly swarm eat right through the paper?* I read all morning, wondering whether my cellmate has died in his cocoon, his occasional breathing sounds reassuring me.

Bullet stops by late afternoon and drops his case paperwork off. He's been charged with Class 3 felonies and less, not serious crimes, but is facing a double-digit sentence because of his prior convictions and Security Threat Group status in the prison system. The proposed sentencing range seems disproportionate. I'll advise him to reject the plea bargain – on the assumption he already knows to do so, but is just seeking the comfort of a second opinion, like many un-sentenced inmates. When he returns for his paperwork, our conversation disturbs my cellmate – the cocoon shuffles – so we go upstairs to his cell. I tell Bullet what I think. He is excitable, a different man from earlier, his pupils almost non-existent.

"This case ain't shit. But my prosecutor knows I done other shit, all kinds of heavy shit, but can't prove it. I'd do anything to get that sorry bitch off my fucking ass. She's asking for something bad to happen to her. Man, if I ever get bonded out, I'm gonna chop that bitch into pieces. Kill her slowly though. Like to work her over with a blowtorch."

Such talk can get us both charged with conspiring to murder a prosecutor, so I try to steer him elsewhere. "It's crazy how they can catch you doing one thing, yet try to sentence you for all of the things they think you've ever done."

"Done plenty. Shot some dude in the stomach once. Rolled him up in a blanket and threw him in a dumpster."

Discussing past murders is as unsettling as future ones. "So, what's all your tattoos mean, Bullet? Like that eagle on your chest?"

"Why you wanna know?" Bullet's eyes probe mine.

My eyes hold their ground. "Just curious."

"It's a war bird. The AB patch."

"AB patch?"

"What the Aryan Brotherhood gives you when you've put enough work in."

"How long does it take to earn a patch?"

"Depends how quickly you put your work in. You have to earn your lightning bolts first."

"Why you got red and black lightning bolts?"

"You get SS bolts for beating someone down or for being an

enforcer for the family. Red lightning bolts for killing someone. I was sent down as a youngster. They gave me steel and told me who to handle and I handled it. You don't ask questions. You just get blood on your steel. Dudes who get these tats without putting work in are told to cover them up or leave the yard."

"What if they refuse?"

"They're held down and we carve the ink off them."

Imagining them carving a chunk of flesh to remove a tattoo, I cringe. He's really enjoying telling me this now. His volatile nature is clear and frightening. *He's accepted me too much. He's trying to impress me before making demands.*

At night, I'm unable to sleep. Cocooned in heat, surrounded by cockroaches, I hear the swamp-cooler vent – a metal grid at the top of a wall – hissing out tepid air. Giving up on sleep, I put my earphones on and tune into National Public Radio. Listening to a Vivaldi violin concerto, I close my eyes and press my tailbone down to straighten my back as if I'm doing a yogic relaxation. The playful allegro thrills me, lifting my spirits, but the wistful adagio provokes sad emotions and tears. I open my eyes and gaze into the gloom. Due to lack of sleep, I start hallucinating and hearing voices over the music whispering threats. I'm at breaking point. Although I have accepted that I committed crimes and deserve to be punished, no one should have to live like this. I'm furious at myself for making the series of reckless decisions that put me in here and for losing absolutely everything. As violins crescendo in my ears, I remember what my life used to be like.

SHAUN'S INCARCERATION CONCLUDES IN PRISON TIME

CHAPTER 1

"I've got a padlock in a sock. I can smash your brains in while you're asleep. I can kill you whenever I want." My new cellmate sizes me up with no trace of human feeling in his eyes. Muscular and pot-bellied, he's caked in prison ink, including six snakes on his skull, slithering side by side. The top of his right ear is missing in a semi-circle.

The waves of fear are overwhelming. After being in transportation all day, I can feel my bladder hurting. "I'm not looking to cause any trouble. I'm the quietest cellmate you'll ever have. All I do is read and write."

Scowling, he shakes his head. "Why've they put a fish in with me?" He swaggers close enough for me to smell his cigarette breath. "Us convicts don't get along with fresh fish."

"Should I ask to move then?" I say, hoping he'll agree if he hates new prisoners so much.

"No! They'll think I threatened you!"

In the eight by twelve feet slab of space, I swerve around him and place my property box on the top bunk.

He pushes me aside and grabs the box. "You just put that on my artwork! I ought to fucking smash you, fish!"

"Sorry, I didn't see it."

"You need to be more aware of your fucking surroundings! What you in for anyway, fish?"

I explain my charges, Ecstasy dealing and how I spent twenty-six months fighting my case.

"How come the cops were so hard-core after you?" he asks, squinting.

"It was a big case, a multi-million dollar investigation. They raided over a hundred people and didn't find any drugs. They were pretty pissed off. I'd stopped dealing by the time they caught up with me, but I'd done plenty over the years, so I accept my punishment."

"Throwing raves," he says, staring at the ceiling as if remembering something. "Were you partying with underage girls?" he asks, his voice slow, coaxing.

Being called a sex offender is the worst insult in prison. Into my third year of incarceration, I'm conditioned to react. "What you trying to say?" I yell angrily, brow clenched.

"Were you fucking underage girls?" Flexing his body, he shakes both fists as if about to punch me.

"Hey, I'm no child molester, and I'd prefer you didn't say shit like that!"

"My buddy next door is doing twenty-five to life for murdering a child molester. How do I know Ecstasy dealing ain't your cover story?" He inhales loudly, nostrils flaring.

"You want to see my fucking paperwork?"

A stocky prisoner walks in. Short hair. Dark eyes. Powerful neck. On one arm: a tattoo of a man in handcuffs above the word OMERTA – the Mafia code of silence towards law enforcement. "What the fuck's going on in here, Bud?" asks Junior Bull – the son of "Sammy the Bull" Gravano, the Mafia mass murderer who was my biggest competitor in the Ecstasy market.

Relieved to see a familiar face, I say, "How're you doing?"

Shaking my hand, he says in a New York Italian accent, "I'm doing alright. I read that shit in the newspaper about you starting a blog in Sheriff Joe Arpaio's jail."

"The blog's been bringing media heat on the conditions."

"You know him?" Bud asks.

"Yeah, from Towers jail. He's a good dude. He's in for dealing Ecstasy like me."

"It's a good job you said that 'cause I was about to smash his ass," Bud says.

"It's a good job Wild Man ain't here 'cause you'd a got your ass thrown off the balcony," Junior Bull says.

I laugh. The presence of my best friend, Wild Man, was partly the reason I never took a beating at the county jail, but with Wild Man in a different prison, I feel vulnerable. When Bud casts a death stare on me, my smile fades.

"What the fuck you guys on about?" Bud asks.

"Let's go talk downstairs." Junior Bull leads Bud out.

I rush to a stainless steel sink/toilet bolted to a cement-block wall by the front of the cell, unbutton my orange jumpsuit and crane my neck to watch the upper-tier walkway in case Bud returns. I bask in relief as my bladder deflates. After flushing, I take stock of my new home, grateful for the slight improvement in the conditions versus what I'd grown accustomed to in Sheriff Joe Arpaio's jail. No cockroaches. No blood stains. A working swamp cooler. Something I've never seen in a cell before: shelves. The steel table bolted to the wall is slightly larger, too. *But how will I concentrate on writing with Bud around?* There's a mixture of smells in the room. Cleaning chemicals. Aftershave. Tobacco. A vinegar-like odour. The slit of a window at the back overlooks gravel in a no-man's-land before the next building with gleaming curls of razor wire around its roof.

From the doorway upstairs, I'm facing two storeys of cells overlooking a day room with shower cubicles at the end of both tiers. At two white plastic circular tables, prisoners are playing dominoes, cards, chess and Scrabble, some concentrating, others yelling obscenities, contributing to a brain-scraping din that I hope to block out by purchasing a Walkman. In a raised box-shaped Plexiglas control tower, two guards are monitoring the prisoners.

Bud returns. My pulse jumps. Not wanting to feel like I'm stuck in a kennel with a rabid dog, I grab a notepad and pen and head for the day room.

Focussed on my body language, not wanting to signal any weakness, I'm striding along the upper tier, head and chest elevated, when two hands appear from a doorway and grab me. I drop the pad. The pen clinks against grid-metal and tumbles to the day room as I'm pulled into a cell reeking of backside sweat and masturbation, a cheese-tinted funk.

"I'm Booga. Let's fuck," says a squat man in urine-stained boxers, with WHITE TRASH tattooed on his torso below a mobile home, and an arm sleeved with the Virgin Mary.

Shocked, I brace to flee or fight to preserve my anal virginity. I can't believe my eyes when he drops his boxers and waggles his penis.

Dancing to music playing through a speaker he has rigged up, Booga smiles in a sexy way. "Come on," he says in a husky voice. "Drop your pants. Let's fuck." He pulls pornography faces. I question his sanity. He moves closer. "If I let you fart in my mouth, can I fart in yours?"

"You can fuck off," I say, springing towards the doorway.

He grabs me. We scuffle. Every time I make progress towards the doorway, he clings to my clothes, dragging me back in. When I feel his penis rub against my leg, my adrenalin kicks in so forcefully I experience a burst of strength and wriggle free. I bolt out as fast as my shower sandals will allow, and snatch my pad. Looking over my shoulder, I see him stood calmly in the doorway, smiling. He points at me. "You have to walk past my door every day. We're gonna get together. I'll lick your ass and you can fart in my mouth." Booga blows a kiss and disappears.

I rush downstairs. With my back to a wall, I pause to steady my thoughts and breathing. In survival mode, I think, *What's going to come at me next?* In the hope of reducing my tension, I borrow a pen to do what helps me stay sane: writing. With the details fresh in my mind, I document my journey to the prison for my blog readers, keeping an eye out in case anyone else wants to test the new prisoner. The more I write, the more I fill with a sense of purpose. Jon's Jail Journal is a connection to the outside world that I cherish.

Someone yells, "One time!" The din lowers. A door rumbles open. A guard does a security walk, his every move scrutinised by dozens of scornful eyes staring from cells. When he exits, the din resumes, and the prisoners return to injecting drugs to escape from reality, including the length of their sentences. This continues all day with "Two times!" signifying two approaching guards, and "Three times!" three and so on. Every now and then an announcement by a guard over the speakers briefly lowers the din.

Before lockdown, I join the line for a shower, holding bars of soap in a towel that I aim to swing at the head of the next person to try me. With boisterous inmates a few feet away, yelling at the men in the showers to "Stop jerking off," and "Hurry the fuck up," I get in a cubicle that reeks of bleach and mildew. With every nerve strained, I undress and rinse fast.

At night, despite the desert heat, I cocoon myself in a blanket from head to toe and turn towards the wall, making my face more difficult to strike. I leave a hole for air, but the warm cement block inches from my mouth returns each exhalation to my face as if it's breathing on me, creating a feeling of suffocation. For hours, my heart drums so hard against the thin mattress I feel as if I'm moving even though I'm still. I try to sleep, but my eyes keep springing open and my head turning towards the cell as I try to penetrate the darkness, searching for Bud swinging a padlock in a sock at my head.

OTHER BOOKS BY SHAUN ATTWOOD

Pablo Escobar: Beyond Narcos

War on Drugs Series Book 1

The mind-blowing true story of Pablo Escobar and the Medellín Cartel beyond their portrayal on Netflix.

Colombian drug lord Pablo Escobar was a devoted family man and a psychopathic killer; a terrible enemy, yet a wonderful friend. While donating millions to the poor, he bombed and tortured his enemies – some had their eyeballs removed with hot spoons. Through ruthless cunning and America's insatiable appetite for cocaine, he became a multi-billionaire, who lived in a $100-million house with its own zoo.

Pablo Escobar: Beyond Narcos demolishes the standard good versus evil telling of his story. The authorities were not hunting Pablo down to stop his cocaine business. They were taking over it.

American Made: Who Killed Barry Seal? Pablo Escobar or George HW Bush

War on Drugs Series Book 2

Set in a world where crime and government coexist, *American Made* is the jaw-dropping true story of CIA pilot Barry Seal that the Hollywood movie starring Tom Cruise is afraid to tell.

Barry Seal flew cocaine and weapons worth billions of dollars into and out of America in the 1980s. After he became a government informant, Pablo Escobar's Medellin Cartel offered a million for him alive and half a million dead. But his real trouble began after he threatened to expose the dirty dealings of George HW Bush.

American Made rips the roof off Bush and Clinton's complicity in cocaine trafficking in Mena, Arkansas.

"A conspiracy of the grandest magnitude." Congressman Bill Alexander on the Mena affair.

The Cali Cartel: Beyond Narcos

War on Drugs Series Book 3

An electrifying account of the Cali Cartel beyond its portrayal on Netflix.

From the ashes of Pablo Escobar's empire rose an even bigger and more malevolent cartel. A new breed of sophisticated mobsters became the kings of cocaine. Their leader was Gilberto Rodríguez Orejuela – known as the Chess Player due to his foresight and calculated cunning.

Gilberto and his terrifying brother, Miguel, ran a multi-billion-dollar drug empire like a corporation. They employed a politically astute brand of thuggery and spent $10 million to put a president in power. Although the godfathers from Cali preferred bribery over violence, their many loyal torturers and hit men were never idle.

Pablo Escobar's Story (4-book series)

"Finally, the definitive book about Escobar, original and up-to-date" – UNILAD

"The most comprehensive account ever written" – True Geordie

Pablo Escobar was a mama's boy who cherished his family and

sang in the shower, yet he bombed a passenger plane and formed a death squad that used genital electrocution.

Most Escobar biographies only provide a few pieces of the puzzle, but this action-packed 1000-page book reveals everything about the king of cocaine.

Mostly translated from Spanish, Part 1 contains stories untold in the English-speaking world, including:

The tragic death of his youngest brother Fernando.

The fate of his pregnant mistress.

The shocking details of his affair with a TV celebrity.

The presidential candidate who encouraged him to eliminate their rivals.

The Mafia Philosopher

"A fast-paced true-crime memoir with all of the action of Good-fellas" – UNILAD

"Sopranos v Sons of Anarchy with an Alaskan-snow backdrop" – True Geordie Podcast

Breaking bones, burying bodies and planting bombs became second nature to Two Tonys while working for the Bonanno Crime Family, whose exploits inspired The Godfather.

After a dispute with an outlaw motorcycle club, Two Tonys left a trail of corpses from Arizona to Alaska. On the run, he was pursued by bikers and a neo-Nazi gang blood-thirsty for revenge, while a homicide detective launched a nationwide manhunt.

As the mist from his smoking gun fades, readers are left with an unexpected portrait of a stoic philosopher with a wealth of charm, a glorious turn of phrase and a fanatical devotion to his daughter.

Party Time

An action-packed roller-coaster account of a life spiralling out of control, featuring wild women, gangsters and a mountain of drugs.

Shaun Attwood arrived in Phoenix, Arizona, a penniless business graduate from a small industrial town in England. Within a decade, he became a stock-market millionaire. But he was leading a double life.

After taking his first Ecstasy pill at a rave in Manchester as a shy student, Shaun became intoxicated by the party lifestyle that would change his fortune. Years later, in the Arizona desert, he became submerged in a criminal underworld, throwing parties for thousands of ravers and running an Ecstasy ring in competition with the Mafia mass murderer Sammy 'The Bull' Gravano.

As greed and excess tore through his life, Shaun had eye-watering encounters with Mafia hit men and crystal-meth addicts, enjoyed extravagant debauchery with superstar DJs and glitter girls, and ingested enough drugs to kill a herd of elephants. This is his story.

Hard Time

"Makes the Shawshank Redemption look like a holiday camp" – NOTW

After a SWAT team smashed down stock-market millionaire Shaun Attwood's door, he found himself inside of Arizona's deadliest jail and locked into a brutal struggle for survival.

Shaun's hope of living the American Dream turned into a nightmare of violence and chaos, when he had a run-in with Sammy the Bull Gravano, an Italian Mafia mass murderer.

In jail, Shaun was forced to endure cockroaches crawling in his ears at night, dead rats in the food and the sound of skulls getting cracked against toilets. He meticulously documented the conditions and smuggled out his message.

Join Shaun on a harrowing voyage into the darkest recesses of human existence.

Hard Time provides a revealing glimpse into the tragedy, brutality, dark comedy and eccentricity of prison life.

Featured worldwide on Nat Geo Channel's Locked-Up/Banged-Up Abroad Raving Arizona.

Prison Time

Sentenced to 9½ years in Arizona's state prison for distributing Ecstasy, Shaun finds himself living among gang members, sexual predators and drug-crazed psychopaths. After being attacked by a Californian biker in for stabbing a girlfriend, Shaun writes about the prisoners who befriend, protect and inspire him. They include T-Bone, a massive African American ex-Marine who risks his life saving vulnerable inmates from rape, and Two Tonys, an old-school Mafia murderer who left the corpses of his rivals from Arizona to Alaska. They teach Shaun how to turn incarceration to his advantage, and to learn from his mistakes.

Shaun is no stranger to love and lust in the heterosexual world, but the tables are turned on him inside. Sexual advances come at him from all directions, some cleverly disguised, others more sinister – making Shaun question his sexual identity.

Resigned to living alongside violent, mentally-ill and drug-addicted inmates, Shaun immerses himself in psychology and philosophy to try to make sense of his past behaviour, and begins applying what he learns as he adapts to prison life. Encouraged by Two Tonys to explore fiction as well, Shaun reads over 1000 books which, with support from a brilliant psychotherapist, Dr Owen, speed along his personal development. As his ability to deflect daily threats improves, Shaun begins to look forward to his release with optimism and a new love waiting for him. Yet the words of Aristotle from one of Shaun's books will prove prophetic: "We cannot learn without pain."

Un-Making a Murderer: The Framing of Steven Avery and Brendan Dassey

Innocent people do go to jail. Sometimes mistakes are made. But even more terrifying is when the authorities conspire to frame them. That's what happened to Steven Avery and Brendan Dassey, who were convicted of murder and are serving life sentences.

Un-Making a Murderer is an explosive book which uncovers the illegal, devious and covert tactics used by Wisconsin officials, including:

– Concealing Other Suspects

– Paying Expert Witnesses to Lie

– Planting Evidence

– Jury Tampering

The art of framing innocent people has been in practice for centuries and will continue until the perpetrators are held accountable. Turning conventional assumptions and beliefs in the justice system upside down, *Un-Making a Murderer* takes you on that journey.

The profits from this book are going to Steven and Brendan and to donate free books to schools and prisons. In the last three years, Shaun Attwood has donated 20,000 books.

ABOUT SHAUN ATTWOOD

Shaun Attwood is a former stock-market millionaire and Ecstasy trafficker turned YouTuber, public speaker, author and activist, who is banned from America for life. His story was featured worldwide on National Geographic Channel as an episode of Locked Up/Banged Up Abroad called Raving Arizona.

Shaun's writing – smuggled out of the jail with the highest death rate in America run by Sheriff Joe Arpaio – attracted international media attention to the human rights violations: murders by guards and gang members, dead rats in the food, cockroach infestations...

While incarcerated, Shaun was forced to reappraise his life. He read over 1,000 books in just under six years. By studying original texts in psychology and philosophy, he sought to better understand himself and his past behaviour. He credits books as being the lifeblood of his rehabilitation.

Shaun tells his story to schools to dissuade young people from drugs and crime. He campaigns against injustice via his books and blog, Jon's Jail Journal. He has appeared on the BBC, Sky News and TV worldwide to talk about issues affecting prisoners' rights.

As a best-selling true-crime author, Shaun is writing a series of action-packed books exposing the War on Drugs, which feature the CIA, Pablo Escobar and the cocaine Mafia. He is also writing the longest ever Escobar biography: *Pablo Escobar's Story*, a 4-book series with over 1,000 pages. On his weekly true-crime podcast on YouTube, Shaun interviews people with hard-hitting crime stories and harrowing prison experiences.

CPSIA information can be obtained
at www.ICGtesting.com
Printed in the USA
LVHW101948051221
705331LV00013B/1960